A Handbook of
Public Speaking

A Handbook of Public Speaking

Richard Letteri

Furman University

Allyn and Bacon

BOSTON ■ LONDON ■ TORONTO ■ SYDNEY ■ TOKYO ■ SINGAPORE

Series Editor: Karon Bowers
Editorial Assistant: Jennifer Trebby
Marketing Manager: Mandee Eckersley
Production Administrator: Beth Houston
Editorial-Production Service: Omegatype Typography, Inc.
Composition and Prepress Buyer: Linda Cox
Manufacturing Buyer: Julie McNeill
Cover Administrator: Kristina Mose-Libon
Electronic Composition: Omegatype Typography, Inc.

Between the time Website information is gathered and then published, it is
not unusual for some sites to have closed. Also, the transcription of URLs can
result in unintended typographical errors. The publisher would appreciate
notification where these occur so that they may be corrected in subsequent
editions. Thank you.

Library of Congress Cataloging-in-Publication Data

Letteri, Richard.
    A handbook of public speaking / Richard Letteri.
        p. cm.
    Includes bibliographical references and index.
    ISBN 0-205-31965-3
    1. Public speaking.   I. Title.

PN4121 .L397 2002
808.5'1—dc21

2001041346

Printed in the United States of America

10 9 8 7 6 5 4 3 2 1   06 05 04 03 02 01

To Gilda Letteri,
my mother, teacher, mentor.

Brief Contents

Chapter 1   *Research*   *1*

    1.1 *Critical Thinking and Listening*   1
    1.2 *Analyzing Your Audience*   5
    1.3 *Selecting Your Topic*   10
    1.4 *Researching Your Topic*   14
    1.5 *Electronic Research*   18
    1.6 *Research Sources*   24
    1.7 *Evaluating Source Credibility*   27
    1.8 *Principles of Interviewing*   29

Chapter 2   *Evidence and Arguments*   *33*

    2.1 *Modes of Proof*   33
    2.2 *Types of Evidence*   38
    2.3 *Forms of Argument*   59
    2.4 *Argument Strategies*   81
    2.5 *Argument Fallacies*   87

Chapter 3   *Visual Aids*   *94*

    3.1 *The Purpose of Visual Aids*   94
    3.2 *Two-Dimensional Aids*   96
    3.3 *Three-Dimensional Aids*   105
    3.4 *Media Aids*   106
    3.5 *Designing Visual Aids*   110
    3.6 *Using Visual Aids*   113

Chapter 4   *Organization*   *117*

    4.1 *General Speech Structure*   117
    4.2 *Introductory and Concluding Statements*   120

4.3 *Thesis Statement and Preview Summary*   127

4.4 *Patterns of Organization*   130

4.5 *Types of Transitions*   134

4.6 *Principles of Outlining*   137

Chapter 5 Types of Speeches   144

5.1 *Principles of Informative Speaking*   144

5.2 *Types of Informative Speeches*   148

5.3 *Principles of Persuasive Speaking*   154

5.4 *Types of Persuasive Speeches*   162

5.5 *Principles of Ceremonial Speaking*   174

5.6 *Types of Ceremonial Speeches*   176

Chapter 6 Style   183

6.1 *Principles of Style*   183

6.2 *Grammar, Composition, and Word Choice*   188

6.3 *Revising Your Style*   193

6.4 *Oral Citations*   194

6.5 *Figures of Speech*   196

Chapter 7 Delivery   202

7.1 *Modes of Delivery*   202

7.2 *Elements of Vocal Delivery*   204

7.3 *Elements of Nonverbal Delivery*   208

7.4 *Enhancing Your Memory*   211

7.5 *Practicing Your Speech*   213

7.6 *Preparing to Speak*   217

7.7 *Reducing Speech Anxiety*   219

7.8 *Responding to Questions*   223

Appendix: Student Speeches   227

Notes   255

Index   269

Contents

Preface   xxv

Chapter **1** *Research*   1

1.1 *Critical Thinking and Listening*   1

   1 Concentrate on the message   2

   2 Maintain a positive attitude and set aside any presuppositions
      you have about the speech's subject   2

   3 Evaluate the evidence and main parts of the speech   2

   4 Listen closely to the language and the delivery
      of the speech   3

   5 Assess the overall qualities of the speech   5

   6 Compare and contrast the speech's main ideas to your own and
      those of other audience members   4

   7 Consider taking notes on the speech   4

1.2 *Analyzing Your Audience*   5

   1 Compare and contrast your audience to a hypothetical universal
      or ideal audience and to the general public   5

   2 Use demographic information to analyze your audience   6

   3 Consider developing a psychological profile
      of your audience   7

   4 Develop a sense of your audience's cultural characteristics   8

   5 Consider where your audience usually obtains its information
      and how these sources would influence their thinking about
      your subject   9

1.3 *Selecting Your Topic*   10

   1 Begin by brainstorming   10

   2 To discover more topics, check reference indexes, browse the
      Internet, and skim through some major newspapers, periodicals,
      and academic journals   11

   3 Generate new topics from those you have already listed   12

   4 After accumulating enough topics, select those that will be the
      most significant and appealing to your audience   12

5 Identify those topics that best fit your speech assignments   13

6 Consider ways to modify a topic to fit the requirements of your
speaking situation   13

7 Determine whether you have the appropriate facilities,
knowledge, and time to research your topic   13

1.4 *Researching Your Topic*   14

1 Develop a list of key terms that will help you gather information
on your topic   15

2 To gather information on your topic, consult encyclopedias,
almanacs, books, other types of reference material, as well as
your librarian   15

3 Use your library's electronic catalogue to search
its holdings   16

4 Search your library's databases and the internet for more specific
and current sources dealing with your topic   16

5 Interview government officials, scholars, professionals,
administrators, experts, and witnesses for their testimonies and
opinions on your topic   17

6 Document your information and its sources   17

7 Begin evaluating your evidence and organizing it
into an outline   18

1.5 *Electronic Research*   18

1 Use your key terms to conduct electronic searches of both
databases and the Internet   19

2 Consider where in the document your key term is most likely to
appear, and conduct a field search in that area   19

3 Consider ways to expand or narrow your search by using search
operators and techniques   19

4 Use your library's computer informational systems to call up
databases with information about your subject   21

5 You can also look for information about your topic by searching
the Internet   21

6 Two other good sources of information on the Internet are
databases and webzines   23

7 Follow the links you find in an electronic source
or document   23

8 Create a bookmark to keep track of web sites that you want
to revisit   23

9 Be sure to document the address of every web site you use, and
cite the web site when giving your speech   23

1.6 *Research Sources*   24

1.7 Evaluating Source Credibility   27

1 Uncover any presuppositions that a source may have about your topic   27

2 Check the credibility of a source   28

3 Always verify a source's claims by double-checking its facts and by comparing the information and arguments found in different sources   28

4 Although you can interpret evidence in ways other than a source presents it, never distort, falsify, or state evidence out of context   29

1.8 Principles of Interviewing   29

1 Set up the interview by contacting the interviewee and briefly explaining your intent   30

2 Prepare for the interview by researching your topic and interviewee beforehand   30

3 Create open-ended questions that will not limit the interviewee's possible responses   30

4 Create a set of specific questions that cover various aspects of your topic   30

5 Arrive on time for the interview, and be courteous   31

6 Even if you are taping the interview, take notes on any specific quotations that may be important   31

7 As the interview goes along, adapt your prepared list of questions to the interviewee's comments   31

8 Encourage the interviewee to elaborate on his or her answers with brief verbal and nonverbal cues   32

9 Do not be confrontational or ask critical questions until the end of the interview   32

10 When ending the interview, summarize the main points that have been covered, and give the interviewee an opportunity to discuss any issue or make any comment that he or she believes is important   32

11 Do not take the interviewee's statements as the absolute truth   32

Chapter 2 *Evidence and Arguments*   *33*

2.1 Modes of Proof   33

1 Logical proof   34

2 Ethical proof   35

3 Emotional proof   36

4 Normative proof   37

2.2 Types of Evidence   38

1 Explanation   38

2 Definition   41

3 Description   43

4 Statistics   45

5 Example   48

6 Narrative   51

7 Analogy   54

8 Testimony   56

2.3 Forms of Argument   59

1 Deductive arguments   61

2 Inductive arguments   68

3 Enthymeme   70

4 Causal arguments   71

5 Argument from signs   72

6 Two-sided arguments   73

7 Legal arguments   75

8 Toulmin's model of argument   78

2.4 Argument Strategies   81

1 Correlative ideas   82

2 Greater and lesser   82

3 Opposites   83

4 Less and more likely (*a fortiori*)   83

5 Crisscross consequences   83

6 Identical consequences and antecedents   84

7 Proportional relations   84

8 Same principle but different actions   84

9 Before and after   84

10 Turning the tables   85

11 Reduction to absurdity (*reductio ad absurdum*)   85

12 Method of residue   86

13 Means-to-ends rationale   86

14 Sustainability   86

15 Best- and worst-case scenarios   86

16 Common maxims   87

2.5 Argument Fallacies   87

1 Hasty generalization   88

2 Accident   88

3 Composition   88

4 Division   88

5 Equivocation   89

6 After this, therefore because of this (*post hoc, ergo propter hoc*)   89

7 Weak analogy   89

8 Appeal to authority   89

9 Appeal to the people (*ad populum*)   90

10 Appeal to tradition   90

11 Appeal to ignorance   90

12 Against the person (*ad hominem*)   91

13 False dichotomy   91

14 Slippery slope   91

15 Straw man   92

16 Red herring   92

17 Complex question   92

18 Begging the question   93

Chapter **3** *Visual Aids*   94

3.1 *The Purpose of Visual Aids* 94

1 Visual aids can clarify complex information   94

2 Use visual aids to illustrate your ideas   94

3 Visual aids are integral to demonstrating your ideas   95

4 Visual aids call attention to important ideas in your speech   95

5 Visual aids allow your audience to recognize the organization of your ideas   95

6 Use visual aids to help you speak extemporaneously   95

3.2 *Two-Dimensional Aids* 96

1 Maps   96

2 Graphs   97

3 Charts   100

4 Pictorial aids   103

5 Handouts   104

3.3 *Three-Dimensional Aids* 105

1 Models   105

2 Mock-ups   105

3 Cutaways   106

3.4 Media Aids 106

  1 Projectors and video aids   106

  2 Audio aids   108

  3 Computer aids   109

3.5 Designing Visual Aids 110

  1 Design your own visual aid   110

  2 Be sure your aid is visible to all audience members   110

  3 Make any writing short, simple, and easy to read   111

  4 When creating a graph or chart to display on an easel, use a strong paper that will support itself   111

  5 Keep colors vivid and simple   111

  6 To help your audience recognize the most significant points, place your most important information in the center of your aid   112

  7 Create design elements that have multiple functions   112

  8 Be sure that all maps, charts, and graphs contain a title and key that denote the information contained in the aid   112

  9 Do not use misleading symbols on your aid   113

3.6 Using Visual Aids 113

  1 Focus each aid on no more than three or four major points   113

  2 Limit your use of visual aids to no more than one-third to one-half of your speech   113

  3 Never use a visual aid that adds little new information, illustrates a minor point, or disrupts the flow of your speech   114

  4 Determine exactly when you will use your aid and how much time you need to discuss it   114

  5 Be sure that you have all of your aids ready at the time of the presentation   114

  6 Practice working with an assistant   115

  7 Prepare transitions that will move you to and from your aid and introduce the purpose of the aid   115

  8 Remember to maintain eye contact with your audience   115

  9 Explain how the information on your aid is organized   115

  10 Always point directly to the item on the aid that you are discussing   115

  11 Consider covering and then removing your aid before and after you use it   116

Chapter **4** *Organization*   117

4.1 General Speech Structure 117

  1 Introduction   117

2 Body   119

3 Conclusion   119

4.2 *Introductory and Concluding Statements*   *120*

1 Shock   121

2 Statistics   122

3 Testimony   122

4 Narrative   123

5 Current event   124

6 Analogy   124

7 Humor   125

8 Rhetorical question   125

9 Affirming a value   126

10 Stating your thesis   127

4.3 *Thesis Statement and Preview Summary*   *127*

1 When creating your thesis statement, ask yourself questions about your speech's subject matter and intent   127

2 Consider the rhetorical purpose of your speech   128

3 Determine the specific purpose of your speech   128

4 Create a working thesis that reflects your rhetorical purpose, your specific purpose, the areas of the topic you want to discuss, and your potential conclusion   129

5 State your thesis in a simple, declarative sentence that makes clear what you will discuss and how you will discuss it   129

6 Make sure the wording of your thesis presents your speech's intent in the clearest, most effective way possible   129

7 Directly follow your thesis statement with a preview summary of the organization of your speech   130

8 Repeat or rephrase your thesis statement throughout your speech   130

4.4 *Patterns of Organization*   *130*

1 Chronological   131

2 Spatial   131

3 Topical   131

4 Deductive   132

5 Inductive   132

6 Parallel   132

7 Climactic   133

8 Anticlimactic   133

9 Cause and effect   133

10 Problem and solution   133

4.5 Types of Transitions 134

  1 Preview transition 134

  2 Review transition 134

  3 Signpost transition 135

  4 Chronological transition 135

  5 Spatial transition 135

  6 Qualifying transition 136

  7 Relational transition 136

  8 Oppositional transition 137

4.6 Principles of Outlining 137

  1 Design your outline or manuscript so that it is easy to read when you are delivering your speech 137

  2 Clearly distinguish between main parts of your speech and between your main points, subpoints, and sub-subpoints 138

  3 Use your outline to reflect a clear symmetrical relationship among your speech's various parts 139

  4 Use each main point to discuss a different issue relating to your topic 139

  5 Use a combination of complete sentences, short phrases, and separate words in your outline 139

  6 Place your oral citations within your outline, and place a bibliography of your sources at the end of your outline 140

Chapter 5 Types of Speeches 144

5.1 Principles of Informative Speaking 144

  1 Arouse and maintain your audience's interest in your topic and speech 144

  2 Consider ways to employ the four modes of proof—logical, ethical, emotional, and normative—to inform your audience about your subject 145

  3 Less is more 146

  4 Strike a balance between the old and the new 146

  5 Be consistent, yet use variety 146

  6 Use evidence and language that is specific and concrete 147

  7 Use transitions, qualifiers, and your vocal delivery to represent your speech's organization and content 147

  8 Be energetic and enthusiastic 148

5.2 Types of Informative Speeches 148

  1 Speech of explanation 148

  2 Speech of definition 149

3 Speech of description   151

4 Speech of demonstration   151

5.3 *Principles of Persuasive Speaking* 154

1 Consider your audience's attitude toward your subject and your thesis statement   154

2 Present strong evidence and rational, sound, and clear arguments   156

3 Increase your persuasiveness by showing your audience that you are trustworthy and hold the same values as they do with respect to your subject   156

4 Appeal to your audience's values and emotional needs   157

5 Relate commonly held beliefs, norms, and narratives to your claim   158

6 Support your claims by stating both general moral or political principles and specific evidence and arguments   158

7 Apply principles and values consistently   159

8 Ask your audience to make small and gradual changes in their thinking or actions   159

9 Use a cost–benefit analysis to weigh the disadvantages of your claim against its advantages   159

10 Make detailed comparisons between things your audience accepts (or opposes) and other things they view positively (or negatively)   160

11 Qualify your claims clearly so you do not overstate them   160

12 Limit the potential criticisms against your claim by addressing these criticisms directly   160

13 Use humor sparingly and always as a means to address your issue   160

14 When motivating your audience to act or when arguing for a program or policy, offer a clear plan for implementing your suggestions   161

5.4 *Types of Persuasive Speeches* 162

1 Classical speech   162

2 Monroe's motivated sequence   165

3 Speech of fact   167

4 Value speech   169

5 Policy speech   171

5.5 *Principles of Ceremonial Speaking* 174

1 Create a ceremonial speech that is short and eloquent   174

2 Adapt your speech to the occasion and to the person, place, or event you are celebrating   174

3 Establish your personal relationship with the honoree   174

4 Consider the emotional needs of your audience, and attempt to fulfill these needs with your speech   175

5 Unify your audience through shared emotions and sentiments   175

6 Amplify the virtues of the honoree by specifically referring to his or her personal qualities, actions, and contributions   175

7 Balance your adulation of the honoree's professional accomplishments with praise for his or her personal achievements   176

8 Do not understate or exaggerate your emotions or praise of the honoree   176

5.6 Types of Ceremonial Speeches   176

1 Speech of introduction   177

2 Speech of presentation   178

3 Speech of acceptance   179

4 Toast   179

5 Testimonial   181

6 Eulogy   181

Chapter *Style* 183

6.1 Principles of Style   183

1 The two most important elements of a good style are clarity and appropriateness   184

2 Use a speaking style consistent with the type of speech you are giving   184

3 Depending on your abilities, choose either the plain style or a combination of the plain, middle, and grand style of speaking   184

4 Create a title that represents your speech's topic and thesis statement in a clear and inviting way   185

5 To help your audience remember your speech's main ideas, repeat your main points and key evidence more often than you normally would in written composition   186

6 Make suggestions and ask questions to extend goodwill to your audience   186

7 Develop a secondary theme or motif or repeat an engaging phrase throughout your speech to embellish your thesis statement and add a literary flair to your speech   186

8 To maintain your audience's attention, add some uncertainty to your speech   187

9 When speaking, never start discussing one idea and then begin another, tangential idea before completing the first idea   187

10 Create a unified, coherent, and emphatic speech   187

6.2 *Grammar, Composition, and Word Choice*   188

1 Although you should speak in a conversational manner, follow the basic rules of grammar and composition when writing and delivering your speech   188

2 Use terms that present your ideas clearly and effectively   189

3 Try to use evidence in the most direct and concise way   190

4 Use active and passive voice and the imperative mood to emphasize ideas in your speech   190

5 Although you may use contractions, do not overuse them   191

6 Use gender-neutral and inoffensive terms   191

7 Always qualify your terms and statements to reflect their size, strength, and importance   191

8 Avoid using phrases such as *I think, in my opinion,* or *I believe*   192

9 Avoid mixing metaphors and exaggerating claims   192

10 State a term or the name of an institution before using its common abbreviation or acronym   192

6.3 *Revising Your Style*   193

1 Before completing your final draft, take a break from writing your speech   193

2 When you begin working on your final draft, concentrate first on revising your speech's overall organization   193

3 After reviewing your speech's overall organization, assess the various parts of your speech   193

4 Enhance the speech's style   193

6.4 *Oral Citations*   194

1 Cite those sources that you quote directly, summarize, or paraphrase   194

2 Use an oral citation to establish the trustworthiness or timeliness of your source   194

3 Be as brief as possible   195

4 Acknowledge your source either before, after, or in the middle of a statement or quotation   195

5 Avoid saying *quote* and *unquote*   195

6 Refer to information gathered from a web site by giving the web site's title   196

6.5 Figures of Speech 196
     1 Alliteration 196
     2 Anadiplosis 197
     3 Anaphora 197
     4 Antanaclasis 197
     5 Antithesis 197
     6 Assonance 198
     7 Asyndeton 198
     8 Chiasmus 198
     9 Climax 198
    10 Enallage 198
    11 Epanalepsis 199
    12 Epistrophe 199
    13 Hyperbole 199
    14 Malaproprism 199
    15 Metaphor 199
    16 Metonymy (Synecdoche) 200
    17 Onomatopoeia 200
    18 Parallelism 200
    19 Polysyndeton 200
    20 Pun 201
    21 Rhetorical question 201
    22 Simile 201

Chapter **7** *Delivery*   202

7.1 Modes of Delivery 202
     1 Extemporaneous delivery 202
     2 Manuscript delivery 203
     3 Impromptu delivery 203
     4 Memorized delivery 204
7.2 Elements of Vocal Delivery 204
     1 Register 204
     2 Tone 205
     3 Rate 206
     4 Volume 206
     5 Enunciation 207
     6 Pauses 208

7.3 *Elements of Nonverbal Delivery* 208

1 Dress 209

2 Posture 209

3 Gestures 209

4 Movement 210

5 Facial expressions 210

6 Eye contact 211

7.4 *Enhancing Your Memory* 211

1 Build your memory by concentrating first on your speech's overall organization, and then on its individual parts 212

2 Do not try to memorize every word of your speech 212

3 To maintain consistency in your speech, remember what you have already said when deciding what to say next 212

4 Use parallel sentences, mnemonic devices, and other rhetorical techniques to help recall your points 213

5 Develop distinctive subpoints that are easy to recall 213

7.5 *Practicing Your Speech* 213

1 Begin by simply reading over your presentation and making revisions or mental notes as to how you want it to sound 214

2 Practice your delivery 214

3 Use a key word outline in some of your early practice rounds to help you memorize parts of your speech and practice explaining ideas and formulating sentences 214

4 Attempt to relate the whole ideas, not just words or sentences 215

5 Practice the vocal elements of your delivery by varying your voice 215

6 Practice your gesturing and the other nonverbal elements of your delivery 215

7 Choreograph any movements that are integral to your speech 216

8 Recognize poor speaking habits, and try to correct them 216

9 Make a conscious effort to control nervous habits 217

10 After practicing your speech several times on your own, deliver it in front of a select audience of friends 217

7.6 *Preparing To Speak* 217

1 Before speaking, find a place to relax and think about your speech 218

2 Prepare your voice by performing a warm-up exercise
or two   218

3 Prepare your body with warm-up exercises   218

4 Establish a comfortable breathing pattern with a few
relaxation exercises   218

5 When you arrive in the room, walk around to become more
familiar with your speaking situation   219

6 Once you are ready to begin, look at your audience to gain
their attention   219

7.7   *Reducing Speech Anxiety   219*

1 You will be more confident and have less speech anxiety if you
are well prepared and practice your speech a great deal   220

2 Have your introduction well prepared so that you
begin strongly   220

3 When you feel yourself becoming nervous, focus on the ideas
in your speech and away from the fact that you are speaking
to an audience   220

4 If your speech anxiety causes you to lose your place or have a
mental block, try summarizing your last point to see if your
summary helps you recall your next point   221

5 Breathe comfortably when speaking   221

6 Avoid increasing your rate of delivery when you
become nervous   221

7 Limit your use of filler words   221

8 If being nervous causes such symptoms as sweaty palms or
shaky hands or legs, try to relax, breathe slowly and deeply,
and move your muscles   222

9 If your mouth and throat become dry, move your jaw back and
forth, swallow several times, and keep your mouth closed before
speaking   222

10 Do not let distractions make you nervous   222

7.8   *Responding to Questions   223*

1 Prepare for potential questions by being as critical as possible
about your speech   223

2 Direct your audience's questions to a point that you were unable
to discuss thoroughly in your speech   223

3 If necessary, take notes on your audience's questions
and comments   223

4 Always answer a question in the clearest, most concise
manner possible   223

5 Maintain a positive demeanor when answering a question   224

6 If a question is unclear, ask the audience member to rephrase it, or try to restate it in terms that he or she accepts 224
7 Respond gracefully to counterarguments, and then show why your argument is stronger 224
8 If you do not know the answer to a question, simply say so 225
9 Never allow your questioner to limit your response 225
10 When necessary, control the question-and-answer period forcefully yet discreetly 225

Appendix: Student Speeches 227

Informative Speeches 227
  Speech of explanation 227
  Speech of demonstration 233
Persuasive Speeches 236
  Mixed speech types 236
  Policy speech 243
Ceremonial Speeches 250
  Speech of introduction 250
  Eulogy 252

Notes 255

Index 269

Preface

As with most instructors who teach the same introductory course every term, I foolishly convinced myself that I could quickly write a public speaking book that my students would find more suited to their needs than the texts I had been assigning. Initially, I believed that in a summer or two I could write a book that was not "needlessly long," "overly simplistic," or "difficult to use when preparing a speech." Now, after all too many years of writing and revising, my hope is that this handbook offers some clear advantages over those books for which I have much new-found respect.

Intent of the Handbook

One of the main goals of an introductory public speaking book is to provide a thorough description of the public speaking process. If done properly, such a description leads directly to fulfilling a second and third goal of teaching students how to speak effectively and think critically. Yet these goals often get obscured as authors confuse a thorough description with a copious one and simplify the complex principles of critical thinking so that they are readily but superficially understood. In preparing this handbook, I sought a way to retain the thoroughness and accessibility of contemporary public speaking books while rectifying their main limitations by presenting the principles of public speaking in a more concise yet rigorous way. Recalling how much I had learned about the critical nature of speaking from my studies of rhetoric, I turned to the classical rhetorical tradition for guidance.

By most historical accounts, the study of public speaking begins with the training of young citizen-orators in the principles and techniques of classical rhetoric. Aristotle states that rhetoric is the art of finding the available means of persuasion for any given case.[1] By persuasion, Aristotle meant not only using arguments to convince an audience, but also informing and moving an audience through explanation and eloquence.[2] As important as the study of classical rhetoric was for preparing citizens to speak in a variety of public venues, rhetoric was also seen as a fundamental component of a student's overall education. By studying all the available means of persuasion, a student would be able to argue opposing positions on an issue and, in the end, understand the issue more clearly and thoroughly.[3] Because rhetoric taught students how to speak on any subject and prepared them for further study in all fields of academic endeavor, educators from the classical period through the Renaissance placed rhetoric at the core of their curricula.

This handbook attempts to reestablish these original goals of public speaking by integrating many of the fundamental principles, strategies, and techniques of classical rhetoric with those of contemporary public speaking and rhetorical theory to teach students how to think critically and speak effectively about issues they will confront both within and outside their public speaking classrooms. However, unlike some public speaking and composition textbooks, this handbook does not offer a historical account of ancient rhetoric, nor does it attempt to rigidly reproduce its original principles and categories.[4] Rather, the handbook adapts the precepts and categories of public speaking from both the classical and contemporary tradition to fit the needs of contemporary student speakers. Moreover, just as it does not adhere rigidly to either rhetorical tradition, neither does it limit its contents to the principles of rhetoric and public speaking. Instead, it takes ideas from such diverse areas of study as logic, composition, moral and political philosophy, and psychology whenever they can contribute to the reader's capacity to think critically, persuade effectively, and speak eloquently.

Design of the Handbook

Along with adapting many of the principles of classical rhetoric to the needs of the contemporary student speaker, I have adapted the design of one of its main pedagogic tools—the handbook. Although many ancient as well as contemporary handbooks fail to live up to their essential function of providing a succinct and well-ordered guide to their subject, when done well, a handbook can be a very instructive and practical instrument of learning. To best represent the public speaking process as a whole, I first arranged the handbook's chapters in the chronological order that one generally follows when preparing a speech. This is not to say, for instance, that a speaker should not think about his or her speech's style or delivery until its evidence or organizational structure has been chosen. To the contrary, a speaker should always be concerned with what words he or she will use to represent a piece of evidence. For the most part, however, choosing what evidence to use in a speech will occur prior to putting the final touches on one's style and delivery.

I divided each chapter into distinct sections that provide a concise summary of the main principles, techniques, and elements of each specific area of public speaking. Thus, if the reader or instructor wants to address the issue of speech anxiety, he or she can go directly to that section and find a separate explanation of its likely symptoms and potential remedies (see Section 7.7). In those instances when an explanation given in one section leads to a discussion of a principle or strategy provided in another section, the handbook provides convenient references (e.g., see Section 7.3) where the reader can find the latter.

To illustrate the main principles or components of public speaking, I try to offer suggestions or examples that demonstrate how to employ each main idea. When possible, the examples presented in the handbook show how former students have applied a principle or used a main element of speech in one of their speeches. At other times, examples have been created to fit the principle, strategy, or component of speaking being explained. Finally, an appendix of students' speeches is provided to show how former students have adapted various principles, forms of evidence, and a host of other techniques to their particular topics. Both a manuscript and outline for each speech are given to provide a better understanding of differences between these two modes of delivery.

The reader must recognize that although the handbook format often makes it appear that the principles and strategies presented in its pages are universal and absolute laws that must be followed unconditionally, *they are not.* As one commentator has noted, for Cicero, the problem with handbooks is that "oratory is not so orderly a business; its rules are never more than rough generalizations that must be tempered by experience and conditioned by the recognition of the changing requirements of real circumstances."[5] To this extent, the precepts offered in this handbook operate as general guidelines that should be modified, combined, or rejected to fit the particular needs of the reader's speech. Thus, for instance, the reader should not hesitate to adopt a technique for showing admiration for someone from the sections on ceremonial speaking when considering how to build the *ethos* of the person who is the topic of his or her informative speech (see Sections 5.2., 5.5, and 5.6).

Whether this handbook accomplishes its goals of presenting the main principles of public speaking in a more insightful and accessible manner than other books is up to the reader to decide. In making a conscious decision to keep the handbook concise, I realize that every detail about the public speaking process and the rhetorical tradition could not be included, nor could I explain everything to the fullest extent possible. I also do not offer much on the various types of speaking that take place outside the classroom. However, I hope that I have provided enough information that the reader can infer what has been left unsaid and use his or her own judgment, that is, think critically, about how to apply the handbook's precepts to speaking situations outside the classroom.

Acknowledgments

I would like to acknowledge the many students who allowed me to reprint their speeches in the handbook. I also want to express my gratitude to my colleagues at Furman University whose contributions to this handbook are noted in its endnotes. A note of appreciation also goes to those colleagues who offered insightful suggestions about the handbook's content and style: Anne Leen, Charles DeLancey, Tom Buford, and Sean O'Rourke. I especially want to thank Linda Julian, Furman University, for editing the manuscript; Kevin Sargent, University of South Carolina, and Cindy Simmons for their general assistance; Debbie Stegall for reproducing the speaking aids; and Illana Fisher for helping prepare the handbook's index and instructor's manual. For their helpful comments as reviewers, I would like to thank Kelby Halone, Clemson University; Beth Lamoureux, Buena Vista University; and Beth Innocenti Manolescu, University of Kansas. Finally, I wish to thank Karon Bowers, my editor at Allyn & Bacon, for giving me the opportunity to publish this handbook.

A Handbook of
Public Speaking

CHAPTER

1

Research

1.1   *Critical Thinking and Listening*

1.2   *Analyzing Your Audience*

1.3   *Selecting Your Topic*

1.4   *Researching Your Topic*

1.5   *Electronic Research*

1.6   *Research Sources*

1.7   *Evaluating Source Credibility*

1.8   *Principles of Interviewing*

1.1 Critical Thinking and Listening

To become a better speaker, you will need to become a critical thinker and listener. Critical listening goes beyond merely hearing the words someone speaks. It entails making a conscious effort to comprehend and evaluate the meaning of the speaker's message. Learning to analyze a **text** (e.g., a speech, written source, Internet site, interviewee, etc.) critically will allow you to gain a greater understanding of a subject and its manner of presentation. Critical thinking and listening include evaluating the information, reasoning, and appeals a source or speaker bases a claim on. Critical thinking and listening also mean paying close attention to how the text is organized and the language it uses. Along with helping you assess a text's strengths and weaknesses, such skills will help you discover your own attitudes, opinions, and presuppositions about the text's subject. In this way, you will become more aware of the limits of your own thinking and be able to view the subject more objectively. By learning how to examine other speakers and writers critically, you can learn how to become a better speaker yourself.

1

The following guidelines outline techniques for developing your critical thinking and listening skills. As a general rule, these techniques will help you not only to judge other speeches but also to assess critically your own speeches as well as the evidence and arguments you find in research sources.

1   Concentrate on the message.

Focus your attention on what is said and how it is said. Do not let things happening around the room distract you. Shut out any noises and other external distractions. Also, keep yourself from daydreaming and thinking about things not directly related to what the speaker is discussing.

2   Maintain a positive attitude and set aside any presuppositions you have about the speech's subject.

Do not stop listening to a speaker just because he or she is talking about something that may not interest you, is saying something that you disagree with, or is not a good speaker. Listening carefully to the speaker will open you to new ideas, new information, and new perspectives on the speaker's subject. At the very least, listening carefully will make you aware of what to avoid doing when giving your speech.

Likewise, do not let your presuppositions or prejudices deter you from listening. Instead, allow the speech to challenge your previous beliefs and understanding of the subject. Filtering a speech through your prior beliefs may cause you to put words in the speaker's mouth. You then may alter what the speaker has actually said to fit your previous understanding or attitude about the subject and thus misinterpret the speaker's point. The main point is to pay close attention to what the speaker is actually saying rather than what you *believe* he or she is or should be saying.

3   Evaluate the evidence and main parts of the speech.

Listen for the thesis statement and the main points of the speech, and determine whether the evidence provided by the speaker supports his or her thesis in a satisfactory way (see Sections 4.1 and 4.3). Decide whether the evidence is meant to explore an idea, express an opinion, or prove a claim (see Sections 2.2 and 2.3). Assess whether the evidence is relevant to the point or claim made, whether it is the most recent evidence and thus most applicable, and whether there is a sufficient amount of evidence presented relative to the significance of the point. Then assess the quality of the evidence: Determine whether explanations and descriptions are clear, whether the examples and statistics are strong, and whether the narratives and testimony are compelling. Also, ask yourself if other evidence would help the speaker support a point. Conversely, determine whether the arguments made are logical or fallacious (see Section 2.5). Assess whether the evidence or arguments are consistent or contradictory, whether each point coheres with the others, and whether the speaker's logical and emotional appeals are reasonable and effective (see Section 2.1). When judging the merits of an argument, consider what values or principles the claims are based on, and whether the claims are overdrawn, unreasonable, or impractical (see Section 2.3).

You also should determine whether the speech's main points are arranged in a clear and logical manner, whether each point is developed thoroughly, and whether the introduction and conclusion use the appropriate appeals (see Sections 4.1, 4.2, and 4.4). Finally, consider whether the sources cited are credible; they should hold no presuppositions, and neither the source nor the speaker should manipulate the evidence to his or her advantage (see Section 1.7).

4   Listen closely to the language and the delivery of the speech.

Ask yourself if the speaker uses the appropriate language style and delivers the speech in the best manner possible (see Sections 6.1, 6.2, 7.1, and 7.2). Consider, for instance, whether the words used are too technical or if the sentences are long and difficult to follow. Similarly, study the speaker's delivery to see whether his or her changes in tone, speed, and volume and use of pauses increase the audience's understanding of the speech's points, or note how an overly monotone delivery limits the audience's understanding. Also, pay attention to gestures and movements the speaker uses, and determine how effective these nonverbal cues are and where additional gestures and movements would help the speaker relay his or her points in a more convincing manner.

As you are assessing what impact the speaker is having on you, watch how the rest of the audience responds to the speaker's language and delivery. If the speaker's wording and delivery are eliciting a positive response, consider which techniques you can incorporate into your own speaking style and delivery. If the wording and delivery are ineffective, ask yourself how you would perform the speech differently to elicit a better response.

5   Assess the overall qualities of the speech.

Although the main intent of each type of speech (informative, persuasive, ceremonial) differs, see whether the speaker strikes the appropriate balance among informing, persuading, and entertaining the audience (see Sections 5.1, 5.3, and 5.5). Evaluate the speaker's ability to explain and describe his or her subject, the analytical clarity of the evidence and arguments presented, and the way in which his or her style and delivery contribute to the overall rhetorical eloquence of the speech (see Sections 2.2, 2.3, 6.1, 6.2, 7.1, and 7.2).

6   Compare and contrast the speech's main ideas to your own and those of other audience members.

Compare the evidence and arguments presented to those you have already heard on this or a related topic (see Sections 2.2 and 2.3). See whether the speech adds to what you already know about the topic, changes your feelings about it, or makes you reconsider any presuppositions, prejudices, or misunderstandings you have about the topic.

Another way to compare your understanding of a subject to the way a speaker interprets it is to try to predict what the speaker will say next.[1] Although you should not hold steadfastly to your previous beliefs, determine whether your logic is consistent with the speaker's. If it is not, assess why the speaker moved in another direction, what his or her choice adds or subtracts from your understanding of the subject, and what his or her decision says about how you and the speaker view the subject differently.

You should also listen carefully to the comments made by other audience members. Their responses may suggest alternative ways to explore the subject and strengthen the speaker's claims. Their positive and negative reactions may also tell you a great deal about how an audience will view the evidence, appeals, and language you plan to use in one of your speeches (see Sections 2.1, 2.2, 6.1, and 6.2).

7   Consider taking notes on the speech.

If necessary, take notes to remind you of the speech's overall structure and its main ideas. Try to write down a brief phrase that indicates each main element or point in the speech's introduction, body, and conclusion (see Section 4.1). You might want to use various abbreviations, such as "personal" for a personal narrative, "two-sided" for a two-sided argument, and "norm" for a normative appeal, to record what type of evidence or appeals the speaker uses (see Sections 2.1, 2.2, and 2.3). You should also indicate whether you agree ("yes") or disagree ("no") with a point and try to paraphrase statements you do not understand or agree with so that you can ask the speaker about them if there is time for questions afterwards.

1.2 Analyzing Your Audience

Your audience's prior knowledge of and opinions about your subject can affect how they receive your speech. Thus, your understanding of your audience's interests, education, and attitudes should play a role in determining the topic you will choose, the thesis you will pursue, and the evidence, appeals, and arguments you will use (see Sections 1.3, 2.1, 2.2, and 4.3). Shaping your speech to fit the demands of your audience in no way means that you should change your position on your subject; rather, analyzing your audience should help you decide the best ways to present your subject and position given your audience's background, concerns, and values.

Listed in this section are some of the main ways that you can analyze an audience. Each approach takes a different perspective on conducting your analysis. Some approaches have obvious similarities; others have distinct differences. Some may be more beneficial than others depending on the information you can find on your audience, the thesis you want to pursue, and the degree to which you want to accommodate or challenge your audience. Thus, it is up to you to decide which method(s) will help you understand your audience and create an effective speech.

Finally, while analyzing your audience can suggest ways to make your speech more appealing, it can also cause problems. For instance, some forms of audience analysis may prompt you to direct your speech's appeals only to that segment of your audience that fits the results of your analysis. Thus, your analysis may cause you to infer incorrectly that what is true of a segment of your audience is true of the whole audience. You may also confront a problem when you find that your audience has so many different backgrounds, values, and interests that it is impossible to determine how to appeal to everyone's particular inclinations. To remedy both of these problems, always make the goal of your analysis to find those values generally shared by you and all the audience members. Then try to find speaking strategies that will accommodate everyone equally, or use various strategies that appeal to different people but do not offend any particular group or member of your audience. By using these types of appeals, you are more likely to build common ground among your audience members while increasing their satisfaction with your speech.

1   **Compare and contrast your audience to a hypothetical universal or ideal audience and to the general public.**

An **ideal** or **universal audience** holds to that ideal set of values that you would hope to find in all rational people.[2] Some characteristics they may have are that they are open-minded and willing to change their thinking if they are given convincing reasons to do so. They would also believe that everyone should be treated fairly, that personal dignity should be respected, and that we should always strive to improve society and balance the needs of individuals and society. They would not hold a particular culture's beliefs as universal, and they would acknowledge and respect differences between people while believing it is possible to find common ground among diverse interests.

By first establishing the character of this ideal audience, you may find those values that your audience already holds or aspires to. You can then make appeals based on these commonly shared values and convictions in an attempt to move your audience to this higher ground. For instance, when giving a speech on the women's suffrage movement, get your audience to equate the right of every citizen in a democracy to choose his or her political representatives to the movement's goal of giving women the right to vote.

The **general public audience** shares the common values and cultural tastes of the society in which its members live. Often, the notion of a general public audience is used to characterize an audience when you do not have specific information about the particular audience you will address. Thus, given the general knowledge you have about your audience, it may be worth considering what values, beliefs, and interests they have and direct your appeals to these preferences (see Section 2.1). However, do not presuppose too much about this audience because you may end up alienating certain audience members that do not hold the same values and beliefs that the general public does. You also should not direct your appeals to those values and beliefs that the general public holds that are nevertheless prejudicial or unreasonable, such as the belief that wealth is a sign of personal achievement.

If you do have some specific knowledge about your audience, you could determine how your particular audience differs from the general public so that you can focus your discussion on their specific inclinations. For example, in a classroom full of potential job seekers, you could narrow your discussion of work discrimination to how interns and entry-level employees are treated unfairly rather than discussing issues relating to the discrimination of elderly employees.

2   Use demographic information to analyze your audience.

A demographic study provides you with data on such characteristics as the age, gender, race, income, and education level of your audience members. Demographic studies are usually done by taking a poll or a survey of potential audience members. The problem with con-

ducting a demographic analysis is that you may not have the time, resources, and training to do one correctly. Therefore, you might just
want to estimate how your audience's demographic characteristics
will influence its reception of your speech based on what you do know
about your audience. You also may find out something about them
from other sources such as a government census, almanac, or a business's or institution's profile of its potential and existing customers
and clients. Check, for instance, if your university's admissions
department has put together a profile of prospective and present
students.

The main intent of a demographic study is to determine how demographic factors may affect your audience's reception of your subject and the claims you want to make. For instance, knowing the
income level of your audience members may help you decide what arguments you would want to pursue when discussing the merits of
providing universal health care. However, be careful about presupposing that because most of your audience has the same background
they think similarly, or that having a particular demographic characteristic will cause them to think in a certain way. Just because wealthy
audience members are likely to have private health insurance policies
does not mean that they would not want the government to provide
the poor with some form of health insurance.

3 Consider developing a psychological profile of your audience.

A psychological study of your audience examines the values, beliefs, and attitudes they may have toward your subject and why they
hold such convictions.[3] Like a demographic analysis, you can gather
information on your audience's values and beliefs by conducting a survey or poll. You could also interview potential audience members.
However, you may just want to spend some time considering what
convictions they may hold and how their ideals and inclinations may
affect their reception of your speech.

Values are usually defined as those fundamental moral or religious principles that shape people's sense of what is right or wrong,
good or bad, and acceptable or unacceptable. People also have political, economic, social, and cultural values such as whether they believe more in strong government or the free market, or whether they
are politically more conservative or liberal. Values often are strongly
held and interrelated. For many people, values establish the fundamental basis for who they are, what they think, and how they act.
Values usually affect a person's beliefs and attitudes. Thus, understanding what values your audience holds will help you determine
such things as what value claims you may want to make or how you

should characterize an honoree's actions in a speech of presentation (see Section 5.6).

Beliefs are ideas, opinions, judgments, or impressions a person may hold about a subject. They can be based on a person's value systems or on personal interest or experience. Beliefs can be relatively strong and affect a person's understanding of a variety of issues, or they can be weak and therefore more susceptible to change. Beliefs may also vary widely among audience members. Thus, it may be difficult to determine what their beliefs are, both collectively and individually. You can influence or change someone's beliefs, especially weaker ones, by providing information that shows how your subject has been misrepresented by others, by associating your subject with a positive belief the audience members hold, or by showing how your subject relates to their personal lives. Questions such as whether scientists should be allowed to conduct experiments on animals, whether corporations should consider both their shareholders' interests and the public good, and whether racism is a major social problem or a prejudice held by a few ignorant people usually hinge on a person's beliefs.

Another part of an audience's psychological make-up you may want to consider is their attitude toward your subject. **Attitudes** are feelings, inclinations, tastes, and preferences. They usually determine whether someone likes or dislikes something. Attitudes may be tied to deeper convictions, set by long-term habits or beliefs, and arise from repeated experiences; or they may be based on an intuition, presupposition, or incidental event. Thus, you may or may not be able to change your audience's attitude about your subject, depending on how strongly it is held. Either way, knowing what attitude your audience holds toward your subject can help you decide how you want to introduce that subject, what examples you may want use, and what goals you want to achieve. For instance, citing an example of a politician who won his election without taking money from special interest groups may change your audience's prior attitude that political lobbies control all politicians. Also, consider how you can use elements of your vocal delivery to change attitudes (see Section 7.2). For example, taking on a sympathetic tone when speaking about the plight of an endangered species may incline your audience to consider your proposal for a sanctuary.

4   Develop a sense of your audience's cultural characteristics.

Become sensitive to how people of different genders, income levels, ethnic and racial backgrounds, and so on may respond to your speech.[4] Also, consider how their gender may influence their reactions to your speech. Because you do not want to offend anyone in your audience unknowingly, try to make yourself aware of how people from diverse cultures or with different cultural interests may view your subject and the evidence, language, and appeals you may use. For instance, some cultures value proving a claim by using factual evidence such as statistics and clear, logical reasoning, whereas people from other cultures are more likely to accept a claim if it is exemplified through a narrative that coheres with their personal experience or stirs their emotions (see Section 2.2). In some cultures the use of hyperbole and metaphor in a speech is generally accepted because these figures of speech show the strength of a speaker's personal conviction or add a poetic element to a speech (see Section 6.5). In other cultures, people expect a speaker to use precise and concrete language (see Sections 7.1 and 7.2). Likewise, some people prefer that a speaker establish a more formal relation to his or her audience, whereas other people favor a more personal rapport. To learn more about various cultures, study their histories and social practices, or interview people who are either from other cultures or very familiar with other cultures.

As with any type of audience analysis, there are two main problems with considering the cultural traits of your audience. The first is that audience members may come from a wide variety of cultural backgrounds, and thus trying to appease everyone may be difficult. In fact, trying to placate one group may cause you to antagonize another. A second problem is that you may end up stereotyping people because they come from a particular culture. Just because someone values his or her own cultural heritage does not mean that he or she accepts every element of that culture or that he or she does not appreciate other cultural views and practices. To solve the problem of speaking to a multicultural audience, use a variety of appeals, forms of evidence, arguments, and delivery techniques so that various members of your audience will recognize their own cultural modes of speaking while being exposed to those of other cultures (see Sections 2.1, 2.2, 2.3, 7.2, and 7.3). Moreover, instead of speaking to a specific group in your audience, establish a common bond among various audience members' beliefs. Try to unify your audience while maintaining sensitivity to the differences among audience members. Above all, avoid **ethnocentrism**—presupposing that your particular culture is the best, that it holds all the correct values, and that other cultures are inferior. Likewise, avoid making prejudicial statements as well as racial, ethnic, and sexist jokes.

5   Consider where your audience usually obtains its information and how these sources would influence their thinking about your subject.

Analyze your audience based on the types of information they normally are exposed to and what media outlets they usually obtain their information from.[5] For example, consider what types of newspapers and periodicals they read, what evening news shows they watch, and what web sites they frequent. Similarly, decide whether they value objective news reporting, watch political pundits debate on television, or listen to talk radio. Also, ask yourself what movies they have seen and what popular novels they have read. Determine how these sources shape their attitudes toward your subject.

Learning about where your audience obtains information may help you shape your speech in a variety of ways. It can help you decide whether you should present a neutral description of your subject or make an impassioned plea for your position, whether to provide evidence from credible periodicals or from a popular web site, whether to relate your subject to an influential editorialist or a public celebrity, or whether to use a quotation from a novel or a line from a popular movie.

1.3 Selecting Your Topic

Although you can create a speech on just about any subject, selecting a good speech topic takes considerable thought and effort. Good speech topics address issues that are not only important and timely, but also are relevant and interesting to your audience. They shed new light on an old subject, address an idea from a different perspective, or take a position on a controversy. In addition, the amount of research material you find on your topic, your ability to create a strong thesis statement, and your development of interesting themes throughout the speech all play a role in turning a good speech topic into a good speech (see Sections 4.3 and 6.1). The following guidelines offer an effective strategy for developing a list of possible topics, choosing one that best fits your speech assignment, and refining your topic's focus so that your audience will find it significant and interesting.

1   Begin by brainstorming.

Develop potential speech topics by listing as many ideas as possible. At first, do not criticize any ideas. Simply write down whatever comes to mind, no matter how general or specific the subject is. Begin by brainstorming on topics that interest you and that you would like to learn more about.

When brainstorming, start with subjects that readily come to mind because they are of personal interest to you. Consider topics that relate to a class you took recently, a trip you plan to take, or a job or internship you hope to obtain. Likewise, list topics that relate to subjects that you always wanted to learn about but were never given the opportunity to study, or a current event that you have been following in the news. Also, write down topics that involve volunteer work you do or a personal hobby you enjoy such as working at an animal shelter or swing dancing.

After exhausting these topics, turn next to more traditional speech topics such as important persons, places, and events. Write down the names of significant individuals in history, politics, or religion. Also, consider doing a speech on your favorite author or artist. Similarly, list the names of major cities, exciting community festivals, or noteworthy monuments or geographical areas you have visited or would like to know more about. You should also consider doing a speech on how some recent scientific research, technological innovation, or archeological discovery has dramatically changed how we will live in the future or understand the past.

You can also develop topics that deal with more practical, everyday concerns such as a new computer software product, a profitable investment strategy, a popular diet plan, or an innovative exercise routine. How to repair a mountain bike, where to take an inexpensive vacation, and what nutritional value various types of ethnic foods have are also speech topics that your audience may find interesting and relevant.

If you are interested in political and social issues, think about topics that concern anything from welfare and educational policy, to health care and environmental concerns, to media violence and teen pregnancy. These speech topics can cover areas as large as international trade, a peace treaty between nations, a worldwide epidemic, and global warming; or areas as small as local city zoning, a truce between neighborhood street gangs, ways to prevent spreading the flu, or your university's recycling program.

Finally, consider topics that are unusual, such as why a manual laborer gave a large amount of money to a charity, or how a famous work of art was discovered to be a forgery. You can also list topics that are sensational or controversial. Such topics can include a well-publicized legal case, a natural disaster, a strange religious belief, or a hotly debated Hollywood movie. Similarly, consider doing a speech on such paranormal phenomena as extrasensory perception or UFOs.

2   **To discover more topics, check reference indexes, browse the Internet, and skim through some major newspapers, periodicals, and academic journals.**

Peruse your library's reference system, databases, and the Internet for potential topics (see Sections 1.4. and 1.5). Skim through printed sources for articles that discuss important issues that you can rework into a speech topic. The research sources listed in this chapter cover a variety of potential subjects for speeches that may interest both you and your audience (see Section 1.6).

3   Generate new topics from those you have already listed.

Start by narrowing topics that are overly broad so that you can thoroughly explore your subject in the time allotted to you. For example, you can limit a speech on campus life to the difficulties foreign exchange students face in a new academic environment. Likewise, rework a speech on health maintenance organizations (HMOs) to one that deals specifically with how many HMO health policies do not pay for mental health care. Also consider reworking older topics into newer ones. For instance, instead of doing a speech on the Italian mafia, focus on the Russian mafia or Colombian drug cartels.

Next, think about how you can turn a topic that is overly general or personal to one that is more unique and significant. Instead of giving a speech on why you are a football fanatic, consider doing a speech on English soccer hooligans. Also think about how you can relate a current event to a matter of continual interest and importance. For example, turn a speech on racism into one about how hate groups are using the Internet to recruit members. Or provide a context for a great piece of literature by discussing those historical events that shaped the author's portrayal of the events and characters in the book.

Finally, consider addressing issues or characteristics of a familiar topic that are not often discussed. In this case, instead of describing the damage caused by a hurricane, debate whether local governments should fix the prices of goods and services after a natural disaster. In addition, try developing alternative ways to interpret a topic. For instance, instead of explaining the political events surrounding a terrorist act, offer a psychological portrait of a terrorist.

4   After accumulating enough topics, select those that will be the most significant and appealing to your audience.

Choose subjects that your audience will find interesting, informative, and entertaining. Just as you ask questions that help you determine which topics interest you, ask whether your audience would find a topic appealing because it affects them personally, because it offers a solution to a significant problem, or because it deals with a controversial topic. In addition, you can engage an audience by discussing new information about a topic. For example, in light of recent DNA studies, your audience may be interested in a speech on Thomas Jefferson's relationship with Sally Hemming. You can also try addressing a common topic from a new perspective. Thus, rather than giving a speech on baseball, give one on why children should not throw certain types of pitches that may injure their underdeveloped arm muscles.

When considering your audience, however, do not underestimate their willingness to listen to a speech about a topic audience members initially view as difficult or unappealing. By discovering interesting evidence and making the appropriate appeals, you can engage even a reluctant audience.

5 Identify those topics that best fit your speech assignments.

After determining which of your topics are the most interesting, consider which topic best fits the type of speech you are assigned to give (see Chapter 5). For an informative speech, look for a topic you can clearly define, classify, or describe. If you are assigned a demonstrative speech, choose a topic that lets you perform an activity relating to it. The best demonstrative topics are those you can break down into clear, distinct steps that your audience can follow easily. When preparing a persuasive speech, choose a topic that entails some controversy or issue on which you can take a position and construct arguments that support your position. For a policy speech, your topic must concern how an organization has failed to deal adequately with a problem or to provide services to its constituents, and your plan to improve the situation.

6 Consider ways to modify a topic to fit the requirements of your speaking situation.

The main components of your speaking situation are the time allotted for your speech, its setting, the mode of your delivery (see Section 7.1), and your audience's attitude toward your topic. Because people's attitudes are often shaped by such things as their age, sex, race, income, values, beliefs, personal interests, and what sources they usually obtain their information from, consider how these factors may influence your audience's reception of your speech (see Section 1.2).

7 Determine whether you have the appropriate facilities, knowledge, and time to research your topic.

Consider whether you can obtain important information and other material relating to your topic. Ask yourself such questions as

- Does my library have the sources I need (see Sections 1.4 and 1.5)?
- Do I have the material that I need for my demonstrative speech (see Section 5.2)?

- Can I obtain media and computer aids for my presentation (see Section 3.4)?
- Who are the individuals I would like to interview for my speech (see Section 1.8)?

Also, although you will learn more about your topic through your research, consider whether you have enough prior knowledge of the topic to understand the evidence and arguments you will find. Ask yourself,

- Do I understand the main terms relating to my topic?
- Will I be able to explain clearly the evidence I find (see Section 2.2)?
- Do I know enough about my topic that I can weigh arguments for or against it (see Section 2.3)?

Last, plan how much time you will need to research, organize, and practice your speech (see Sections 1.4, 1.5, 7.5, and Chapter 5). Consider making a schedule that designates how much time you will need to do library research, conduct interviews, and gather additional materials for your speech (see Section 1.8). Then determine how much time you will need to complete your outline or manuscript and how long it will take to practice delivering your speech. You must also set aside some time to evaluate your speech critically. When evaluating your speech, ask yourself questions such as

- Are there better ways to introduce or conclude my speech (see Sections 4.1 and 4.2)?
- Do any of my main points lack strong supportive evidence (see Section 2.2)?
- Do the various parts of my speech fit together into a unified whole?
- Have I chosen the best words, phrases, and sentence structures for expressing my point (see Sections 6.1 and 6.2)?

If you answer "no" to any of these questions, you will need to take the time to do some additional research or rewrite your speech.

1.4 Researching Your Topic

Once you have a general idea of what your topic will be, you are ready to begin your research. Although some topics may require you to pursue your research differently, one of the best ways to discover information on your topic is first to look for general background material on your topic and then pursue more recent and specific sources. The research strategy given here follows this basic process.

1 Develop a list of key terms that will help you gather information on your topic.

Create a preliminary list of important issues, ideas, facts, people, and dates that you will want to discuss in your speech. One way to develop this list is to employ the journalistic technique of asking questions about the who, what, where, when, why, and how of your topic.[6] For example, ask such questions as the following:

- Who are the most important people relating to my topic?
- Who are the premier authorities on my topic?
- Who is affected the most by my topic?
- What is the best way to define my topic?
- What are the most important issues relating to my topic?
- What are the important facts relating to my topic?
- What are the main organizations and associations that deal with my topic?
- What are the main newspapers, periodicals, academic journals, and so on that discuss my topic?
- Where are the places that are most affected by my topic?
- When was my topic born or created, or when did it happen?
- When did people become interested in my topic?
- Why is my topic important to people?
- Why is my topic controversial?
- How has my topic changed through time?
- How does my topic relate to people's immediate concerns?
- How does my topic relate to other important issues?

Use your answers to these questions to create the key terms you will use to search the various sources described next.

2 To gather general information on your topic, consult encyclopedias, almanacs, books, other types of reference material, as well as your librarian.

Become better acquainted with your topic by first going to research sources that present a general overview of your subject. Both general and specialized encyclopedias are good places to find background information such as historical facts and definitions relating to your topic (see Section 1.6).

An encyclopedia also can provide you with other types of helpful information. For instance, how an encyclopedia divides your topic into subject areas can suggest ways to organize the main points of your speech. Moreover, pay close attention to how an encyclopedia explains your topic. Because an encyclopedia is written for a general reading audience, the terms and writing style it uses may suggest ways to present your topic that your audience can easily understand. Also, most encyclopedias offer a brief but authoritative bibliography that may contain additional sources for your speech.

Other reference sources, such as almanacs and statistical abstracts, may provide additional information about your topic (see Section 1.6). These sources organize statistical data in a variety of ways. For instance, they can provide information on the scope of your topic, how it has changed over time, or the ways it is classified by region, gender, or race. You can find almanacs and statistical abstracts, as well as encyclopedias, in your library's reference section, on a database, and on the Internet.

Finally, after doing some preliminary research, ask a librarian to help find information on your subject. Librarians know their library's holdings better than anyone and have helped people conduct research on most every subject. Their suggestions can help you to find more information as well as to use your time in the library more efficiently.

3 Use your library's electronic catalogue to search its holdings.

Your library's electronic catalogue system indexes the books, news periodicals, academic journals, government documents, videotapes, and other research materials in its present collection. Use your key terms, particularly the names of the authors, titles of books, and possible subject headings to search for materials pertaining to your topic. You should also combine various key words with the search operators and techniques listed in Section 1.5.

4 Search your library's databases and the Internet for more specific and current sources dealing with your topic.

Databases are electronic indexes that provide either references to sources or the actual sources themselves, be they articles published in newspapers, periodicals, or academic journals, transcripts from radio and television shows, or government documents (see Sections 1.5 and

1.6). The Internet also provides access to many of these same sources as well as to a host of web sites maintained by media outlets, private individuals and associations, scholars, and government agencies. Thus, both databases and the Internet provide access to a variety of sources that discuss a vast array of subjects. Moreover, using databases and the Internet can help you find some of the most specific and up-to-date information concerning your topic.

5   Interview government officials, scholars, professionals, administrators, experts, and witnesses for their testimonies and opinions on your topic.

An interview may provide you with unpublished recent or personal information that cannot be obtained elsewhere (see Section 1.8). In addition, audiences appreciate the extra effort it takes to acquire this information. If you are going to interview someone, make sure that you complete most of your research beforehand so that you appear knowledgeable about your subject and so that you prepare an effective list of interview questions.

6   Document your information and its sources.

Use a separate note card or sheet of paper for each piece of evidence. Placing each piece of evidence on a separate note will allow you to arrange your evidence in your outline more easily.

When conducting your research, take notes on all the relevant information. You do not have to copy information verbatim. Rather, you can save time by summarizing long passages and commonly known information and by paraphrasing information that you will not quote directly. Remember, however, to avoid plagiarizing from your original sources (see Section 6.4).

To save time and ensure accuracy, you might want to photocopy those sources that contain a great deal of pertinent information. When retrieving information from a database or a web site, you may be able to transfer the information onto a computer file (or send it to your e-mail box), and then print it out. Once you have the information as it appeared originally, you can then, literally or electronically, cut and paste information onto note cards.

Another important way to document your source is to indicate whether you have summarized (S), paraphrased (P), or directly quoted from (" ") the source. In addition, consider using headings to suggest where you might use the information in your speech (e.g., "Introduction," "First main point") or what function it might serve (e.g., "Anecdote," "Evidence against the status quo").

Finally, make sure you copy all the relevant bibliographic information pertaining to the source of your information, such as the author, title, volume number, date, publisher, and page numbers.

7   **Begin evaluating your evidence and organizing it into an outline.**

After completing your initial search, determine what your strongest, most credible evidence is, and then begin determining what your main points and subpoints will be (see Sections 1.6, 2.2, and 4.1). Omit any evidence that is weak, overly technical, and irrelevant to the overall purpose of your speech. Nevertheless, do not select only that evidence which fits your working thesis statement (see Section 4.3). Rather, change your thesis to fit the evidence you have found.

Next, determine which organizational structure will allow you to arrange your evidence most effectively, and arrange your information accordingly (see Sections 4.1, 4.4, 5.2, 5.4, and 5.6).

Last, as mentioned earlier, realize that when preparing and practicing your speech, you may discover that you need additional material, such as a strong quotation or statistic, to support a point (see Section 1.4). Hence, be prepared to look for more information whenever necessary.

1.5 Electronic Research

Computers are powerful research tools that can provide unparalleled access to information. One of the first research tools you should consider using is your library's electronic catalogue, which lists those sources found in its holdings (see Section 1.4). More than likely, your library also makes available various **databases** that index bibliographic references, abstracts, and full texts of information sources. Your university or library may also provide you with access to the **Internet,** or **World Wide Web,** which contains a variety of sources including everything from free web sites maintained by private individuals or interest groups to commercial sites supported by major media outlets.

Although electronic research can provide quick and easy access to information, be careful: The Internet is still in its infancy and thus does not provide the scope of reliable information found in printed sources. Even full-text articles found in databases often are limited to the most recent dates. Moreover, it can be difficult to assess the reliability of an Internet source. Thus, ask yourself what incentives are in place to ensure that the information you have found is as accurate and truthful a possible. A news organization such as CNN.com is likely to strive to meet the standards of journalistic accountability; however, a private individual or an advocacy group may disregard these standards in pursuit of a personal or institutional agenda (see Section 1.7). It also is easy to be overwhelmed by the vast quantity of information available through electronic sources. The best solution to these problems is to learn good search skills. The research strategy that follows offers a reliable approach to gathering evidence from electronic sources.[7]

1   Use your key terms to conduct electronic searches of both databases and the Internet.

Often, the same terms you use to find printed sources will help you retrieve documents from electronic sources (see Section 1.4). The most helpful key terms for conducting electronic research are the names of authors, publications, organizations, and words that generally relate to your topic.

2   Consider where in the document your key term is most likely to appear, and conduct a field search in that area.

The area of the electronic documents you want to search is called a **field.** Field searches are usually conducted in such areas as a source's author (or sponsor), title (or name), publisher (or server), or subject. However, different electronic research tools, such as a library's electronic catalogue or a search engine, may use different terms and symbols to conduct a search. For instance, you may use "AU= (author's name)" to search for an author in one index, but use "A (author's name)" in another. Hence, you may need to consult the tool's Help file to determine the correct protocol to conduct your field search. In most cases, however, you will want to use the Keyword field because this search covers every part of the documents it indexes.

3   Consider ways to expand or narrow your search by using search operators and techniques.

Most search tools use a common system of operators and techniques that allow you to combine key terms in ways that will either broaden or narrow your search. Listed here are some of the main search operators and techniques that you can use to conduct research in a database or on the Internet.

Search Operators

And.   By combining key terms with "and," you can limit your search to only those records that contain both terms.

> **EXAMPLE:**   *celebrities and paparazzi*

Or.   Placing the search operator "or" between key words allows you to expand your search to all the documents that contain either word.

> **EXAMPLE:**   *militia or white supremacist groups*

And/Or.   By simply using two or more words together without any search operators, you will first retrieve documents containing both words and then those records that contain one or the other word. Because this operator will call up documents that contain only one of the terms, be aware that toward the bottom of the list you may find many records that are unrelated to your subject.

> **EXAMPLE:**   *free agency contracts*

Not.   The operator "not" limits your search to one key word but not another. Use this operator when there may be issues related to your topic that are more commonly addressed but do not relate to your specific interests.

> **EXAMPLE:**   *immigration not illegal*

Search Techniques

Nesting.   If you are unsure which key terms or what combination of key terms you should use, you can combine, or "nest" key terms together using parentheses. This technique will direct your search to information listed under a variety of headings.

> **EXAMPLE:**   *(organic or herbal) and (medicine or therapy)*

Truncation.   If related key terms may appear in slightly different forms, truncate the key term by using its root word followed by an asterisk or question mark. Truncating your key word allows you to find any text that has that part of the word in it. However, avoid truncating your term so narrowly that it calls up a range of terms that are not related to your subject. For example, the truncated key term *comm** would call up *communism, commodity, community,* and *communication.*

> **EXAMPLE:**   *porn** for *pornography* and *pornographic*

Combined Search.   You can combine search operators and techniques to find very specific or general information on your subject. Just remember to follow the rules for each kind of operator and technique you use.

> **EXAMPLE:**   *(manic or depress*) in ti* for *manic depressive, depression,* and so on in the title

4   **Use your library's computer informational systems
     to call up databases with information about your subject.**

Databases are collections of printed texts that include such information as bibliographic citations, abstracts, complete articles from
periodicals and academic journals, television news transcripts, and
government documents. Although most databases you will find in
your university's library should be credible because they have been
through some form of editorial or academic review, this is not always
the case for those databases found on-line. Regardless of where you
find the database, you should check it for its credibility (see Section
1.6). To search a database, use your list of key terms as well as search
operators and techniques.

When conducting a database search, concentrate on gathering information from the most recent and authoritative sources listed. Peruse these sources to find which provide the most valuable information,
refer to the most credible authorities, and offer the most insightful
commentary on your topic. Although many different databases are
available, Lexis-Nexis and First Search are two commonly found in libraries (see Section 1.6).

5   **You can also look for information about your topic by
     searching the Internet.**

Although the Internet contains a seemingly endless amount of information, some subjects are not covered as well as others. In general,
web sites can provide useful information on daily news events, government services, popular culture, political and social movements,
and business activities. Here again, however, you must consider the
web site's credibility because some do not contain the most objective
information or critical analysis on academic subjects such as historical events, art movements, economic trends, and public policy. Newspapers and weekly magazines, government agencies, fan clubs, and
advocacy groups maintain web sites. Many encyclopedias and almanacs also publish web sites that reprint some if not all their printed
text, though you may have to pay a fee to access them. Two standard
ways to access information are through a browser or a search engine.

Using a Browser to Retrieve Information from the Internet.   A
browser is software that provides access to web sites. A **web site** is an
electronic document on the Internet that offers text, graphics, and links
to other web sites (or parts of the same web site) and other forms of
electronic communication. The two most common browsers are
Netscape Communicator and Microsoft Internet Explorer, both of
which can be downloaded for free from the Internet.

A browser uses a search engine to look for web sites on any topic you choose. You can also go directly to a particular site if you know its electronic address, or **URL (Uniform Resource Locator).** There are three main parts to a URL:

protocol	site and domain name	directory path
http://	www.time.com/	opinion

Protocol.   The letters *http* stand for hypertext transfer protocol, which is the standard set of commands used to browse the Internet.

Site and Domain Name.   This part of the URL directs the browser to the server (a computer) where the web site is stored. It contains three main parts, separated by periods: The prefix *www* stands for the World Wide Web, next is the abbreviation for the domain or computer server that stores the web site, and finally a suffix tells you what type of organization maintains the computer server. Some of the most common domain suffixes are *.edu* (educational institution), *.com* (commercial enterprise), *.gov* (government agency), and *.org* (nonprofit organization). Other suffixes may refer to the state, as in *.nv* (Nevada), or the country, as in *.nl* (Netherlands), where the server is located.

Directory Path.   The directory path is the name of the specific directory or subdirectory that stores the computer file or web page you are seeking.

Using a Search Engine to Retrieve Information from the Internet.   A search engine is a free computer program available on the Internet that can access any type of information found on the Internet, including web sites, databases, and chat groups. No single search engine catalogues every site on the Internet; however, each will provide you a list of all the sites it has found.

Most search engines now categorize their listings under such headings as *Finance, Politics, Sports, E-mail,* and *Downloads.* These headings break down into further subheadings that allow you to narrow your search. Search engines also scan all the documents in their holdings for the search term you select. In most cases, search engines are set to perform a keyword search, unless you decide otherwise by changing the search field.

Popular search engines include Alta Vista (http://www.altavista.digital.com), Google (http://www.google.com), Lycos (http://www.lycos.com), and Yahoo (http://www.yahoo.com), but there are many others. Almost every search engine claims to be the fastest and most comprehensive, but they are close enough in capability that you should choose one based on personal experience and trial and error.

6   Two other good sources of information on the Internet are databases and webzines.

There are now databases on the Internet that provide volumes of information from many different media outlets, encyclopedias, statistical abstracts, and government agencies. One of the main on-line databases is Refdesk.com (http://www.refdesk.com), although several other very good databases also index a wide variety of information (see Section 1.6). You should also consider researching some of the many well-established **webzines** published solely on the Internet. One of the best and most credible is *Salon Magazine* (http://www.salon.com), which discusses a range of political, social, and cultural issues.

7   Follow the links you find in an electronic source or document.

Although search tools help narrow your search for information, they do not catalogue every document. Consequently, when you find a good source on the Internet or in a database, pay close attention to the links it provides to other documents. Most of the time you can recognize a link because it is underlined or colored differently, or your mouse arrow will turn into a hand icon when you place your mouse on the link. By following the links from one source to another, you will often discover valuable information you did not expect to find.

8   Create a bookmark to keep track of web sites that you want to revisit.

A **bookmark** will store a web site's URL so that you can return to it more quickly. To create a bookmark, most browsers will use these same commands: Call up the web site, and click on the Bookmark heading in your browser's menu. Then scroll down to Add Bookmark and double click. To return to a bookmark, simply click on the same Bookmark heading, scroll down to the name of the web site, and then click.

9   Be sure to document the address of every web site you use, and cite the web site when giving your speech.

A printout of a web site usually places its URL in the upper right-hand corner of the page. When you are taking notes from a web site, remember to write down its address. When giving your speech, remember to refer to the web site with an oral citation (see Section 6.4).

1.6 Research Sources

The following list provides the names of assorted publications and indexes that contain information on a variety of topics.[8] This list is by no means comprehensive; rather, it offers a sampling of sources written for a general audience and that are generally accepted for academic use. These publications cover many political, economic, social, cultural, scientific, and regional issues from a variety of perspectives. Many of these newspapers, periodicals, encyclopedias, abstracts, and books of quotations also maintain web sites that can be found on the Internet (see Section 1.5). If you would like to obtain more specific information on your topic or you are researching a specialized topic, such as a specific ethnic culture or an area of biochemistry, you may need to consult a specialized encyclopedia or scholarly journal on the subject.

NEWSPAPERS

Atlanta Constitution	*Boston Globe*
Chicago Tribune	*Christian Science Monitor*
Dallas Morning News	*Denver Post*
Los Angeles Times	*Miami Herald*
New York Times	*Philadelphia Inquirer*
Wall Street Journal	*Washington Post*

NEWS AND CURRENT EVENTS PERIODICALS

The American Prospect	*The Atlantic Monthly*
Christianity Today	*Commentary*
Consumer's Guide	*Ebony*
Foreign Affairs	*Foreign Policy*
George	*Harper's*
The Humanist	*Mother Jones*
The Nation	*The National Review*
The New Republic	*Newsweek*
The New Yorker	*The New York Times Review of Books*
Ms.	*Psychology Today*
Rolling Stone	*Sojourners*
Society	*Spin*
Sports Illustrated	*The Weekly Standard*
Time	*US News & World Report*
World Politics	*World Press Review*

ECONOMIC AND BUSINESS PERIODICALS

Business Week	*The Economist*
Forbes	*Fortune*
Inc.	*Money*

SCIENCE, TECHNOLOGY, AND ENVIRONMENTAL PERIODICALS

Database	*Discovery*
National Geographic	*Natural History*
Nature	*Omni*
PC World	*Popular Science*
Scientific American	*Smithsonian*

ENCYCLOPEDIAS

Collier's Encyclopedia	*Encyclopedia Americana*
Encyclopaedia Britannica	*Encyclopedia of American History*
Encyclopedia of World History	

BIOGRAPHIES

Biography Index	*Current Biography*
Dictionary of American Biography	*Dictionary of National Biography*
Who's Who in America	*Who's Who in the World*

ALMANACS

Facts on File	*The Information Please Almanac*
People's Almanac	*The Statesman's Yearbook*
The World Almanac and Book of Facts	

BOOKS OF QUOTATIONS

Bartlett's Familiar Quotations	*Columbia Worldbook of Quotations*
The Oxford Dictionary of Quotations	

DICTIONARIES

The Oxford English Dictionary	*The Oxford Dictionary of English Etymology*
Webster's Dictionary of English Usage	

GOVERNMENT DOCUMENTS AND INDEXES

Congressional Quarterly Almanac

Congressional Quarterly Weekly Report

Congressional Record

Historical Statistics of the United States

Public Papers of the Presidents

Shepard's Acts and Cases by Popular Names

Statistical Abstract of the United States

United States Congressional Serial Set

United States Law Week (index)

United States Supreme Court Decisions

United States Statutes at Large

NEWS AND CURRENT EVENTS DATABASES

CQ Researcher

Dow Jones Interactive

Fact.com

Lexis-Nexis

Newsbank Infoweb

ProQuest

DATABASES OF ACADEMIC AND PROFESSIONAL JOURNALS

EBSCOhost

Expanded Academic ASAP

JSTOR

Project Muse

Wilson Omni File

DATABASES FOR SPECIAL TOPICS

Art Index (Art)

Art and Humanities Citation Index (Arts and Humanities)

Applied Science and Technology (Science and Technology)

Cambridge Scientific Abstracts (General Science)

Dow Jones Interactive (Business and Finance)

Fact Search (Statistical Data)

Medline (Health and Medicine)

MLA (Modern Language Association) (Literature and Film Criticism)

PAIS (Public Affairs Information Service) (Social Science and Public Affairs)

Sociofile (Social Sciences)

NON-SUBSCRIPTION DATABASES

Bartley.com (http://www.bartley.com)

FedWorld.gov (http://www.fedworld.gov)

FrontPage Magazine (http:www.frontpage.com)

Refdesk.com (http://www.refdesk.com)

Newslink (http://www.newslink.org)

1.7 Evaluating Source Credibility

One of the most important factors to consider when determining what evidence you will use in your speech is the credibility of its source. Evaluating credibility requires that you continually maintain a critical perspective toward the material you are reading. The following guidelines provide some preliminary criteria for evaluating the legitimacy of an author and source and the information contained in a document. By exposing a bias, presupposition, or faulty evidence in a source, you will be more able to assess the strengths and weaknesses of a source's claim. Remember, however, that two sources may have a legitimate disagreement about the facts relating to your subject. Thus, you will need to analyze critically the merits of each source's evidence and arguments (see Sections 2.2 and 2.3).

1   Uncover any presuppositions that a source may have about your topic.

Consider whether an author or publication has any biases that prevent it from giving a cogent analysis of your topic. First, determine whether a source has a political agenda that may influence its interpretation of your subject. Second, check whether the author has any personal or political biases that would influence his or her analysis of your topic. At the same time, examine your own belief system to see whether you have any personal inclinations that limit your own understanding of the topic.

Uncovering such biases can be as easy as reading the description that accompanies the author's name, or asking a librarian, instructor, or avid reader in your subject area about a publication's general character. If a group publishes the document, try to find a description of its agenda by researching the group in an association index or encyclopedia. You can also find a general description of many publications and their publishers in William A. Katz and Linda Sternberg Katz's *Magazines for Libraries: For the General Reader and School, Junior College, College University, and Public Libraries.*[9]

Because anyone can post a web site, assessing the credibility of information found on-line is very important. Some web sites may offer a brief description of the individual or association that maintains the site. If there is no such description, check the links it has to other web sites to find information about the author's affiliations and biases. Whether the site provides links to credible or standard sources of information or to sites maintained by biased or disreputable organizations will tell you a good deal about its reliability. At the bottom of its homepage, most sites also list the name or e-mail address of an author or association responsible for a web site. If no e-mail address is given, you often can find one by going to View in your browser's menu and opening up the web sites' Source Information Window. Once you find an e-mail address, send a message asking for more background information about the web site's information and author. You also can assess a web site's credibility by checking its links to other texts. Web sites with links to reliable sources may maintain higher standards for providing accurate and objective information.

2   Check the credibility of a source.

Your evidence should come from the most reliable and authoritative sources. Some sources, such as books, pamphlets, studies, and web sites that are not subject to critical review by authorities in their field, may be biased or unscholarly.[10] Hence, you should not use information from these sources in your speech.

You also should avoid using sources published by institutions having an extreme ideological agenda. You can usually recognize such publications by their bombastic rhetoric, by their prejudicial reporting and analysis, and, in many cases, by the poor quality of their design. Do not be deceived by appearances, however, for the visual appeal of some web sites sometimes obscures weak content. These publications are not usually referenced in scholarly or mainstream periodicals, journals, or books. If a source is never mentioned in other articles and books, you should be a bit suspicious about its credibility.

Finally, because awards and ratings for web sites often consider their graphic design, accessibility, or popularity and not their accuracy, objectivity, and thoroughness, such honors may not be the best sources to gauge a web site's credibility. Two credible publications that review web sites are *Choice* and *Chronicle of Higher Education*. In addition, The Argus Clearinghouse (http://www.clearinghous.net) rates subject guides that index individual web sites for content.

3   Always verify a source's claims by double-checking its facts and by comparing the information and arguments found in different sources.

Determine whether a source has misrepresented facts, omitted evidence, or exaggerated its claims in pursuit of a particular agenda. One way to verify a source's evidence and claims is to compare its facts and interpretations with those presented in other sources. If the facts appear differently in various sources, you may want to mention this discrepancy while relying on the more impartial and authoritative source. For instance, use government data instead of data published from a private, for-profit research facility that may have a particular agenda.

Finally, remember that a single piece of evidence can legitimately be interpreted in various ways. For instance, one authority can claim that the chances of a nuclear meltdown occurring in a power plant are negligible and that the benefits of nuclear power outweigh the risks. Critics of nuclear power, however, might claim that the potential devastation caused by one meltdown would be so great that any chance is unacceptably high. Thus, you must exercise your own judgment when you encounter different interpretations of the same evidence.

4   Although you can interpret evidence in ways other than a source presents it, never distort, falsify, or state evidence out of context.

One of the most common instances of stating evidence out of context is when an article presents both sides of an issue and you characterize one of the arguments as the source's conclusion, when it is actually the opposing argument.

If you believe that the evidence presented in a source leads to a conclusion different from the one given, you should point out the error in its argument and then explain why you interpret the evidence differently. However, you should never intentionally distort, falsify, or omit evidence to fit your objective. Similarly, always check to make sure that your sources have not done the same.

1.8 Principles of Interviewing

Interviews are one of the most fruitful, yet underutilized, sources of information for a speech. When deciding whom to interview, consider whom you have access to that is considered an authority on your topic. For instance, consider interviewing professors, government officials, citizens, businesspersons, artists, and so on in your area who have expertise in your subject. Also talk with individuals who can provide critical information not found in written sources, especially in the case of topics about a local concern or an administrative matter that has few public records. In addition, interview someone who may provide personal testimony that cannot be obtained elsewhere. Although you can conduct a telephone interview with someone not in your area, always try to interview someone local in person. Regardless of where or how you do the interview, follow these guidelines.

1   **Set up the interview by contacting the interviewee and briefly explaining your intent.**

Contact the interviewee and ask permission to conduct the interview. State your purpose and what topics you would like to discuss. Tell the interviewee how much time the interview will take. In general, keep your interview in the range of twenty minutes to one hour. Finally, ask if you can takes notes or tape the interview.

2   **Prepare for the interview by researching your topic and interviewee beforehand.**

To avoid asking needless questions and make yourself professional and competent, research your topic first and read any articles, books, or critical reviews written by or about the interviewee. You may also want to read past interviews he or she has given, or talk with some of the interviewee's colleagues or friends who can provide insight into the interviewee.

3   **Create open-ended questions that will not limit the interviewee's possible responses.**

Do not restrict the interviewee's potential answers by asking simple yes–no or either–or questions, or by forcing him or her to adhere to your terms or definitions. Instead, allow the interviewee to answer your questions in the manner he or she thinks best. Such open-ended questions allow the interviewee to express his or her thoughts and opinions rather than simply confirm your prior beliefs. For instance, instead of asking, "Is it better to invest in stocks or mutual funds?," ask, "What do you think is the best investment strategy for the young investor?" Also, make sure your questions are clear and specific; they should allow the interviewee to recognize easily what is being asked, and they should address one issue at a time.

4   **Create a set of specific questions that cover various aspects of your topic.**

After brainstorming about potential questions, choose the most important ones, and then organize them in a sequence that allows the interviewee to discuss your topic in a logical, step-by-step process. Ask the interviewee to discuss important facts about your topic first, and then turn to his or her ideas and opinions about it. For instance, ask the interviewee to explain how his or her career began, how it progressed, and what he or she will do next. Then ask about the purposes and goals, the advantages and disadvantages, and the strengths and weaknesses of his or her work. Next, turn to more practical concerns, such as the size of the interviewee's budget and staff, the time needed to complete a project or determine its results, and the number of people his or her institution or project will serve or affect. Then ask the interviewee to discuss important but neglected issues, respond to critics, and offer personal comments about his or her own work.

5   Arrive on time for the interview, and be courteous.

As with any other formal meeting, dressing appropriately and conducting yourself appropriately will make a good impression and increase your credibility.

Before starting the interview, introduce yourself and try to establish a friendly rapport with the interviewee. You may want first to congratulate the interviewee on a recent accomplishment or briefly mention a mutual acquaintance or interest.

Then begin the interview by stating your purpose and noting what you plan to cover in the interview. Confirm the time allotted and his or her permission to take notes or tape the interview. Finally, ask the interviewee to make you aware of any comments that he or she would like to keep off the record.

6   Even if you are taping the interview, take notes on any specific quotations that may be important.

If you are not taping the interview, summarize everything that is said, and transcribe any significant quotations. You may not recognize the significance of a comment until sometime after the interview, so keep a record of everything. If you are taping the interview, you should still transcribe specific quotations that you may want to refer to later in the interview.

7   As the interview goes along, adapt your prepared list of questions to the interviewee's comments.

Begin your interview with your prepared list of questions, but then allow the interviewee to establish the direction of the interview, and modify your questions accordingly. For instance,

- If the interviewee's answer can be tied to a question that comes later in your list, then jump to this question.

- If the interviewee wants to discuss an issue that is not on your list, invent a question that will allow him or her to discuss the issue further.

- If the interviewee's answer is unclear or unsatisfactory, ask a second question that focuses attention on the part of the answer that needs clarification.

- If the interviewee starts to talk about an unrelated matter, get him or her back on track by tying the interviewee's remarks to one of your prepared questions or by politely asking if you can move on to your next question.

8   **Encourage the interviewee to elaborate on his or her answers with brief verbal and nonverbal cues.**

Use short interjections, such as "yes" or "I see," and clear nonverbal gestures, such as a puzzled look, to encourage the interviewee to discuss his or her ideas more thoroughly. Also, read the interviewee's nonverbal feedback for clues about where to take the interview. Watch for signs of agreement, enthusiasm, or uneasiness that will help you direct your questions and interpret the interviewee's responses.

9   **Do not be confrontational or ask critical questions until the end of the interview.**

If you are argumentative, the interviewee may not answer questions openly. However, if you would like the interviewee to respond to criticism, or if he or she is dodging a question, you can ask a direct question that will limit the interviewee's potential answer. For instance, ask a question such as, "How do you respond to critics who have said . . . ?"

10   **When ending the interview, summarize the main points that have been covered, and give the interviewee an opportunity to discuss any issue or make any comment that he or she believes is important.**

Before concluding the interview, restate some of the interviewee's most important comments, and ask the interviewee to verify your understanding of the statements made. Then simply ask a closing question like, "Is there anything else that you believe would be important to my speech?" Finally, thank the interviewee for his or her time and ask if you can contact the interviewee again if you need to clarify a response or ask any follow-up questions.

11   **Do not take the interviewee's statements as the absolute truth.**

It is unlikely that the interviewee will recall perfectly all the various facts, names, and dates that he or she discussed, so check his or her statements for accuracy. Remember too that, like most people, the interviewee will have certain inclinations and biases that will shape his or her opinions. Consequently, maintain a critical perspective on your interviewee's comments as you would any other source of information.

2

Evidence and Arguments

2.1	Modes of Proof
2.2	Types of Evidence
2.3	Forms of Argument
2.4	Argument Strategies
2.5	Argument Fallacies

2.1 Modes of Proof

The four modes of proof described in this section represent the main ways that you can use evidence and arguments in a speech. Although proofs are often defined as the logical way you use evidence and structure an argument to prove a claim, proofs also employ evidence to support and clarify a point, build your credibility as a speaker, tie your claim to a widely held social value, or stir your audience's emotions. Thus, regardless of whether your intent is to inform, persuade, or move your audience, these four modes of proof characterize the various strategies for presenting evidence based on logical, ethical, emotional, and normative **appeals.**

Although you can use all four modes of proof in any type of speech, you must determine what types of proofs will best enhance your audience's understanding of your subject or acceptance of your claim. For instance, you may want to present scientific evidence and arguments to show the need for new environmental regulations; however, your audience may be better persuaded by a psychological appeal to the need for human contact when, for example, you are arguing against putting prisoners in solitary confinement for extended periods of time.

You will also need to consider when is the best time to employ a particular type of proof. Typically, ethical proofs that build your credibility as a speaker are first presented in your introduction, and then logical proofs, which must be supported by factual evidence and elaborate forms of reasoning, are given in your speech's body. Your conclusion then consists of both ethical appeals that remind your audience of your credibility, and emotional appeals that are meant to have a lasting effect and move your audience to action (see Section 4.1).[1] However, you should deviate from these guidelines when necessary. For instance, you can establish a strong logical basis for your claim by beginning your speech with statistical data outlining the severity of the problem you are trying to solve (see Section 4.2). You should also recognize that sometimes you could fulfill the aims of two or more modes of proof simultaneously. For example, by telling a personal story of how you were helped by a nonprofit organization, you could both build your credibility and stir your audience's emotions.

In addition to the various types of evidence and arguments, your organization, style, and delivery can function as a mode of proof. A well-ordered speech has tremendous logical appeal, whereas a sympathetic voice can sway your audience's emotions.

The brief explanations given here merely provides a preliminary look at the various ways to construct proofs and make appeals based on the types of evidence outlined in this chapter. You will find many more strategies for constructing proofs throughout this chapter and the rest of the handbook (see Sections 5.1, 5.3, and 5.5).

1   Logical proof.

Appeals based on *logos*, or logical proof, target your audience's need to hear strong evidence and rational arguments relating to your topic.[2] Such proofs help you explicate a topic or verify a claim. Thus, logical proofs such as explicit definitions, thorough explanations, vital statistics, and well-drawn analogies help your audience gain a better sense of your topic's main properties. Logical proofs also consist of arguments that provide evidence from which you draw a conclusion about your topic. In a persuasive speech, you can use evidence to convince your audience either to reinforce or change what they do or how they think about your topic. For instance, by citing how an authority reinterprets your subject based on new research, you can argue that a traditional interpretation is inadequate while providing evidence for a new and better one. Though ceremonial speeches are meant to honor and entertain, they too can be supported by logical appeals. For example, you can present a personal story as clear evidence that the honoree has certain redeeming qualities.

To appeal to your audience's desire for logical clarity, use precise and clear language and carefully organize your speech. Audiences will recognize the logical character of a well-structured deductive or two-sided argument as well as that of a speech closely following the policy speech design (see Sections 2.3 and 5.4).

EXAMPLE

Those who support the present state flag of Georgia claim that the change in 1956 was made to commemorate the one-hundred-year anniversary of the Civil War that was then just five years away. As Tom Opdyke of the *Atlanta Constitution* states, "The more recognizable battle flag was chosen to replace the flag of the Confederacy because it was the flag people associated with the war." However, according to Eric Harrison and Edith Stanley of the *Los Angeles Times,* it is more likely that the General Assembly made the changes to the flag "in the wake of the historic *Brown vs. Topeka Board of Education* school desegregation case." There is strong evidence to support such a claim. For instance, Marvin Griffin, the Governor of Georgia in 1956 said, "Georgia will have separate public schools or no public schools." Griffin, along with ten other Southern governors, signed the "Southern Manifesto," an anti-integration statement in the mid 1950s. Moreover, according to the *Atlanta Journal*'s Mark Sherman, the then House of Representatives leader made this curious comment about the state flag in 1956: "This [flag] will show that we in Georgia intend to uphold what we stood for, will stand for, and will fight for." Consequently, as Numan Brantley, a professor of Georgia history at the University of Georgia argues, "I have never found a reference to the intent of the time, but given the context of the legislation and the atmosphere, there had to be racial implications."[3]

2 Ethical proof.

You can develop your *ethos,* or speaker's credibility, by proving that you are trustworthy, moral, and have good intentions.[4] Establishing each characteristic of your *ethos* demands that you represent your relation to your audience in several ways. To establish your trustworthiness, you will need to show that you have researched and thought critically about your subject. Referring to your research sources, tying your subject to a personal experience, and offering a fair assessment of how others view your subject are just three ways to gain your audience's confidence and respect. Another way to express your strong moral character is to tie your claim to an ethical value that you hold in common with your audience. You also can show moral integrity by speaking with sincere emotions. For example, if you compassionately describe how your proposal for family-leave legislation will allow people to care for their loved ones at a difficult time, your audience may view you and your proposal as humane and sympathetic. Finally, by providing your audience opportunities to weigh evidence on their own, asking them questions, and using humor, you can extend goodwill to your audience and represent yourself as an amiable person.

To develop your credibility, you should show not only that you and your audience share similar moral convictions, but also that you are an ethical speaker. Being an ethical speaker entails that you are truthful and trustworthy. To this extent, you should never attempt to distort evidence, use fallacious reasoning, manipulate your audience's perceptions and emotions, or alter your views just to win an argument or appease their beliefs (see Sections 2.2, 2.3, 2.4, 4.3, and 5.3). Instead, you always should make sure that the way you state your evidence coheres with its presentation in its original source; that you have done your best to produce a logically valid argument; that the emotional response you are trying to elicit is justified; and that you sincerely believe in your claim while making an effort to present evidence and arguments in a way that will incline your audience to view your subject more clearly and favorably. Although you may think that your audience would never be able to disprove the veracity of your evidence or the sincerity of your emotions, you should never underestimate what they already know about your subject, what they may ask about after your speech, and what cues they may observe that suggest your dishonesty.

EXAMPLE

Today, I am going to tell you about my family's relationship with young Abraham Lincoln, starting with my great, great, great, great uncle Jack Armstrong and ending with his son, Duff. I will focus on two stories: the first is a tale of the fistfight my Uncle Jack had with Lincoln, and the second is the story of how Lincoln, the lawyer, defended Duff against the indictment of murder. Although I frequently heard these stories when I was growing up, it was interesting for me to actually verify them when I did research for this speech. Thus, the tale I will weave today not only comes from a long line of Armstrong storytellers but also from Carl Sandburg's *Abraham Lincoln: The Prairie Years and the War Years, Lincoln's New Salem,* by Benjamin Thomas, and *With Malice Towards None,* by Stephen Oates.[5]

3   Emotional proof.

You can also create proofs that stir your audience's emotions through ***pathos***.[6] Whereas logical arguments appeal to your audience's ability to reason, emotional appeals are directed at such psychological impulses as fear, anger, pride, and compassion. Making an emotional appeal can increase your audience's personal involvement with your subject as well as tie positive emotions to your position or negative ones to an opposing position. One of the most effective ways to stir your audience's emotions is to use vivid, passionate language when telling a story, describing a scene, or presenting an example. Impassioned testimony, shocking statistics, and arguments based on your audience's desire for personal security, equal opportunity, and just punishment also can evoke strong emotions.

> **EXAMPLE**
> One school prayer proposal offered by Representative Ernest Istook of Oklahoma is to leave the decision of the type of school prayer to the local community and school board. This may seem appropriate if you are a member of the majority religion in the school district and the school board chooses a daily prayer from that religious belief system. But let's reverse the circumstances. How would you feel if your child went to a school with a predominantly Jewish or Islamic student body? Would you want your child to have to sit quietly every morning while the rest of the students read out loud from the Torah or the Koran?[7]

4   Normative proof.

Normative proofs are based on commonly accepted social values and norms as well as myths and stories on which your audience base their understanding of themselves and society.[8] Such proofs can refer to common social beliefs or guidelines for personal behavior, such as when you explain the enduring relationship of two people who have been separated for a long time by saying, "absence makes the heart grow fonder" or by reminding your audience that "you can't get blood out of a turnip," when arguing why international banking institutions should forgive the national debts owed to them by developing countries. You also can develop such proofs from a classical myth, Biblical story, American folktale, Hollywood movie, or urban legend. The purpose of such proofs is to tie the story's characters and its moral lesson to your subject so that you represent your subject as familiar or morally worthy (or suspect). Consider, for instance, telling the story of a group of recent immigrants who left their homeland with the hope of finding a better life in the United States or how a group of greedy stock investors suffered the same fate as Gordon Gekko did in *Wall Street*.

> **EXAMPLE**
> According to *Legends of the Outer Banks* by Charles Harry, Blackbeard was seven feet tall and wore pigtails in his beard that were tied with red ribbons. When attacking a ship, Blackbeard would light slow-burning matches that were tied to his hat and pigtails. He did this so that the smoke would create a fiery haze around his huge body that would intimidate even the toughest sailors. Needless to say, it worked. For as legend tells us, Blackbeard roamed the Outer Banks for years and took whatever riches he wanted.[9]

2.2 Types of Evidence

Evidence is information that you gather from your research and present to your audience in your speech. Evidence can perform a variety of functions in a speech: It can help you explore your subject's main qualities and characteristics; give you a means to discuss your subject's purpose and significance; it can elucidate your subject's history and its influence on society; and it can provide you with the support needed to make a claim about your subject. Listed in this section are eight of the main types of evidence along with some of their main subtypes. Although every form of evidence has its strengths, they each also have their weaknesses. Thus, as you do your research, you will need to judge the merits of each piece of evidence you gather and determine whether you should use it in your speech. Once this decision is made, you must decide how and when you will use it. By studying the definitions, explanations, and strategies that accompany each type of evidence examined here, you can learn powerful strategies for assessing and presenting evidence (along with effective ways to combine various types of evidence) so that you can learn how to create the most effective speech possible.

1   Explanation.

An explanation is a statement or group of statements that addresses how or why something occurs. It can clarify your subject by analyzing such things as its historical evolution, its main components and their functions, or its primary causes and effects. The length of your explanation will depend on the degree to which you need to explore your subject. You can organize your whole speech around a series of explanations, as in the case of examining the many activities of the brain, or you can simply formulate one specific point, such as a major influence on an author's writing. Either way, your explanation should not just state your point, but should explicate it by offering an analysis of its main characteristics or component parts. For example, when discussing a religious ritual, do not simply state what each step of the ceremony is, but explain how its various symbols, ornaments, and procedures give meaning to the ritual.

Regardless of what you are explaining, always focus on the main issues or parts of your subject, and avoid getting bogged down in discussing minor points or characteristics that may have less importance or take too long to explain. If your explanation is very abstract and complicated, illustrate it with a concrete example, or use an analogy to compare it to something more familiar. You can also clarify a point by stating it in very practical terms. For instance, you could explain how virtual reality allows architects to change a building's design and compute its structural needs more easily than would an actual model.

Three types of explanation are comparison, division, and interpretation.

Comparison. A comparative explanation identifies the similarities and differences between two ideas or objects. Comparative explanations are usually made when you are comparing something new to something old, something unique to something more typical, or two ideas or objects that are not obviously different. Other, more poetic, forms of comparison are metaphors, similes, and analogies (see the following and Section 6.5).[10] When making a comparison, first look at general similarities and differences between two entities, and then focus on comparing and contrasting some of their more specific characteristics. For instance, you could make a general comparison between how Caucasians and African Americans view race relations differently in the United States, and then give more specific comparisons between how each group views the police, the legal system, and the mass media.

> **EXAMPLE**
> In general, both the anorexic's and bulimic's obsession with staying thin results from many of the same social factors; the media's portrayal of Twiggy or the "waif" as the ideal body type, and the pressure exerted by family, friends, and colleagues to maintain a slender appearance. However, their dissimilar eating practices emerge from the different personalities of those suffering from each disorder. While the anorexic is usually a perfectionist who prides herself on controlling her behavior and reaching her goals, the bulimic is more compulsive and outgoing. To this extent, the anorexic maintains strict control over what she eats and, therefore, eats very little, while the bulimic eats compulsively and for immediate pleasure. Thus, while the anorexic's diet consists of foods having very few calories, such as apples, celery, lettuce, coffee, and diet soft drinks, the bulimic is more likely to binge on junk food, like cookies, candy, and potato chips.[11]

Division. An explanation by division is made by breaking down a subject and analyzing its various parts or types.[12] When distinguishing your subject's main parts, explain how each part functions individually and then in combination so that the whole can be understood more fully. If you are exploring various types of the same thing, such as different forms of communication on the Internet, first explain what they have in common, and then make clear the characteristics that make each type unique. You can also reverse the process of division by presenting the different elements of your subject first and then combining or assimilating them into a whole. Consider explaining by division when exploring a complex social issue, a large government agency, or a complicated scientific reaction.

EXAMPLE

For your compost pile to decompose properly and provide nutrients essential to plant life, it must have four ingredients. The first are organic materials containing complex nitrogen and carbon compounds. In the decomposing process, complex compounds will break down and change into simple nitrogen and carbon compounds that help plants grow. Some good sources of complex nitrogen compounds are discarded fruits and vegetables, while dry leaves, corn stalks, and shredded newspapers will provide complex carbon compounds. The second ingredient, microorganisms, does most of the decomposing by breaking down the complex compounds into simple compounds. Microorganisms, such as bacteria, fungi, and worms, can be bought at a garden shop or added by putting already rich soil into the compost pile. To keep your microorganisms alive, your compost pile will need plenty of the last two essential ingredients, water and air. To make sure that you have enough water and air, simply add water and mix your compost pile whenever it is dry.[13]

Interpretation.   An interpretation moves beyond the simple assertion of facts and offers a substantive analysis of the important issues and themes relating to a subject. Thus, when interpreting your subject, do not just state what your subject's main elements are, but tell what they mean, represent, or signify. For instance, do not simply say the symbol of the Tao represents the changing universe, but explain how its use of color, circles, and other design elements exemplify various opposing forces that create our changing universe. Another strategy of interpretation is to first explain each of the passage's main words, clauses, or sentences separately and then combine these parts to explain what the passage means as a whole.

Often, an interpretation compares your explanation of a subject to how others explain it. Usually, this type of interpretation begins by stating the relevant facts and issues associated with the subject. You then offer a critical analysis of other interpretations that you deem inadequate or faulty. (In this way, an interpretation is often considered to be an argument.) Finally, you should give a series of explanations, examples, and arguments that advance your interpretation.

EXAMPLE

One of the arguments used by the Catholic Church to prevent women from becoming ordained priests is that Jesus chose all males as his disciples. However, one has to look no further than the Bible, the Church's own source of authority, to find examples of women acting as disciples.

In John 7:42, Jesus encountered a Samaritan woman who went to draw water from a well where Jesus sat. Christ revealed himself to her as the Son of God, and the woman then went into the city to tell others. According to John, "Many Samaritans from that city believed in him because of the woman's testimony." Clearly, this passage illustrates how the woman acted as a disciple by proclaiming what Christ related to her and by converting others to believe in his word.[14]

2   Definition.

A definition is a statement or group of statements that establishes the meaning of a term or phrase by clarifying the main ideas, objects, or characteristics the term refers to. When creating a definition, clearly state the essential characteristics of the object or idea to which the term refers, and show how these characteristics distinguish it from other similar objects or ideas.[15]

You can create a definition by analyzing a term's linguistic parts, explaining its essential causes and effects, or showing why one meaning of the term is preferable to another. You also can refer to synonyms or give a term's denotative (i.e., standard or literal) meaning and its connotative (i.e., suggestive or indirect) meaning. For instance, the denotative definition of a politician is "someone seeking a position in representative government through the election process," whereas its connotative definition might be "someone who would do anything to gain political power and control over the government's purse strings."

When defining a term, do not rely solely on standard dictionary definitions, which may sound overly simplistic or vague. Rather, consult encyclopedias and discipline-specific dictionaries that offer more elaborate and refined definitions (see Section 1.6). However, as with any type of evidence, avoid using overly technical language when defining the term; instead, simplify your language.

Some of the best times to use a definition are when introducing an uncommon term, correcting the misuse of a term, or distinguishing one term from another. You should also give a brief definition of a term that is not central to your point but is nevertheless unfamiliar to your audience. For example, you might say, "the staccato, or quick and brief, yet powerful, movements of the belly dancer."

Definitions also can provide support for an argument or proposal. For instance, the way you define a fetus and the point at which life begins can have major implications for how your audience views abortion. Likewise, how you define poverty will determine who is qualified to receive certain welfare benefits. The point is that arguments concerning controversial issues often depend on how certain terms are defined. Thus, if you can get your audience to accept your definition, you can build on it throughout the rest of your speech. To this extent, how you define a term can help persuade your audience to accept a claim you are making. You also may want to define a term that is normally viewed negatively in a positive way so that your audience will accept it more readily. Conversely, by defining a law, value, or code of behavior, you can present in a negative light someone who has violated its precepts.

Definitions can be etymological, categorical, or oppositional.

Etymological definition. An etymological definition shows how a term's meaning has developed through time. By examining a term's original meaning, an etymological definition can help you interpret how a term is used correctly as well as differentiate it from other terms that have a similar meaning. Presenting a term's etymology also can help you reclaim a term's lost meaning or relay to your audience the term's continued significance and adaptability to present needs.[16] There are three common ways to define a term etymologically: (1) by analyzing its root, prefix, and suffix; (2) by exploring how its usage differs within various languages, historical periods, geographical locations, or social groups; and (3) by comparing its parts and origins to those of other similar terms. When possible, weave these definitions together so that your audience gains a fuller appreciation of the term's history and meaning.

EXAMPLE

Biases against the left hand appear in many different languages. In French, left is *gauche,* meaning ugly or uncouth. In Anglo-Saxon, left is *lyft,* meaning weak or useless. In Latin, *zona-sinistrata,* is a disaster area. In Russian, *nalyevo,* is a black market operator. The *Random House College Edition Dictionary* even defines left-handed as "clumsy and awkward!"[17]

Categorical definition. A categorical definition explains how a term is either similar to or different from other members of its class or subclass.[18] In other words, a categorical definition distinguishes a term from other terms from which it differs, or associates the term with similar terms. Categorical definitions help your audience recognize the size and scope of your term relative to those of similar terms. In most cases, categorical definitions show how a term embodies characteristics of a larger class; contrast a term to other terms within the same class; or describe the similarities between a term and other members of its subclass.

EXAMPLE

There are two standard terms for describing a vegetarian; *vegan* and *lacto-ovo vegetarian.* Lacto-ovo vegetarians eat no meat products but do eat dairy products such as cheese, milk, and eggs. Vegans do not eat any animal products whatsoever. Most vegetarians are lacto-ovo vegetarians because dairy products provide a rich source of calcium, protein, and other vitamins.[19]

Oppositional definition. An oppositional definition defines a term by indicating what it is not. The actual meaning of the term is not stated directly but is inferred from how it differs from the oppositional definition. Oppositional definitions are commonly used when a term is difficult to define or when you want to contrast a term with another that has a clearly negative connotation.

EXAMPLE

A typical example of a Connecticut Yankee is its former governor Lowell Weicker. Weicker ran for governor as an independent because he realized that the people of Connecticut wanted a governor who was not conservative enough be a Republican but not liberal enough to be a Democrat.[20]

3   Description.

A description is a statement or series of statements that creates a vivid picture of your subject's main characteristics and qualities. When introducing your subject, do not give just its name, but describe its main properties so that your audience gains a clearer understanding of its main attributes. A description also can explore important facts relating to your subject. One strategy for using a description is to combine it with an explanation of the main functions of a subject's various parts. Thus, when giving a speech on tennis, describe how each part of new type of tennis racket is designed and then explain how each of these parts can enhance a player's power or control. You can also combine a description with an analogy. For example, create a series of analogies that illustrate the similarities and differences among the stance, grip, and swing used in tennis, golf, and baseball.

Descriptions can be either pictorial or objective.

Pictorial description. A pictorial description is what you normally give when asked to describe something. A pictorial description creates a mental picture of your subject. When constructing a pictorial definition, try to get your audience to visualize, understand, and experience the object you are describing. Use graphic language to bring out the look, feel, taste, sound, and smell of your subject, and use emotive terms to evoke certain feelings from your audience.[21] In addition, describe elements peculiar to your subject rather than those it has in common with other similar things; emphasize qualities and actions that have immediate and strong effects, rather than those that are inconsequential and develop slowly; and use clear, contrasting terms such as *vibrant* and *dull* or *rigid* and *supple.*

EXAMPLE

Located on the north wing's first floor, the Old Supreme Court Chamber sits next to the Senate wing of the Capitol. The Chamber's classical European design represents enduring, historical values. Its columns, archways, and frescoes reflect the ideals of the European republican tradition, while its deep maroon carpet and royal blue accents fill the room with an aura of respect for our nation's highest court. To represent our uniquely American heritage, the Chamber's crown molding and furniture display more traditional, American symbols like eagles, corn ears, wheat stocks, and even tobacco plants. The Chamber is arranged like most other courts with a bench for the judges, two lawyers' tables, and a jury box. However, one of its most prominent features is the five-feet-high bar that separates the judges from the rest of the proceedings. The only persons who were allowed to cross this bar to confer with the judges were lawyers. Because those aspiring to become lawyers yearned for the opportunity to approach the bench, the successful completion of their legal exams has become known as "passing the bar."[22]

Objective description.   An objective description offers a litany of facts relating to your subject. This description may entail such factual evidence as your subject's size and scope as well as other forms of statistical information. Objective descriptions can present a brief account of your subject's evolution, depict your subject's main qualities, or portray the different characteristics of its main subtypes.

The main difference between a pictorial and an objective description is that the latter attempts to provide an impartial and unbiased description of the concrete facts relating to your subject. Hence, consider using an objective description when you want to rid your audience of any preconceived ideas or emotional attachment to your subject, or when you want to establish your own objectivity. Once your audience has accepted this description as factual, you can then go on to construct an argument or appeal to their emotions.

EXAMPLE

According to the U.S. Justice Department, domestic violence is the leading cause of injury to women, more so than muggings, stranger rapes, and car accidents combined. Although an act of domestic violence occurs every seven seconds in the United States, officials believe that only one-tenth of actual cases are reported. Domestic violence usually follows a similar cycle of abuse. First, there is the "tension building" phase in which small occurrences such as requesting money or not serving a meal to a husband's liking escalate into a series of tension-release episodes. Feeling a sense of responsibility to their marriage and children, the woman usually stays in the relationship and blames herself for the problem. The second phase is the "acute battering incident," which involves a series of actual physical or emotional assaults. Next, the couple moves into the "hearts and flowers" phase, where the batterer feels remorse for his actions and becomes loving to the abused. He promises never to hurt her again, and she believes him, hoping that the situation will change. However, unless the batterer receives help, the cycle often repeats itself with increasing frequency and severity.[23]

4   Statistics.

Statistics are any measurement or set of measurements that explains or describes a subject or its main properties. A statistic can be an aggregate, average, ratio, percentage, correlation, or any other form of quantitative information.

Because statistics represent your subject in very clear and concrete ways, they are considered a strong form of evidence. However, given the vast array of statistical information available, you must determine which statistics provide the most relevant information on your subject. You also need to find the best way to state this information. Three highly effective ways to present statistics include (1) showing the rate at which an entity changes over time; (2) representing an entity's aggregate total and then dividing it into its per capita or individual rate; and (3) comparing statistical data on two entities that are literally or figuratively alike. Thus, when discussing the cost of presidential campaigns, you could first show the increasing amount of money spent on campaigns in the last four elections; second, state how much total money was spent by a candidate in the last election and the average amount spent on each vote; and third, compare the amount of money spent on political television advertisements to the amount spent on laundry soap commercials in the same year.

Use the same statistical measurement when comparing similar things. For instance, when discussing racial prejudice in business, compare the percentage of African American lieutenants and generals in the army to the percentage of those who are vice-presidents and presidents in private corporations. Use different measurements when comparing unlike things. In a speech on teenage pregnancy, for example, you could state the total number of teenage mothers in the United States, the percentage of these mothers who graduate from high school, and finally, their average incomes. Using different measurements allows your audience to identify each measurement easily with its specific point of reference.

Although statistics have their advantages, they also have disadvantages. Statistics may sound objective and scientific, but they can also make you appear cold and impersonal. Moreover, audiences find it difficult to distinguish and remember a large number of statistics. Unless your intent is to achieve a strong effect by overwhelming your audience with statistical data that support your point (rather than having them remember or assess the data critically), limit the number of statistics you present at one time. Also, to increase support for your claim, state what the data mean (i.e., how they should be interpreted) rather than making your audience figure out what the data imply.

Also consider complementing any general statistic with a particular example or narrative. This technique allows you to restate your statistical information in more concrete terms. Sometimes, you may want to get your example from the experiment or survey from which the statistics were collected. If possible, try to supplement your statistics with a true and moving story to balance your analytical proof with an emotional one.

Finally, it may sometimes be necessary to give a simple, nontechnical explanation of how the data were collected. You may also want to use a graph to illustrate complex statistical comparisons (see Section 3.2). In addition, because many people believe that "statistics can prove anything," try to increase the credibility of your statistics by citing a reliable source and by backing your statistics with authoritative testimony (see Section 1.7). Also, always remember to round off large numbers.

Statistics can be either descriptive or inferential.

Descriptive statistics.   Like a description of a person or place, descriptive statistics present a picture of your subject by representing it in quantitative terms. For instance, they provide various measurements that illustrate a subject's (or population's) most significant qualities, such as its size or frequency, or they allow your audience to recognize how something has changed over time. Aggregate amounts, ratios, percentages, and averages are all types of descriptive statistics.

When citing an average, be sure to use the type of average that offers the best description of your subject. The most often cited average is the **mean,** which is found by adding up all the figures and then dividing that number by the number of figures collected. Sometimes the arithmetic mean may be skewed because it includes extremely high and low scores. Thus, it may represent a number that is larger or smaller than the **mode,** or the number that is found most often within a population. The **median** is the number that has one-half of the figures above it and one-half below it. The difference among these types of averages can be very significant. The difference between a mean household income of $42,500 and a median income of $34,000 would be very significant if you were arguing whether most middle-income Americans would be affected by a new tax rate for those making $38,000 and above.

> **EXAMPLE**
> According to *National Wildlife,* the average American uses 749 pounds of paper products a year. By recycling just one ton of paper, which is less than the amount used by three people in a year, we could save 7,000 gallons of water, three cubic yards of landfill space, and seventeen trees.[24]

Inferential statistics.   Inferential statistics provide support that leads to a claim that goes beyond the evidence collected.[25]

Statistics can be used in two ways to infer a claim. The first is a **soft inference.** In this case, you offer a measurement or statistical calculation pertaining to one population as the basis for a claim about another. Here, your claim does not rest on a thoroughly scientific analysis of statistical data. That is, you do not perform an analysis on the statistics themselves, but use the data about one population to infer a claim about another. The most common type of soft inference is a **survey** or **poll** that asks questions about a subject to a sample population from which you draw conclusions about how the whole population will behave in the future or how a similar population will react to similar stimuli.

The second type of statistical inference is a **scientific inference.** This inference entails more scientific methods for analyzing data. Although there are many different methods for collecting and analyzing inferential statistics, two methods are most often cited in mainstream publications and speeches. The first method, a **correlational study,** measures the relationship between two variables. A correlation does not imply a causal relation whereby one variable causes a reaction in another. Rather, a correlation tells you whether two variables are related and the direction of the relationship. For instance, a correlational study can investigate whether a relationship exists between the scores made on the Scholastic Aptitude Test (SAT) and scores on the Intelligence Quotient (IQ). A positive correlation indicates that people with higher SAT scores tend to have higher IQ scores and that the two tests do measure similar intellectual abilities. A negative correlation showing that people with higher SAT scores have lower IQ scores is evidence that the two tests do not measure similar intellectual abilities. A noncorrelation finds that there is no relationship between what people score on these tests and thus calls into question the ability of either test to indicate academic aptitude or intelligence. The second method, the **experimental method,** studies the effect of a variable on one group in comparison to the normal reactions of a control group in which the variable has not been introduced or has been introduced at a different level. A test that studies the effectiveness of a new medicine exemplifies this method.

It is important to remember that because most types of inferential statistics use a sample to represent an overall population, there is always the possibility of a discrepancy between the sample and the population. In cases where this **sampling error,** or **margin of error,** is significant, be sure to acknowledge and account for it.

EXAMPLE

The University of Alabama Medical Center recently did a study of nineteen heart attack victims. Of the nineteen, seven received CPR within five minutes of their attack while the other twelve got no help until the ambulance arrived. Of the seven who received help quickly, only one died and one was left with brain damage, while the other five returned to normal health. Yet of the twelve who did not receive CPR immediately, six died, five were left with brain damage, and only one returned to a normal life. So as you can see, CPR does make a difference.[26]

5   Example.

An example illustrates a particular instance of your subject. Although it offers only one account of your subject, an example can make your subject more clear and vivid.[27] An example can clarify your subject by providing compelling supplementary details to an abstract explanation, complicated definition, or large statistic. A well-described example also allows your audience to visualize your subject more vividly and, through use of impassioned language, may lend your speech strong emotive appeal. To be effective, an example must clearly relate to the point you are making and portray the main characteristics that you are trying to illustrate.

When choosing an example, make sure that it is relatively current and distinct, yet typical enough so that your audience readily associates it with other, more common examples. If you cite an example to illustrate a general point, describe the example in sufficient detail so that your point is clear. For instance, do not simply say that the art, literature, and music of a historical period were influenced by the cultural movements of their time. Rather, cite specific examples of artists' work, and explain how their subject matter represents the values or goals of those movements.

Although an example may be easy to find or create, it may not be effective. Do not use an overly simplistic example that offers little insight into your point or a stereotypical one that relies on a common-sense belief that may be untrue. If a well-known example contradicts your example or refutes your claim, explain why it is unusual or an exception to a general rule.

Finally, make clear how an example functions in your speech; that is, state what type of example it is through such qualifying phrases as "the best example" or "a typical example." The types of examples described in this section are factual examples, hypothetical examples, and case studies.

Three main types of examples are factual examples, hypothetical examples, and case studies.

Factual example.   A factual example illustrates a real person, object, or event. It not only confirms the existence of something but, if described with clear and vivid details, also helps your audience recall or imagine similar instances. Use factual examples to get your audience to empathize with a real person or to allow them to reexperience a real event.

> **EXAMPLE**
> It happened in my ninth-grade algebra class. I sat toward the back of the classroom with the rest of the girls. As I was listening to my teacher's lecture on concave and convex lenses, I suddenly heard my name. "Convex lenses are like what Marilyn Monroe has," he said, "while concave lenses are like what Hayden has." This remark was just one example of the many negative comments my teacher would make to his female students. These statements not only humiliated us, but caused many of my friends to shy away from classroom activities in the hope that similar remarks would be kept to a bare minimum.[28]

Hypothetical example.   A hypothetical example creates an imaginary situation that allows your audience to visualize what might happen under similar circumstances. A hypothetical example does not illustrate something that actually occurred, but rather something that is possible. When using a hypothetical example, make sure it is consistent with the known facts about your subject.

The best time to use a hypothetical example is when a factual example is not available or when you want your audience to focus on the general characteristics of the example rather than the particular people, places, or objects. Thus, by presenting a hypothetical example of how someone could travel through Europe on just thirty dollars a day, you can direct your audience's attention to the way they could travel inexpensively and not on where an individual actually went, where he or she stayed, and what he or she did.

You should always identify a hypothetical example as such. However, if you want the example to appear realistic and have a strong emotional effect on your audience, give the example first and then identify it as fictitious.

EXAMPLE

Take, for instance, a hypothetical welfare recipient in the state of Pennsylvania. On the one hand, if she goes on welfare, she can receive about $4,800 in Aid to Families with Dependent Children (AFDC), $2,700 in food stamps, and $3,000 of Medicaid benefits for a total of $10,500 a year. On the other hand, if she takes a full-time minimum wage job, she would earn approximately $9,500 plus possible overtime and keep one-third of her food stamps. However, it is more than likely that her job will not provide her with the same health care benefits as Medicaid, and she would still have to find day care for her children.[29]

Case study.   A case study is a factual example that illustrates a subject in such a characteristic manner that it is worthy of detailed analysis. Case studies take on different forms depending on their field of inquiry. There are three prominent types of case studies: (1) a research study whose findings establish a body of knowledge or a model for conducting further research on a subject; (2) a prototypical example of a successful (or unsuccessful) program that either has been copied or is deemed worthy (or unworthy) of imitation; and (3) a precedent-setting legal case that provides the basis for further legal rulings.

When discussing a case study, try first to state its subject and intent; second, explain its experimental procedures, programmatic guidelines, or method of interpretation; and third, and most importantly, summarize its main characteristics, findings, and implications.

EXAMPLE

Atlanta's homeless shelter, Cafe458, is one very successful example of how the problems of the homeless can be solved if they are provided a variety of essential services. Upon opening its doors, Cafe458 found that eighty percent of the people they served were addicted to drugs or alcohol. To rectify this problem, they not only instituted a Drug and Alcohol Recovery Program but, in addition, offered participants reading programs, General Educational Degree (GED) courses, and job and housing opportunities. As a result of the Cafe's willingness to address the many needs of the homeless at once, Dr. Harold Braithwaite of Morehouse College found that the Cafe's clientele had an eight percent relapse rate compared with the ninety percent average for government-run addiction programs.[30]

6   Narrative.

A narrative is a story that illustrates a point through the depiction of the story's various parts. It can be real, as in the case of your own personal story, or fictitious, as in a folktale. A narrative can depict anything from the most grandiose event, to an everyday experience. A narrative can tell the story of a battle between monumental forces, a hero's courageous odyssey, the struggles of a small town against a big corporation, or a young person's coming of age.

Narratives serve many different functions. They can represent an abstract value, exemplify a common cultural belief, or simply describe someone's personal experience. Regardless of the events it portrays, a narrative must allow the audience to experience vicariously the events described, empathize with its characters, and recognize the moral implicit in the story.[31]

A narrative does not provide analytical evidence or necessarily lead to a generalization. However, it can be an effective form of evidence if it adheres to the principles of **narrative rationality.** Audiences, having heard many stories, use narrative rationality to judge the merits of your story. There are three main principles of narrative rationality.

First, a narrative must have a **structure.** That is, it must have a beginning that introduces its setting and characters; a middle where its plot unravels, a conflict emerges, or the character's personality or motive is shown through his or her actions; and an end that depicts how conflict is resolved, describes the consequences of the characters' actions, and reveals the moral of the story. Having narrative rationality, however, does not mean that your story must proceed chronologically. Rather, it means only that each part must appear at some point in your speech. You may even want to tell the story out of its chronological order initially to bewilder your audience and then to later surprise them when you weave the story together.

Second, a narrative must be **coherent.** That is, the story's various parts must fit together logically. There should be a clear reason why an event took place in a particular setting, why a character acted the way he or she did, or perhaps, why the conflict depicted was inevitable. Moreover, the story should be as concise as possible. You should leave out of the story that which can be said implicitly, but present those elements of the story, such as the description of a character's action or an event leading up to a conflict that **foreshadow** what will happen in the story. Such foreshadowing gives your audience evidence they will need to know to make sense of your story's development and conclusion.

Third, the narrative must be **consistent** with other stories that your audience has heard and their personal experiences. Unless your intent is to surprise your audience, the story should be plausible and thus similar to other stories they have encountered. That is, the story's characters, plot, moral, and so on should be recognizable from books they have read, movies they have seen, or stories they have heard. This consistency will make the story more believable and, as with other types of normative appeals based on stories or myths, presenting a story consistent with others your audience knows allows them to see their world, their values, and themselves reflected in the narrative (see Section 2.1).

To convey the structure, meaning, and sentiments of the narrative properly, consider how you should use your vocal delivery to tell the story (see Section 7.2). For example, you may want to lower your tone when describing a sinister character, increase your speed when reaching the story's climax, or raise your volume when portraying a character's passionate commitment to a value or cause.

The three main types of narratives are personal narratives, reports, and anecdotes.

Personal narrative.　A personal narrative is a story about an actual experience someone had that is related to your subject or point. A personal narrative should contain an account of the facts that verify what took place, express the sentiments that were brought on by the experience, and explain what insights into your subject were gained as a result of the experience.

A personal narrative can also recount your own experience. For some audience members, describing your own experience increases your credibility; for others, it calls into question your objectivity. One way to eliminate the latter disadvantage is to tell the narrative in the third person until you reach an opportune point in the story, or even later in your speech, to reveal your role.

EXAMPLE
In my sophomore computer class, a girl named Angelita sat down beside me. She had never used a computer before. In fact, she knew very little English. When I asked my classmates who she was, they snickered and told me she was a "migrant kid." By Halloween, Angelita was gone. It was the end of the tomato season in Ohio and time for her family to move on. Two years later as I was sitting in my senior English class, I turned to my right and saw Angelita sitting next to me once again. This time I got to know her a little better. We were in the same group for a class project and I tried to help her through Shakespeare. As I was leaving school one day to attend a special college program, I saw Angelita leaving too. She told me that she too left school early every day because she worked in a canning factory from noon until 11:00 p.m. From there, she said she would go home and do her homework until 2:00 a.m. Then she would wake up at 6:00 a.m. to catch her school bus. I remember thinking, "No wonder she could never stay awake in class!" One day, Angelita took me

home with her. It was like entering a different world. The camp was at the end of a long path in the middle of a cornfield. Four plain army-like barracks lined the path. All I could see were weeds, gravel, old cars, an old barn, and lots of children. The camp was two miles away from my house, yet I had never noticed it before. Most people in my hometown had not seen it either. Most, like me, did not want to see it.[32]

Report.   A report is a story documenting an event or series of events. Like a newspaper article, a report describes concisely who is involved, what happened, where it took place, and why the event occurred. The events reported often are given chronologically so that their temporal progression is clear. As with any narrative, when constructing your chronology, make sure to introduce all the important factors and events affecting the story's conclusion.

Most importantly, a report should give a relatively objective account of a story. Hence, within the report itself, exclude or limit any personal opinion, judgment, or interpretation relating to the facts. Give your opinion only afterwards, along with any other explanations and arguments you would like to make.

EXAMPLE

The controversy over sexually explicit and violent lyrics in rap music first arose in Los Angeles during the summer of 1992. Rapper Ice-T was denounced for his song "Cop Killer," in which the rapper, in an act of revenge against racist cops, takes on the persona of a man who guns down a police officer. Days after the song was released, politicians, police unions, and conservative groups throughout the country pressured Time-Warner, Ice-T's record company, to take the album off the market and terminate the rapper's recording contract. Thus far, Time-Warner has resisted removing Ice-T's record, but pressure continues to mount against the company.[33]

Anecdote.   An anecdote is a short story, amusing observation, or engaging comment that relates to your subject or point. As with most narratives, an anecdote can represent a larger value, principle, or ideal than the point you are making, or it can simply depict a particular incident or offer an observation that relates to your point.

Anecdotes are often used in the introduction or conclusion of a speech to stimulate your audience's interest in your topic, add humor to your speech, or caution your audience against viewing your subject from a single perspective.

EXAMPLE

During the Prime Minister's last visit to Russia, John Major asked Boris Yeltsin to say a word about how things were going in Russia. "Good," the Russian President said. Surprised by the brevity of Yeltsin's answer, Major responded, "Well, could you tell me a little more, maybe say two words about how things are in Russia?" "Not good," Yeltsin replied.[34]

7   Analogy.

An analogy is a comparison made between two objects or ideas so that your audience's previous knowledge of the one provides a basis for understanding the other. Like comparative explanations, metaphors, and similes, the intent of an analogy is to lead your audience to infer that the one idea or object is similar to the other (see Section 6.5).[35]

Analogies work best when based on something that is well known or directly related to your audience. For instance, when discussing inflation, you can compare how the Federal Reserve attempts to set interest rates low enough to prevent inflation but high enough to avoid overspending, to how a doctor tries to prescribe enough medicine to cure a patient but not so much that the patient suffers an overdose. Similarly, you can create an analogy by comparing the national percentage of men who suffer from prostate cancer to the number of men in your audience who, by proportion, would potentially acquire the disease. You could also describe the relative sizes of a star and a planet by comparing them to more familiar objects such as a basketball and golf ball.

An analogy can also be an argument when its intent is to prove that two things are similar and thus will react to an external stimulus in similar ways. For example, you can argue that one midwestern state should enact a welfare-to-work program similar to that in an adjacent state because the states have similar populations, unemployment problems, and economies.

When constructing an analogy, make sure that the two entities have more similarities than differences. Otherwise, someone can refute your analogy by pointing out the significant differences between the two entities or by comparing the object or idea being explained to something with more similar traits. Also, never construct analogies that are overly simplistic, overused, or overdrawn. Avoid comparing political subjects to Nazi atrocities, McCarthyism, or Watergate unless the comparison is absolutely warranted. Such overdrawn comparisons are usually inaccurate and often are perceived as groundless exaggerations.

Finally, when creating an analogy, use terms such as *like, such as,* or *similar to* in order to establish the similarities between the two entities.

Analogies can be either literal or figurative.

Literal analogy.   A literal analogy is a comparison of two or more objects or ideas having overtly similar characteristics. For instance, you can use a literal analogy to compare, say, two cities or two aerobic activities that share common attributes. Most of the time, literal analogies work by either comparing the attributes of a familiar object or idea to those of an unfamiliar one, or by predicting how one entity will act under certain conditions based on how a second, similar entity acted under similar conditions.

When creating a literal analogy, make sure the two ideas or objects are of equal stature and that you are comparing their main characteristics. If they do not share any major attributes, your analogy may be considered weak. If necessary, qualify your analogy by accounting for any dissimilar characteristics. In cases in which you are simply associating some minor, secondary qualities of two ideas or objects, clearly qualify your analogy so that you are not perceived as claiming a stronger similarity between the two.

EXAMPLE

One of the most important advantages of the European Union is the free movement of goods. Under the U.S. Constitution, states are prohibited from placing tariffs on interstate commerce. Thus, goods imported into the United States can be taxed only once at our national borders and not again when they arrive in any particular state. In the same way, the European Community seeks to prohibit individual countries from taxing imported goods as they cross the internal borders of the continent's twelve different nations. Therefore, goods imported into the European Community would be taxed only once at its collective border.[36]

Figurative analogy.   A figurative analogy compares two ideas or objects that have distinctively different, overt characteristics but nevertheless share similar qualities or act in similar ways.

There are two main forms of figurative analogies. In the first form, two common objects or ideas are compared to exemplify some common principle underlying both. Some classic examples of this type of figurative analogy include comparing a political election to a horse race, an athletic event to a military battle, or the stages of life to the four seasons. In the second form, a complex or unfamiliar entity is compared to one found in nature or everyday life. When creating this type of analogy, consider which characteristics of the unfamiliar object can be associated with those of the more common one. An analogy between things that are not commonly compared may offer an original way for the audience to understand your point. For instance, you can compare the way a sculptor must work with his or her material's unique texture and flaws to how a person conducting a small group meeting must be sensitive to each member's special gifts and weaknesses.

Because the basis for comparing two entities with a figurative analogy is more metaphorical than logical, it is usually considered a weaker form of evidence. However, because of the novel way figurative analogies express similarities between unlike things, audiences often find them interesting and appealing.

EXAMPLE

In the opening scene of *Triumph of the Will,* Hitler's plane calmly glides above the clouds over Nuremberg. As Wagner plays in the background, Riefenstahl turns her camera to the medieval streets of Nuremberg. When the plane lands, thousands of Germans are waiting to greet Hilter with open arms. Smiling, Hitler emerges from the plane and is driven through the hordes of devoted Germans to the first Nazi Party convention. The analogy Riefenstahl is making is unmistakable: Hitler, like a god, has descended from the heavens into the holy German city of Nuremberg to lead his people into the promised land of the Third Reich.[37]

8   Testimony.

Testimony is a direct quotation by someone who is either an authority on your subject, a witness whose personal experience provides insight into your subject, or considered a trusted source of social wisdom. Testimony often provides another person's account of your subject; hence, it can take the form of any type of evidence or argument. Moreover, testimonial statements that show that another person's understanding of a subject is similar to your own can build your credibility.

Testimony can be authoritative, lay, or nominal.

Authoritative testimony.   Authoritative testimony is a statement or group of statements given by a credible authority or expert. The best time to use authoritative testimony is when explaining a causal relationship, justifying a value or principle, making a prediction, offering a solution to a problem, advocating a policy proposal, or giving an opinion that goes against another authority or your audience's prior beliefs. Another effective way to use authoritative testimony is when you find an authority who, on most related issues, takes an opposing view but agrees with you on the issue at hand.

When giving authoritative testimony, first provide the expert's credentials with respect to the subject, and then succinctly quote or summarize his or her most important statements. Do not quote the authority at length. Needlessly restating everything that an authority said or wrote makes it appear as if you are relying too heavily on one research source or one person's opinion. Instead, gather information from a variety of sources and use only the authority's strongest statements.

Even though someone is considered an authority, you still must check his or her statements for their accuracy, objectivity, recency, and consistency with other evidence. Also, do not use an authoritative quotation that is simple or trite and does not lend any further insight into your topic. The only exception to this rule is when you want to show that the authority holds the same popular opinion about your subject as your audience does. Moreover, do not mistake a personal experience for authoritative knowledge. To be considered an authority, a person must have credentials relating to the subject. If these credentials are not given, you may want to check his or her educational background, professional training, and affiliations with academic, research, and professional institutions (see Section 1.7).

EXAMPLE

Gun control laws also do not always reduce crime. With over 20,000 gun laws across the country, gun-related crimes are still rising. Gary Kleck, a Florida State University criminologist, studied nineteen different types of gun control laws in U.S. cities with populations of 100,000 or more people and found that "waiting periods have no statistically significant effect on homicides, assaults, robberies, rapes, and suicides." According to Franklin Zimring, a law professor at the University of California-Berkeley, "research . . . shows that many laws do not significantly diminish the number of guns used in violent crimes." A partial weapons ban "will not affect the crime rate. Neither will the Brady Bill," says Northwestern University law professor Daniel Polsby. "Nobody will ever credit this kind of regulation with reducing any lawless or socially destructive behavior. It's pure gesture, pure theater."[38]

Lay testimony. Lay testimony states the opinion, expresses the feelings, or recalls the experience of someone who has some personal relation with a subject. Hence, use lay testimony to reflect someone's personal involvement with or sentiments about a subject.

In cases where an individual expresses how he or she has been positively or negatively affected by the experience, lay testimony can have a strong emotional appeal with your audience. However, the person's ability to offer a firsthand account of your subject does not mean that he or she is an expert in the subject. In fact, the individual may not have studied the subject at all and may have certain positive or negative biases toward your subject that prevent him or her from discussing your subject fairly. Hence do not define these statements as authoritative or use them as a basis for explaining or arguing a point.

EXAMPLE

I would like to conclude with part of a letter sent to Greenpeace from a young girl in Sarajevo. She says, "I am writing to you in the hope that you remember a fourteen-year-old girl, Martina from Sarajevo, who used to write to you about ecological problems that Sarajevo citizens were confronting. I still keep above my bed a Greenpeace poster that gives a warning in seventeen different languages about the extinction of, for me, the most wonderful creature—the dolphin. I also want you to know that Greenpeace has lots of friends here, and there are people who think of the environment and a better future, although we are in the winds of a war."[39]

Nominal testimony.　　Nominal testimony is a general statement made by a well-known person that can be related to your subject.[40] The person providing the testimony may have no expert knowledge of your subject or any direct experience with it. Instead, nominal testimony relies on the "good name" of the person and the general belief that he or she possesses a unique insight into people and the world. Thus, although he is not an authority on art or child development, Einstein's famous quote, "Imagination is more important than knowledge," could be used to justify an increased emphasis on the arts in elementary education.

Since nominal testimony relies on general observations made by famous people, it is not always necessary to cite the specific date or other bibliographic information with an oral citation. In addition, although audiences often have a strong emotional response to statements from famous people, nominal testimony is not a reliable form of evidence for backing specific claims because the source lacks authoritative expertise.

EXAMPLE

"To endure is all." Shakespeare's statement from *King Lear* may sound pessimistic, but he raises an important point. In America today we seem convinced that technological progress and economic growth are unquestionably good things. However, many environmentalists suggest that we should learn how to endure nature and live within our limited resources, rather than try to master and defeat with technologies and programs that try to control nature and use it to our immediate advantage. With this in mind, I want to argue that we should adopt a forestry policy that allows forest fires that do not threaten life and property to burn freely and run their natural course.[41]

2.3 Forms of Argument

An argument is a group of statements that consists of two parts: premises and a conclusion. An argument's **premises** provide evidence that support its conclusion or reasons for believing the claim. The **conclusion** is the claim you are trying to establish with your premises. The difference between an explanation and an argument is that an explanation tries to clarify your subject through elucidating its characteristics or parts, or exploring issues related to it, whereas an argument presents evidence from which a claim about your subject can be logically inferred.

The point of an argument is to present evidence in such a manner that it leads logically to your conclusion. Determining what evidence and argument form to use to prove a conclusion will depend on the subject you are addressing, the claim you are making, and the character of your audience and what appeals, evidence, and arguments they will respond to favorably (see Sections 1.2, 2.1, 2.2, 2.3). Consider, for instance, whether your audience would be more inclined to accept an argument based on concrete facts, lucid explanations, or empirical descriptions relating to your subject; whether they would prefer an argument based on your personal convictions or on authoritative testimony; or whether they want to hear about the moral, political, legal, social, scientific, or aesthetic principle on which your claim is based (see Sections 2.1 and 5.3). In this last instance, you must determine which principle provides the best standard or values for addressing your claim while agreeing with your audience's generally held convictions about how one should approach your subject and similar subjects. For instance, should you appeal to such values as pursuing one's self-interest, gaining material wealth, allowing for individual freedom, following the letter of the law, seeking efficiency, or representing the best elements of humanity such as virtue, courage, and beauty? Or should you appeal to practicing moderation, fulfilling everyone's basic needs, providing security, seeking the social good, adhering to the spirit of the law, producing the highest quality, or depicting the darker or more unconventional character of human psyche or culture (see Sections 5.3 and 5.4)? Finally, you must consider what form of argument will allow you to combine your evidence and appeals to create the strongest argument. Consider whether your general evidence leads to a particular claim, whether a group of particular facts you have presented establishes a general claim, whether a set of causes has your stated effect, whether the sign you describe indicates that something exists or will occur, or whether the facts you have gathered about a case show that a law has been violated.

After choosing your evidence and the form of argument on which you want to build your conclusion, you will need to consider the best way to present your argument. One option is to present your premises before your conclusion. This strategy is often used when your audience is prone to disagree with your claim and thus would be more likely to accept it after hearing your evidence. Presenting your premises first allows your audience to follow the chain of reasoning leading to your conclusion and does not make them immediately suspect your conclusion. Another option is to state your conclusion before your premises. There are three reasons for following this strategy: (1) to reinforce your audience's previous agreement with your claim; (2) to shock your audience with a bold, unsupported conclusion that will entice them to listen carefully for your evidence; and (3) to provide your audience with the proper context for understanding the complicated evidence and logic that leads to your claim. When presenting an argument built on detailed evidence and complex logic, you can choose to present either the premises or conclusion first.

Along with the way you present an argument, the order in which you present your arguments can affect how well your central claim or thesis statement is received (see Section 4.3). You should consider several strategies for organizing arguments. If you have certain arguments that are weaker than others, begin with a strong argument to win your audience over immediately, place your weaker ones next, and then conclude with your strongest arguments so that these arguments will have a long-lasting positive effect. When your audience is unfamiliar with your subject, first offer evidence and arguments that they may have heard before, and then give the lesser known ones. If most of your audience oppose your position, make them more receptive by beginning with arguments based on values, analogies, and authorities they agree with. Next, move to those arguments they may have a hard time accepting, and finish your speech with the strongest arguments. To build a complex argument based on several other arguments, arrange your arguments in a clear, logical order to establish the veracity of two or more statements that you then use as premises for a more advanced claim. Remember to use clear transitional statements to indicate how you are, first, presenting evidence to establish each premise and, second, combining these premises to build your argument and infer your final claim (see Section 4.5).

Finally, because various audience members will find different forms of arguments more or less appealing, you should consider using a variety of arguments in your speech. Presenting different types of arguments allows you to support the weak appeal of one argument with the strong appeal of another. Each of the following forms of argument is distinguished by the type of premises and reasoning process it uses to support a claim. Study the following descriptions to determine which form of argument best suits your evidence and the claim you want to make. Recognize, however, that each form of argument has its strengths and weaknesses, and no one form of argument is considered the absolute best.

1   Deductive arguments.

Deductive arguments are defined in two ways.[42] The first definition is an argument that moves from a general statement to a specific claim. Take, for instance, the argument, "Because all consumers want the best product for the best price, and you are all consumers, all of you want the best product for the best price." This argument tries to establish an inferential relationship between the first premise, which makes a general statement about all consumers, and the second premise, which offers a statement about a particular group of consumers. Because every member represented in the second premise is included in the members of the first premise, the conclusion follows.

The advantage of forming a deductive argument based on this principle is that it requires you to establish a universally accepted principle as a basis for making an inference about something particular. When giving a speech about global warming, for instance, first establish the generally accepted scientific principle about global warming, and then apply the principle to a particular aspect of global warming, whether it be how global warming melts the polar icecaps, damages crops, or entraps pollution in the atmosphere.

A second definition of a deductive argument is an argument in which the conclusion is intended to follow necessarily from the premises. This definition stresses the author's attempt to establish an undeniable claim, rather than the types of premises and conclusion used. In a way, these two definitions are two sides of the same coin. That is, whereas the latter stresses how a necessary inference is made between the premises and conclusion, the former maintains that moving from the general to specific is the clearest way to show a necessary inference.

However, the difference between these two definitions is that, according to the latter, a deductive argument does not always move from a general premise to a specific claim. Take, for instance, the argument "Because all cigarettes contain carcinogens, and all carcinogens are a health risk, all cigarettes are a health risk." This argument contains all universal statements and still is deductive. Hence, regardless of what types of statements you use, if your intent is to show that the premises provide all the evidence needed to prove the conclusion and that your conclusion follows necessarily (i.e., logically from your premises), your argument is deductive.

To this extent, the advantage of using a deductive argument is its intent to present all the necessary evidence so that your conclusion follows without reservation. However, you must always make sure that your deductive argument is **sound**—that is, that its premises are true and its structure is **valid** (i.e., its conclusion is implied necessarily by its premises). For example, the argument "Since all good Americans believe in God, and all of you are good Americans, I can definitively say that all of you believe in God" has a valid logical structure, but its premises are questionable.

Although deductive arguments have their strengths, they also have some weaknesses. First, you must carefully construct your deductive arguments. As shown in the following subsection on hypothetical syllogisms, simple changes in the way you state your premises may change the logical implication you are making and thus render your argument invalid. A second weakness is that certain types of evidence do not lend themselves to being premises in a deductive argument. For instance, statistical data, examples, and predictions support a claim only to a certain degree; thus, you should not attempt to create a deductive argument based on such evidence.

This is not to say that arguments based on empirical evidence are not as good as deductive arguments or that they have no audience appeal. Rather, it implies only that if you want to take advantage of the force of a deductive argument, you must choose suitable evidence. Thus, you should construct deductive arguments from definitions, principles, or values that are generally accepted as true. Also, recognize that just because your argument is deductive does not mean it cannot be refuted. In fact, other speakers can create another valid, deductive argument that leads to a different conclusion.

Finally, to indicate when you are making a deductive inference from your premises, consider using terms such as *necessarily, certainly, absolutely,* and *definitely* to establish the unconditional relationship between your premises and conclusion.

The four types of deductive reasoning are the syllogism, categorical syllogism, disjunctive syllogism, and hypothetical syllogism.

Syllogism.   A syllogism is a deductive argument consisting of two premises and a conclusion, where the conclusion is intended to follow necessarily from the premises. The main strength of a syllogism is that it usually is brief, to the point, and easy to follow. Hence, if you can state your argument in terms of the clear and precise language of a syllogism, your audience is more likely to accept your conclusion. However, one of the syllogism's main weaknesses is that it is often difficult to fit the complex evidence related to some subjects into the syllogism's rigid form. Often, your subject necessitates the use of more detailed and subtle language and reasoning. In this case, you may want to establish the evidence for each of your premises and then summarize or restate that evidence in the simpler, more direct form of premises and then proceed to infer your conclusion.

EXAMPLE

All citizens are given the right of free speech under the Constitution. Some citizens have extreme views about the government. Nevertheless, the Constitution gives these citizens the right to speak out against the government.

Categorical syllogism. Like a syllogism, a categorical syllogism is made up of two premises and a conclusion; however, there are some basic rules for constructing and determining the logical validity of a categorical syllogism.[43] The first rule is that a categorical syllogism's premises and conclusion must be made of (or must be simplified into the form of) a **categorical proposition.** Categorical propositions are either **universal propositions,** such as "All S is P" or "No S is P," that state something definitive about every member of their subject term in relation to their predicate term, or **particular propositions,** such as "Some S is P" or "Some S are not P," that state something definitive about only some members (or at least one member) of the subject term in relation to the predicate term.

The second rule is that categorical syllogisms can be made up of three terms only. No term can appear twice in the same premise or more than twice in both premises. In addition, each term must appear at least twice within the premises and conclusion.

Hence, the third rule is that one of the premises' subject or predicate terms must appear in each of the premises and provide the inferential link between the two premises. This **middle term,** then, does not appear in the conclusion. The conclusion will state the relationship between the two terms remaining from the premises and logically related by the middle term. Thus, for example, when creating an argument defending continued funding for arts in public schools, you might want to construct the following categorical syllogism, which has a valid form, but whose premises must be verified as true if the argument is to be considered sound.

EXAMPLE

All imaginative people are artists.	All Q are P.
All children are imaginative people.	All S are Q.
Therefore, all children are artists.	Therefore, all S are P. (valid)

The fourth rule for categorical syllogisms is that the middle term must be **distributed** in one of its premises. The middle term is distributed only when one of the categorical syllogism's premises says something about all the members of the middle term. To fulfill this requirement, the middle term can be taken from three of the four types of categorical propositions: (1) the subject term of the universal proposition "All S is P" but not its predicate term, because the proposition does not say something definite about all of its members; (2) either the subject or predicate term of the universal proposition "No S is P," because both the subject and predicate terms define all their members in relation to the other term; or (3) the predicate term of the particular proposition "Some S are not P," which says that every member of the predicate is not a member of the subject. Since the particular proposition "Some S is P" distributes neither its subject or predicate term, a categorical syllogism that consists of two "Some S is P" premises will be invalid.

EXAMPLE

Some imaginative people are artists.	Some Q are P.
Some children are imaginative people.	Some S are Q.
Therefore, some children are artists.	Therefore, some S are P. (invalid)

The fifth rule of categorical syllogisms is that a term distributed in the conclusion must be distributed in the premises. This is so because if the premises do not contain information about every member of the term, the conclusion would have no basis for saying something about every member of the term.

EXAMPLE

All artists are imaginative people.	All S are P.
Some imaginative people are children.	Some P are Q.
Therefore, all children are artists.	Therefore, some Q are S. (invalid)

The sixth rule of categorical syllogisms, which deals with the relationship between positive and negative propositions, can be stated in two parts. First, for a syllogism to be valid, at least one of the premises must be a **positive categorical proposition:** "All S is P" or "Some S is P." Second, if the conclusion is a **negative categorical proposition,** such as "No S is P" or "Some S are not P," then one of the premises must be negative. Conversely, if the conclusion is positive, at least one premise must be positive. The reasons behind this rule are that, in the first instance, arguments based on negative premises never provide enough information about the members of its subject or predicate terms to infer anything. In the latter instance, such arguments would be invalid because you can never infer anything negative in a conclusion if your premises present only positive information, and you can never infer something positive if you present only negative information.

EXAMPLE

Some imaginative people are not artists.	Some Q are not P.
Some children are not imaginative people.	Some S are not Q.
Therefore, some children are artists.	Therefore, some S are P. (invalid)

Another way to test the validity of a categorical syllogism is to substitute members (classes, species, etc.) of the animal kingdom for the argument's subject and predicate terms. If you create a syllogism using the same propositional forms that has two true premises and a false conclusion, then you know the form is invalid. Remember that this technique can prove only that a syllogism is invalid.

EXAMPLE

All republicans are pro-lifers.	All reptiles are animals. (True)
No republicans are pro-union.	No reptiles are mammals. (True)
Therefore, no pro-lifers are pro-union.	Therefore, no animals are mammals. (False) (invalid)

Disjunctive syllogism. A disjunctive syllogism contains two premises, one that is an "either X or Y" proposition; the other that is the negation of one of the disjuncts, "X" or "Y"; and a conclusion that affirms the other disjunct. A disjunctive syllogism divides your subject into two possible alternatives and, by negating one of them, allows you to infer the other. Thus, you can use a disjunctive syllogism when your subject allows for only two possible choices. However, beware of creating a false dichotomy that does not recognize that both choices, as well as some other choices, are possible (see Section 2.5).

EXAMPLE

Either we begin enforcing product liability laws so that people can sue corporations for producing faulty merchandise, or we eliminate these laws and run the risk of people being injured or taken advantage of by businesses. Since it is unacceptable to allow businesses to cheat or harm consumers, we should begin enforcing product liability laws.

P or Q.

Not Q.

Therefore, P. (valid)

Hypothetical syllogism. A hypothetical syllogism is a deductive argument that contains a **conditional statement,** an if **(antecedent)** . . .

then **(consequent)** proposition, as one of its premises.[44] The conditional statement establishes a hypothetical relationship between the antecedent and the consequent; hence, it is sometimes called a **conditional syllogism.** The second premise either affirms or denies the antecedent or the consequent. The conclusion then either affirms or denies the other part of the conditional statement not addressed in the second premise.

Stated differently, conditional statements are so named because both the antecedent and consequent express the conditions under which the other exists. Such conditions admit to degrees of interdependence; that is, one condition can precede, indicate, require, influence, be a reason for, or be a correlate to the other condition. The antecedent and consequent of a conditional statement cannot be interchanged unless they are **biconditional**—that is, both must be true for either one to be true. Such is the case for a statement such as "There will be significant health care reform if and only if Democrats take both houses of Congress." This statement proposes that both conditions of having health care reform and having Democrats control Congress must be true for either to be true. However, to say "If the Republicans remove the antiabortion plank from their platform, then they will win the House" is not the same as saying "If the Republicans are to win the House, they must remove their antiabortion plank from their platform." The difference is that with the former statement, the antecedent of removing the antiabortion plank provides one condition (i.e., **sufficient condition**) for winning the House while leaving it possible to win the election by other means, whereas the latter statement holds that the only way (i.e., **necessary condition**) they can win the House is by removing the antiabortion plank. Thus the wording of your premises is very important in a hypothetical syllogism.

There are two basic rules for creating a valid hypothetical syllogism. First, by **affirming the antecedent** of a conditional statement with the second premise, the conclusion can affirm its consequent. The reason this argument is valid is that the second premise, the antecedent, provides all the evidence required to infer the consequent. Thus, although it may be true that other antecedents may bring about the consequent, by affirming the antecedent, you have provided sufficient evidence for the consequent. This form of hypothetical syllogism often is used to state the relationship between a hypothesis and the evidence proving the hypothesis.

EXAMPLE

If people do some type of moderate aerobic exercise for thirty minutes every other day, they will reduce the risk of heart disease.

The individuals we studied performed moderate aerobic exercises for thirty minutes every other day.

Therefore, we found that people who perform moderate exercise for thirty minutes every other day will reduce their risk of heart disease.

If P, then Q.

P.

Therefore, Q. (valid)

On the other hand, by affirming the consequent with the second premise, the antecedent cannot be inferred, because the antecedent may occur because of another antecedent not mentioned in your conditional proposition.

EXAMPLE

If people do some type of moderate aerobic exercise for thirty minutes every other day, they will reduce the risk of heart disease.

The individuals we studied reduced their risk of heart disease.

Therefore, the people we studied performed moderate exercise for thirty minutes every other day. (Invalid because no evidence is given that they performed moderate exercise for thirty minutes a day. It may be the case that the group studied was able to reduce their risk of heart disease by some other means.)

If P, then Q.

Q.

Therefore, P. (invalid)

The second rule of hypothetical syllogisms is that by **denying the consequent** in your second premise, you can deny the antecedent in your conclusion. This argument is valid insofar as anytime you have evidence that your consequent does not exist, you can infer that your antecedent does not exist. Said differently, the argument is valid because your conditional proposition establishes that *if* the antecedent did exist, so too would your consequent. However, your second premise provides evidence that your consequent does not exist; hence, neither does its antecedent.

EXAMPLE

If people do some type of moderate aerobic exercise for thirty minutes every other day, they will reduce the risk of heart disease.

The individuals we studied did not reduce their risk of heart disease.

Therefore, the people we studied did not perform moderate exercise for thirty minutes every other day.

If P, then Q.

Not Q.

Therefore, not P. (valid)

However, you cannot deny your antecedent in the second premise and then infer that your conclusion does not exist. Just because your antecedent is not present does not mean that your consequent cannot exist. Here again, the reason the following inference is invalid is that your consequent can occur as a result of another antecedent not mentioned in your argument.

EXAMPLE

If people do some type of moderate aerobic exercise for thirty minutes every other day, they will reduce the risk of heart disease.

The individuals we studied did not perform some type of moderate aerobic exercise for thirty minutes every other day.

Therefore, the people we studied did not reduce their risk of heart disease. (Invalid because it may be the case that the people studied were able to reduce their risk of heat disease by other means.)

If P, then Q.

Not P.

Therefore, not Q. (Invalid)

2 Inductive arguments.

Like a deductive argument, an inductive argument is defined in two ways.[45] The first definition is that an inductive argument moves from particular instances to a general claim. Here, individual pieces of evidence are gathered that, when combined, allow you to say something general about your subject. Thus, this argument is inductive: "After cigarette prices were raised by a dollar or more, many local stores experienced a significant drop in the number of teenagers trying to buy cigarettes. Hence, it is likely that the increased price is having the positive effect of reducing the amount of teenage smoking." Because the first premise does not account for all stores, it lacks universality. Consequently, it forms the basis of an inductive rather than a deductive argument.

A second definition of an inductive argument is one in which you intend to show that the conclusion *probably* follows from the premises. That is, the premises of an inductive argument do not supply all the necessary evidence to prove the conclusion, but they attempt to provide enough evidence for one to infer a probable conclusion. An inductive argument thus requires a "leap of faith" from the evidence to the conclusion.

Inductive arguments are judged by the weight of the evidence provided in their premises. Those inductive arguments supported by a great deal of evidence are considered **strong,** whereas those without much evidential support are considered **weak.** To indicate that you have provided a good deal of evidence for your conclusion, use terms and phrases such as *probably, it is likely,* and *it is reasonable to conclude* to qualify your conclusion.

The main strength of an inductive argument is that your evidence is usually concrete and empirical, and the reasoning process involved is rather straightforward and commonsensical. However, inductive arguments have several weaknesses: They take more time to develop, they lack the logical rigor of a deductive argument, and their strength may be undermined by other instances not addressed in your argument. Thus, when making an inductive argument, be sure that you account for enough instances to make the argument strong and that you explain the reason why any exceptional instances do not undermine your claim.

In general, arguments based on causality, generalizations, and predictions, as well as those based on statistical data such as a poll or survey, are considered inductive arguments. In all of these cases, such arguments cannot provide all the evidence needed to prove your claim conclusively.

An inductive argument can use either generalization or specification.

Generalization.   With a generalization, one can infer a general claim from either general or specific premises. Generalizations usually provide a series of specific instances that attempt to prove something about a whole group. Such generalizations are often based on a great deal of empirical data.

> **EXAMPLE**
> In the 1980s many of the biggest and most influential Wall Street investment firms were fined for illegal trading practices. Therefore, many other investment firms also probably participated in these illegal practices.

Specification.   With this type of inductive argument, one can infer a specific claim from either a general statement, a particular instance, or series of particular instances. Such arguments are effective because the claim being made is about a specific entity rather than a large group. Therefore, you are not making a general claim, but rather a specific claim based on evidence from other specific instances or from some general information. An effective technique of specification is to give a list of specific examples (usually three) as your premises that lead to an assertion about a similar thing.[46] To strengthen the association between your premises and conclusion, give a detailed description of the similarities between each of the things discussed in your premises and your conclusion.

EXAMPLE

After America wins a war, it often elects the military leader who commanded its troops to its presidency to help stabilize the country in its post-war period. After the Revolutionary War, George Washington, general and commander-in-chief of the Continental Army, was elected as the nation's first president. Then, after the Civil War, Ulysses Grant, general of the Union forces, was elected president of the reunited country. Similarly, after World War II, Americans voted for Dwight Eisenhower, supreme commander of the Allied forces. Hence, if either Colin Powell, chairman of the Joint Chiefs of Staff during the Persian Gulf War, or Norman Schwarzkopf, commander-in-chief of Operation Desert Storm, wanted to become president, either military leader would have had an excellent opportunity to win the 1996 presidential election.

3 Enthymeme.

An enthymeme is an argument that leaves a premise or its conclusion unstated.[47] The missing premise or conclusion is often a generally held fact, definition, value, or belief that is left implicit because it is unnecessary to state what your audience already knows or presumes is true. Such is the case for the following argument because it does not define civil unions as the marriage of two people of the same sex: "State laws that do not recognize civil unions are unconstitutional because they do not allow homosexuals to pursue right to life and liberty as provided for them by Article Fourteen of the U.S. Constitution."

An enthymeme can be either a deductive or inductive argument. In fact, an enthymeme can take any form of argument listed in this section. Many times, an enthymeme is an abbreviated syllogism that omits one of its premises, an argument from a sign that does not explain how the sign represents its referent, an argument that claims that an example is member of a larger group without clearly stating which of the example's characteristics are shared by group's members, or an argument based on a probability that does not provide a description of the probable relation or correlation. Here again, such statements should be omitted only when they are readily apparent to your audience, as in the claim "The results of the 2000 presidential election in Florida are a clear sign that your vote does matter!"

Because the enthymeme is a concise form of argument, it has the advantage of being brief and direct. Additionally, insofar as an enthymeme asks your audience to provide the missing premise or conclusion of your argument, it allows your audience to participate in creating your argument and inferring your conclusion. In this manner, it builds your credibility by offering them the opportunity to help formulate your argument. An enthymeme also may increase your credibility because it implicitly asserts a value that your audience already holds.

However, an enthymeme that attempts to conceal a faulty premise may cause you to lose credibility. For instance, to say, "It would be unwise to elect a woman as president because a president has to conduct war and negotiate with foreign leaders," implies the stereotype that "Women, by their nature, are less aggressive and forthright than men." Another disadvantage of an enthymeme is that you cannot always count on your audience to accurately provide the missing premise. Consequently, you always should provide sufficient evidence for your argument so that your audience infers what you are trying to imply.

> **EXAMPLE**
> Because Congress has to approve any campaign reform bill and because there is an election this fall, it is highly unlikely that a campaign reform bill that will substantially limit contributions from lobbyists and political action committees will become law at any time in the near future.
>
> (Suppressed premise: Members of congress who benefit from campaign contributions will not vote for a bill that would limit the funds available to their reelection campaigns.)

4   Causal arguments.

Causal arguments make a claim about a cause-and-effect relationship between two objects, variables, or processes. In a causal argument, you can argue from cause to effect or from effect to cause. In general, a causal argument is considered a type of inductive argument because causality can never be proven absolutely. This is true regardless of whether your argument deals with a scientific, psychological, social, or any other type of causal relationship.

Because so many factors can contribute to a causal relationship, you need to offer a good deal of strong evidence to verify your causal link. For instance, you may want to explain why two or three possible causes do not produce an effect, and then show why a fourth cause is responsible for it.

There are several other ways to strengthen causal arguments. First, briefly refer to any minor causes and effects before explaining the most important causes. Second, begin your explanation of the causal chain with its first primary cause. Third, do not confuse a cause-and-effect relationship with a correlation. Remember that a correlation shows a correspondence between the growth or decline of two things, but it does not prove that one thing actually caused the other to increase or decrease in size. Likewise, make sure that the cause and effect are not merely related temporally, but that the cause does actually produce the effect. Fourth, determine whether other causes could produce the same effect or whether the causes you cite can also produce a different effect. For instance, although legalizing marijuana may cause the crime associated with marijuana to decrease, it may not cause an overall decrease in crime. Rather, marijuana dealers may just begin to traffic in other illegal drugs.

Finally, determine whether the alleged causes and effects increase or decrease in proportion to one another. If they do not, another factor may play an equal or even more significant role within the causal relationship. For example, if you are trying to establish a causal relationship between violence and the media, you may want to investigate whether there is the same relationship between violence and the media in foreign countries that show the same television shows and films. If there is no evidence of such a relationship in these foreign countries, consider whether there is another factor, such as the number of handguns or the decline of family values, that, either separate from or in combination with the media, causes violence in the United States.

EXAMPLE

According to a study by literacy expert B. A. Quigley, minority students tend to drop out of literacy programs for two reasons: They either find the content of the program irrelevant to their lives, or the values of the reading material are in conflict with their own. For instance, Native Americans often find their tribal values in conflict with literary materials that reflect western definitions of success. This may explain why the illiteracy and drop-out rates of Native Americans are higher than the national average. Consequently, multicultural approaches to education are not just attempts at political correctness; rather, they are a valid attempt to correlate literary education to the real experiences of minority students.[48]

5   **Argument from signs.**

An argument from signs is one in which the existence or occurrence of one entity is taken as a sign that another entity also exists or will occur. Such arguments often are based on repeated experiences, common patterns of behavior, and other visible indicators. For example, repeated observations of an individual's unwillingness to go swimming can be a sign of an earlier traumatic experience with water. When the description of the sign is not necessary to include because it is readily apparent to your audience, you may consider leaving this statement of description out of your argument as you would in an enthymeme.[49] Such is the case for the argument, "With no signs that the heat will diminish, coupled with only the exceptional cloud sighting, it is now time for southern California to begin drastic measures to conserve energy and water." Here, it is assumed that constant high temperatures and lack of clouds are signs of continued high temperatures and lack of rain, which may cause increased demand for electricity and water.

Arguments from signs also can show how a sign symbolically represents something. For instance, increased sales of trinkets portraying angels can be a sign of people's renewed desire to find spiritual meaning in their lives. Such arguments, along with arguments from anecdotal observations or prophetic statements, are often based on personal conjecture, little experience, or mystical revelations and thus have limited logical appeal, although they may have strong normative or rhetorical appeal (see Section 2.1).

When creating an argument from a sign, find a variety of signs that point to your claim. For instance, a person may exhibit a variety of signs indicating that he or she is contemplating suicide, such as suddenly becoming euphoric after being depressed, giving away private possessions, and insisting on having a gathering of close friends. You should also analyze whether a sign functions in the same way in similar objects or activities. For example, failure to meet obligations, a drop in job performance, and symptoms of withdrawal are all signs of being addicted to either alcohol or another chemical substance such as cocaine. Thus, base your argument on signs that clearly and consistently indicate the claim you are inferring.

Finally, do not overstate your case by implying that a sign *causes* an object or relationship to exist. Remember, a sign can imply the existence of an object, act, or relationship, but a sign does not directly influence or cause the entity it represents. Possible exceptions to this, however, are when you can show how an economic index has directly affected people's purchasing habits or how a political poll has influenced people's voting.

EXAMPLE

If you suspect that a woman is a victim of domestic violence, you should look for some common signs of physical and mental abuse. In most cases, these victims will have very low self-esteem, they will continually make excuses for their abusers' behavior, and they will avoid any social contact with friends and family members in order to hide the bruises sustained from being hit.[50]

6 Two-sided arguments.

A two-sided argument presents arguments on both sides of an issue.[51] Because two-sided arguments can incorporate any form of argument, they sometimes are considered as a strategy for organizing arguments in your speech rather than as a form of argument.

Whereas in most cases you research both sides of an issue but use only those arguments that support your position, a two-sided argument allows you to present both sets of arguments. You should use a two-sided argument when your audience holds an opposing view or when they are familiar with an opposing one. In either case, failure to address the counterargument may appear as an attempt to avoid it.

The advantage of a two-sided argument is that it allows you to present each argument's strengths and weaknesses. By approaching each side in a fair and balanced way and conceding some of the opposing argument's basic principles or facts, you can increase your trustworthiness.

When using a two-sided argument, do not simply refute the weaker, opposing arguments. Focusing on weak arguments may reduce your credibility as a speaker, particularly if your audience is already familiar with a stronger one. Rather, try to refute the strongest opposing arguments so that your audience has no alternative but to accept your claim.

One of the clearest ways to construct a two-sided argument is first to state the opposing argument; second, refute it; and third, offer the supporting evidence and claim for your argument. Another effective way to build a two-sided argument is to indicate how an opposing argument can be turned against itself and used in support of your position. For instance, an argument claiming that a flat tax would reduce the need for tax lawyers can be turned around to show how this tax would increase attorneys' roles in finding ways to shelter people's money in corporate stock options and retirement plans. This method shows that your arguments provide a deeper insight into your subject than do the opposing arguments. If the two sets of arguments do not relate directly to each other, simply state the opposing arguments first and your arguments second, and then explain why your arguments as a whole outweigh the opposing ones.

Finally, recognize that when you present two-sided arguments, your audience may have a difficult time determining which arguments you are advocating. This is especially true when your initial intent is to appear neutral. Thus, remember to use clear transitional statements when moving from an opposing argument to one you are advocating (see Section 4.5).

EXAMPLE

Proponents of the North American Free Trade Agreement (NAFTA) claim that the new trading bloc will significantly increase U.S. exports to Mexico. They argue that if trade barriers are lowered, Americans will buy more Mexican goods. This, supposedly, will cause more Mexican workers to have jobs as well as money to spend on American goods.

American producers will then hire more American workers to produce goods for export to Mexico.

Yet critics of the agreement raise some very important issues. One main area of contention, states the *Christian Science Monitor,* is Mexican wages. Critics argue that with the average Mexican worker making somewhere between one to two dollars an hour, NAFTA provides U.S. firms with an irresistible incentive to relocate their production facilities south of the border. Consequently, many critics believe that Mexico should be required to institute a minimum wage comparable to that of the United States to discourage a substantial loss of American jobs. A second issue involves Mexican labor standards. Critics of NAFTA fear that American firms may move to Mexico to avoid laws that, in the U.S., protect the safety and health of workers. Abiding by strict labor laws costs U.S. companies money, an expense these firms would not have to pay in Mexico, where companies can legally employ child labor. A third criticism involves NAFTA's lack of environmental regulations. Here too there is great potential that American firms will move south to take advantage of weak regulations. The Maquiladora sectors along the Texas–Mexico border already are a testament to the environmental destruction caused by American companies that have dumped chemicals into uncovered ditches and rivers. Robert Benson, professor of international environmental law at Loyola Law School, estimates that even a partial cleanup of the environmental damage already done could be as high as fifty billion dollars, about the same amount of money that NAFTA proponents tout would be gained by NAFTA's increase of exports.[52]

7 Legal arguments.

A legal argument deals with some form of legal reasoning or interpretation of the law. There are two ways to construct a legal argument. First, a legal principle or right can serve as a norm or standard for dealing with something that is not an issue before a court. For instance, when discussing how to maintain a healthy marriage, you can refer to the legal principle that an individual is "innocent until proven guilty" and thus, marriage partners should presume their spouses' innocence before accusing them of infidelity and then allow their spouses to address the accusation. Similarly, you can argue that, as in a legal court, your university's disciplinary council should have the "burden of proof" to show that a student has violated the university's policy of academic dishonesty rather than mandating that the student prove his or her innocence. The problem with this mode of argument is that your audience may be reluctant to accept a legal argument as a basis for a nonlegal issue.

The second and most often used type of legal argument applies to court proceedings. In this instance, either you can make arguments about a case that is coming to trial and give evidence as to how you believe it should be judged, or you can address a case that a court has already considered and assess the merits and problems of its ruling.

To inform yourself better about what evidence you will need to find on legal issues relating to the case, consider outlining your argument according to the doctrines of *stasis* and *loci*.[53] Together, finding the *stasis* and *loci* of the case will help you examine the relevant questions, issues, evidence, and arguments related to that case. *Stasis* identifies where you want to "take a stand" on the legal issue you are arguing. To begin, you will need to consider whether you want to argue that the alleged facts relating to the legal case are actually true. You then move to consider that if the facts are true, can you argue that they actually violate the law? Next, you should try to determine whether there are other laws that should be considered, extenuating circumstances that would show that the defendant's actions were warranted, or whether the punishment fits the crime. Where you take your stand on the legal case will depend on where you find your strongest evidence for or against the issues relating to the relevant facts, laws, and circumstances surrounding the case.

Loci provides you ways "to locate" the evidence and arguments that you will use to support the arguments on which you will take your stand on the case. Although you may have some sense of which evidence and arguments you will use, you still should collect as much evidence as possible pertaining to all the possible arguments you could make pertaining to your case. Start by finding evidence on the events and actions under investigation. Gather facts as to whether the action actually occurred, who engaged in the action, and what events led to the action. Also, consider whether the evidence comes from reliable sources, whether there is conflicting evidence, and whether there are different interpretations of the facts related to the case. If it is a criminal case, collect evidence that will show that the accused actions were intentional, impulsive, or based on extenuating circumstances and whether he or she had the means to engage in the action. You even may want to consider the reliability of the witnesses and evidence. Next, gather information and arguments regarding the applicability of the law to the case. Study the definition of the law and determine if the accused's actions actually violate the law. Then determine whether there are ambiguities in the law that can be exploited, or whether the accused was acting under the belief that his or her actions were protected by other laws that supercede the law he or she is accused of violating. Also, collect evidence on how other similar cases were judged with respect to the law under consideration. If a ruling has been made on the case you are arguing, find out whether legal scholars considered the ruling or sentence fair and whether the ruling sets a legitimate precedent for future cases. Finally, try to determine the amount of harm done by the accused and whether the punishment fits the crime.

To find information on a legal case or issue, use the name of a case, plaintiff, or defendant or a key word relating to the legal issue to search the applicable indexes. If it is a recent case, go to *U.S. Law Week;* if it is a Supreme Court case, go to *United States Supreme Court Decisions.* Knowing the case citation also will allow you to search the database Lexis-Nexis, which provides the most comprehensive pool of information on court cases and legal opinions. To help determine the issues related to the evidence, law, and ruling related to the case, examine the opposing arguments of the defendant and prosecutor (or plaintiff) as well as the judge's opinion. In the case of the Supreme Court, read the reasoning of the majority and dissenting opinions. You also should study any outside analyses of these opinions that you can find. When assessing these opinions, realize that the issue or ruling may have changed over time and may not hold the same significance as the original ruling. If this is true, the analyses should contain references to other cases that have affected the evolution of the original ruling. If necessary, study and incorporate the analyses of these cases into your argument.

Once you analyze all this information, you will need to take a position on the case. Remember that you are not limited to agreeing with the ruling or the majority opinion. Rather, you can agree with parts of the ruling, side with the minority opinion, or create your own interpretation of the ruling.

Legal arguments have several important advantages and disadvantages. Using legal arguments can indicate your understanding of the law, your ability to apply legal doctrines to specific issues, and, in some cases, your willingness to think independently. The disadvantages are that they can take a great deal of time to construct and that discussions of legal issues can become mired in legal jargon. Consequently, try to find ways to express your arguments both concisely and clearly.

EXAMPLE

The 1969 case of *Tinker vs. Des Moines Independent Community School District* does not appear to provide a legal basis for finding that mandatory school uniforms is unconstitutional. In this case, students who wore black armbands to protest the Vietnam War were suspended because they violated the school dress code. The federal district court judge upheld the suspension, arguing that the school's interest in maintaining an environment conducive to learning outweighs the student's right to free speech. However, the Supreme Court overturned this ruling, arguing that students do not fall outside the bounds of the Constitution once they enter a school building. They are afforded the same rights of free speech as adults, and schools are not permitted to single out controversial topics and prohibit discourse on them. What is most relevant about this decision with respect to the issue of school uniforms, however, is that the majority opinion specifically states that this was an attempt to ban a specific speech act and that the Court found no evidence that suggested that wearing armbands disrupted the school's goal of providing an environment conducive for learning. Hence, insofar as a school uniform policy mandates that uniforms must be worn by all students, it does not selectively restrict any one student's or group of students' right to free speech.[54]

8   Toulmin's model of argument.

Toulmin's model of argument delineates what he understands as the main components that are present or implicit in every argument, regardless of the type of argument or its subject matter.[55] To this extent, it represents a universal, general, or metatheoretical model of all the possible types of arguments, including those described in this section. When constructing an argument, consider how you can use these various components to build a strong argument. Also, consider which components you must state clearly and which you can leave implicit. Toulmin's model of argument has six main components (see Figure 2.1):

Grounds.   Grounds are the evidence presented in support of a claim. Grounds consist of all the various types of evidence given in Chapter 2, such as explanations, descriptions, statistics, examples, analogies, and testimony. Each piece of evidence used as grounds is weighed according to its own merits as well as its relationship to your argument's warrant and claim.

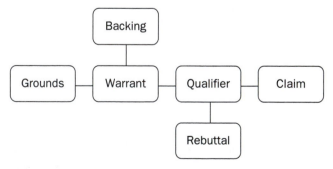

FIGURE 2.1   *The Six Main Components of Toulmin's Model of Argument*

Warrant.   A warrant is the stated or implied principle or value that establishes the inferential relationship between the grounds and the claim. In other words, the warrant provides the basis for drawing the conclusion from the evidence. Warrants can be rules of formal logic, the laws of science, or, as in legal arguments, the statutes on which a legal ruling is based. They can also be social norms, moral values, political ideals, commonsense beliefs, analogies, authoritative appeals, and signs. In this sense, warrants can have logical, moral, or normative appeal. Moreover, an argument can have more than one warrant. For instance, a deductive argument can have both a moral and logical principle as its warrants.

When constructing an argument, determine whether you have strong evidence, such as authoritative testimony or opinion polls, that supports the warrant; whether you are using the strongest warrant to support your claim; whether the value or principle stated as your warrant is in conflict with other values or principles; and whether you can show that supporting a different warrant would have negative results. When two possible warrants may relate to your argument, consider which warrant is more significant or holds a higher position within your audience's hierarchy of values. In some arguments, you may have to consider which of these is the stronger warrant: Following the majority will or protecting minority rights; fostering individual freedoms or achieving social equality; adopting the most efficient means to an end or following a moral means; and producing the greatest quantity or the best quality product. Similarly, determine whether your warrant can be applied consistently to ideas or entities similar to your subject. For example, if your warrant states that single-sex classes provide a more nurturing environment for young women, consider whether we should also have separate classes for African American boys for a similar reason.

Backing.   Backing is the information acquired from history, science, or an everyday experience. Your argument's backing provides evidence from past case studies, legal rulings, policies, research, experiments, and experiences that justifies your warrant. By providing additional support for your warrant, backing strengthens the warrant's ability to tie your grounds to your claim.

Rebuttal.   A rebuttal is a statement or group of statements that places limitations on your claim. In general, a rebuttal anticipates any objections to your claim. The rebuttal allows you to acknowledge those instances or circumstances under which your claim may not hold, and it gives you the opportunity to address any potential criticisms against your claim. When constructing your rebuttal, be sure to account for those grounds, circumstances, and alternative warrants that may undermine your argument. Refer to these limitations by using a phrase such as *on the condition that, the only caveat is,* or *except in the case of.* Although it is wise to present a rebuttal to your argument, be sure to explain how these instances or circumstances may weaken your argument but do not refute its fundamental claim.

Qualifier.   A qualifier is a statement or phrase that represents the degree of certainty attached to a claim. A qualifier indicates the relationship among your evidence, warrant, backing, and claim. When determining which qualifier to use, consider the strength of your argument's components and reasoning.

Qualify your claim unconditionally only if your argument is irrefutable. If not, use a conditional qualifier that suggests the degree to which rejoinders or exceptions can be put forth against your argument. For an unconditional claim, such as those made in a deductive argument, use qualifiers such as *necessarily, certainly,* and *definitely;* and for conditional claims, such as those made in an inductive argument, use qualifiers such as *presumably, it is very likely that,* and *in all probability.*

Claim.   A claim is the conclusion of your argument that you want your audience to accept. In other words, your claim is what you are trying to prove in your argument based on the support your grounds, warrant, and backing offer for the claim. Whether your grounds, warrant, and so on lead your audience to infer your claim, or whether they more generally incline your audience to agree with your claim, getting your audience to agree with your claim is the goal of an argument. Although your claim can assert an explanation, definition, opinion, or theory, in general, a claim usually is classified as either a factual, valuative, or policy claim.

A **factual claim** asserts that something did, does, or will exist. Grounds for a factual claim usually consist of forms of empirical evidence (such as statistics or examples) and testimony that are either observable or verifiable. When making a factual claim, make sure that your grounds are sufficient, accurate, and typical. Factual claims are the basis of the persuasive speech of fact (see Section 5.4).

A **valuative claim** asserts a value or shows how a value relates to a specific issue. Among other types of judgments, it can state that an action, belief, or principle is either right or wrong, good or bad, or just or unjust. When making a valuative claim, make sure that your grounds sufficiently support your claim, your warrant is clearly defined, and your grounds and warrant lead to your claim rather than to another value. Also, make clear that your claim results in good consequences and that rejecting your claim would result in negative consequences. Establishing a valuative claim is fundamental to the persuasive speech of value (see Section 5.4).

A **policy claim** asserts that a particular policy will rectify a problem or will perform a task better than the present policy or an alternative one. A policy claim must have strong evidential support showing what the problem is, why the present policy is inadequate, how your policy can work, and what additional benefits your policy offers. It also must be linked to a warrant that indicates why your policy is effective, good, or just. When making a policy claim, do not overstate the potential results of your policy. Qualify your claim correctly, and use a rebuttal to indicate under what circumstances your policy would not achieve its intended results. The description of the policy speech offers further suggestions on how to substantiate a policy claim (see Section 5.4).

EXAMPLE

The general record of the Vietnam War and our engagement in Somalia offers us some good advice about entering into wars of foreign countries [*backing*]. If a war in a foreign country is a civil war with little bearing on our interests and our engagement adversely affects our situation at home, we should not intervene [*warrant*]. The Bosnian War is a civil war. Its outcome will have minor economic effects on the United States. Moreover, our intervention may be for an extended period of time, and many troops may die there. As the body bags begin to pile up, many citizens will demand that we withdraw while others will insist that we stay the course [*grounds*]. Consequently, [*qualifier*] unless the North Atlantic Treaty Organization (NATO) or the United Nations affirms a resolution calling for a multinational military force to intervene in Bosnia [*rebuttal*], the United States should not enter the Bosnian War on its own [*claim*].[56]

2.4 Argument Strategies

Listed in this section are a variety of argument strategies that you can use to establish a claim. Many of these strategies were formerly called either *topoi* (Greek) or *loci* (Latin) and were defined as the topics or locations of potential arguments related to your claim.[57] In many instances, what were once considered argument strategies are now generally referred to as a form of evidence or argument (see Sections 2.2 and 2.3).

There are also many specific *topoi* or argument strategies that originate in classical rhetoric or have been developed since that time and are used commonly but not listed here. For instance, arguments that praise those who came before us because they thought and acted more virtuously than we do, or arguments that look to a better world in the future because of scientific advancements are common argument strategies. Likewise, arguments that appeal to the audience's commonsense understanding of a subject, that appeal to individuals to sacrifice for the greater good of the society, or that indict another speaker for manipulating the audience in order to please them are longstanding argument strategies. The list of potential argument strategies that relate to specific claims is endless.

Most of the strategies listed here have a general format that you can use to argue a variety of subjects. Many of these strategies provide techniques for constructing arguments based on generally accepted moral values, commonsense beliefs, and logical principles. Thus, arguments based on these strategies have the advantage of appearing reasonable, ethical, and prudent.

However, these strategies have two potential weaknesses. First, insofar as all of these argument strategies have relatively equal merit, one strategy could be refuted by another quite easily. For instance, a before-and-after argument made against a politician who broke a campaign promise not to raise gasoline taxes can be countered by a same-principle-but-different-actions argument showing that because the standard of living has increased since the election, the new tax does not increase the overall amount of taxes people pay in relation to what they earn. Second, because these strategies are based on abstract principles, they may be refuted by factual evidence. For instance, although you may use the crisscross-consequences argument to argue that prohibiting people from doing something may cause them to want to do it more, there may not be evidence that, say, placing restrictions on tobacco and alcohol sales will cause people to smoke and drink more.

1   Correlative ideas.

A correlative-ideas argument holds that if some idea or act is equal to another, then the second merits the same treatment as the first.

EXAMPLE

If you argue that incoming legislators should be limited to serving no more than twelve years in office, then you would agree that incumbents should serve no more than twelve more years after term-limit legislation is signed into law.

2   Greater and lesser.

A greater-and-lesser argument compares ideas or entities based on their relative strengths and weaknesses. This argument strategy is often used to compare the merits of two or more ideas, courses of action, or policy proposals.

EXAMPLE

My policy for fixing welfare is fairer than the policy that would eliminate any safety network for the unemployed, yet it is tougher than those policies that continue to allow able-bodied recipients to live off the government when they could be working.

3 Opposites.

An argument from opposites contrasts the good qualities of one thing to the bad qualities of another. Other opposites that establish a clear contrast between two things are the just and unjust, objective and subjective, rational and irrational, wise and ignorant, courageous and fearful, and progress and decline.

EXAMPLE

In my opinion, a good news reporter provides the background necessary for a reader to understand a story and then gives an objective account of the event he or she is covering. A good reporter does not always look for the "dirt" related to a story, although he or she should be critical when the situation calls for it. A bad reporter provides no context for a story, offers biased explanations, and believes that "the only news is bad news."

4 Less and more likely *(a fortiori).*

A less-and-more-likely argument is based on the belief that if something is true of the lesser, then it is truer of the greater. This strategy also argues that if something is true when it is less likely, it is even truer when it is more likely.

EXAMPLE

If someone is capable of committing murder, then surely he or she is capable of lying in a court of law. For this reason, jurors are unlikely to convict a gangster based on the testimony of a Mafia turncoat who has entered the Witness Protection Program in exchange for his testimony. If he has already committed murder for his crime boss, what would prevent him from lying for the government when it promises to protect him for the rest of his life?

5 Crisscross consequences.

Crisscross consequences is an argument that encourages or discourages an action because the action will yield consequences opposite to what is expected.

EXAMPLE

If you place labels on video games to warn parents about the video's violent or sexually explicit content, you will only spark interest in these games, and children will want to play them even more.

6   Identical consequences and antecedents.

This argument is based on the reasoning that if two consequences are the same, their antecedents are the same.

EXAMPLE

It is probably the case that the same computer hacker entered the government and the university's computers because both entrances show a similar modus operandi.

7   Proportional relations.

A proportional-relations argument asserts that the same criteria for judging one thing should be used to judge another, similar thing. In other words, it is an argument that consistently applies a principle or value to similar things. This strategy is often used to make the argument that if one wrong action is equal to another, both persons deserve the same criticism or punishment.

EXAMPLE

After the Oklahoma City bombing, the liberal press and liberal politicians went to great lengths to condemn conservative talk show hosts and politicians for, as they argued, using bombastic rhetoric that inspired members of right-wing organizations to engage in terrorist acts against the government. However, after it was reported that the Unabomber may have chosen some of his victims from a hit list produced by left-wing environmental groups, you did not hear these same journalists and politicians denounce these groups for their vitriolic propaganda. This type of selective reporting and condemnation is just another example of the myopic attitudes of the liberal press and liberal politicians.

8   Same principle but different actions.

This argument claims that although a different situation may cause one's action to change, one's principle can remain the same.

EXAMPLE

I will vote for either a Democrat or Republican, depending on which candidate supports the needs of small business.

9   Before and after.

A before-and-after argument is directed at an opponent who has changed his or her position on something once an event has occurred or certain conditions have been met.

EXAMPLE

In 1996, congressional Republicans maintained that if President Clinton's budget plan would balance the budget in seven years, they would work with the president to end the gridlock in Washington over the budget and the federal deficit. However, when President Clinton submitted a budget that balanced the budget in seven years, the Republicans began placing new conditions on the president. Consequently, both parties quit trying to reach an agreement. The Republicans' behavior showed that they were never interested in a balanced budget, but only in pursuing their own political agenda.

10 Turning the tables.

Turning the tables is an argument that uses what an opponent has said against your position to refute his or her claim. Similarly, the strategy shows where your opponent says one thing but does the opposite.

EXAMPLE
Clarence Thomas has taken a strong public stance against affirmative action, arguing that it causes minorities to rely on the government and become less ambitious. However, there are many instances in which Clarence Thomas's own career has been advanced by affirmative action policies. In fact, most legal scholars maintain that Clarence Thomas was not the most qualified person to replace Thurgood Marshall as a Supreme Court Justice. Nevertheless, George Bush appointed him because he was both a conservative and an African American.

11 Reduction to absurdity (*reductio ad absurdum*).

A reduction-to-absurdity argument proves its conclusion by offering a series of objections to the conclusion that eventually show the absurdity of not accepting the conclusion. Thus, by showing the problems with thinking that a conclusion is unacceptable, you characterize it as acceptable.

EXAMPLE
Let us agree, for the moment, that we should define the "western canon" exclusively as those writings or works of art produced by western authors and artists. Thus, any texts created by nonwesterners should not be taught in our general survey courses in literature, philosophy, art, and so on. Does this mean that students have nothing to learn from Mahatma Ghandi or Salman Rushdie? Should we not study the Egyptian sculpture that influenced the early Greeks or the Japanese paintings that influenced the Impressionists? Of course, no one, not even a purist, would make these claims. Consequently, we must develop a different set of criteria for deciding what texts and authors should be placed in the canon and taught in our universities.

12 Method of residue.

The method of residue is an argument strategy whereby you refute all other possible claims that do not cohere with the evidence, which leaves you with the claim you endorse. This strategy is best used when there are only a limited number of possible claims that can be refuted or supported. Disjunctive syllogisms use this strategy of argument (see Section 2.3).

EXAMPLE
Because both the Republican and Democratic Parties are controlled by special interest groups, the only way that we can eliminate the influence of lobbyists and Political Action Committees (PACs) is to start a third party whose finances are not beholden to special interests.

13 Means-to-ends rationale.

When using the means-to-ends rationale, one argues either that a worthy end should not be achieved by dishonest or unethical means, or that it is acceptable to reach a good end by any means necessary. This strategy can also claim that the long-term results of your ideas, actions, or policies should be considered over their short-term gains, or vice versa.

EXAMPLE
Although schools should strive to increase students' scores on national aptitude tests, schools should not orient their instruction to prepare students for these tests. Focusing on test scores may cause school administrators to remove from their curriculum certain topics and methods of instruction that help develop students' general thinking skills and overall understanding of the world when teachers take time away to prepare students for these tests.

14 Sustainability.

The sustainability argument holds that an environment or system should never be altered to the extent that it would be unable to regenerate itself. This strategy is often used in defense of preserving an ecosystem or institution threatened by outside forces.

EXAMPLE
If we decide to cut the budget of the National Endowment of the Arts completely, the arts programs that it supports probably will lose the matching funds that private donors contribute. This loss may cause many programs to end. Hence, when we want to refund these programs, they may no longer exist.

15 Best- and worst-case scenarios.

This argument strategy gives a set of predictions forecasting what the most positive and negative outcomes of an action or policy may be.

EXAMPLE

For every one-percent increase in interest rates, we can expect a five- to seven-percent decrease in the number of homes bought and sold in the real estate market.

16 Common maxims.

Common maxims are arguments based on generally agreed upon commonsense beliefs, ethical principles, social norms, or standards of conduct. Such arguments often are considered a type of normative proof (see Section 2.1). Traditional sayings such as, "A penny saved is a penny earned" and, "A bird in the hand is worth two in the bush" are common maxims that can provide a rationale or warrant for a claim. Similarly, proverbs and adages such as, "Anything that can go wrong, will" and, "You never want to make the perfect the enemy of the good" can underscore a prescription for action. Although these maxims are generally accepted as true, many people consider arguments based on commonsense beliefs weak because they are vague, overused, and lack any direct factual support.

EXAMPLE

One of the clearest reasons why the death penalty should be abolished can be taken directly from Scripture: "Thou shall not kill." Now surely I hear my detractors crying, "No, you can't say this because of the separation of church and state!" However, my reply is simply this: Although this commandment is originally part of a religious doctrine, it articulates a principle that is not supported by religious convictions alone. It is also a universal moral standard by which all people should abide. Consequently, all citizens and governments regardless of their religious affiliation should uphold the principle "thou shall not kill."

2.5 Argument Fallacies

A fallacy is a defective argument that results from a deceptive premise or illogical reasoning. Hence, you should avoid using these arguments and recognize when others do use them.

When attacking a fallacious argument, you should clearly explain its faulty characteristics. In cases where a single argument contains several different fallacies, point out each faulty premise or inference as clearly as possible. Although sometimes it is easy to identify a fallacious argument, other times it is more difficult. For instance, although some people may consider it justified to point out the flaws of a politician's character, others may consider it a fallacious "attack on the person" that avoids dealing with his or her political ideas. Similarly, individuals may disagree as to whether a statement is the legitimate testimony of an authority or a fallacious appeal to authority. If someone might consider that you are presenting an argument fallacy, call attention to the potential criticism and then explain why your argument is valid and not fallacious in this case.

To help you recognize when someone is making an illogical appeal, study the following list of common fallacies:[58]

1   Hasty generalization.

A hasty generalization is an inductive argument that provides little evidence for its claim. The argument's general conclusion usually rests on an inadequate number of instances or cites examples that do not represent the claim being made.

> **EXAMPLE**
> After talking with a few classmates, I found that they too were shut out of all the science courses offered for nonscience majors. Hence, the university should offer more courses in geology, biology, chemistry, and physics for the nonscience major.

2   Accident.

An argument by accident is based on a valid principle but one in which the principle is applied incorrectly to a particular example or issue. In some instances, the problem with the argument is that it neglects to consider some overriding factor such as an extenuating circumstance, higher principle, or more important law.

> **EXAMPLE**
> In America, we have the right to free speech. Therefore, tabloid newspapers have the right to print anything they want about celebrities and politicians, regardless of its truth.

3   Composition.

Composition is an assertion made about an entire group that is true only about its parts.

> **EXAMPLE**
> Every element of the federal budget proposal will help some part or group of people in the country. Because it will help so many people and parts of the country, the new budget proposal is a good piece of legislation.

4   Division.

Division is an assertion made about all the parts of a thing but that is true only about the whole.

EXAMPLE
Because of its rich oil fields, not only is Kuwait a very rich country, but so too are its citizens.

5   Equivocation.

Equivocation is an argument that uses the same term in two different ways so that the inference drawn in the argument is illogical.

EXAMPLE
The Beatles should be considered classical musicians because their songs are classics.

6   After this, therefore because of this (*post hoc, ergo propter hoc*).

This type of argument misconstrues two events that occur sequentially as cause and effect. The argument tries to assert a causal relationship, when in fact, one thing simply happened after the other.

EXAMPLE
Since the Great Society's expansion of the welfare state, there has been an increase in the use of illegal drugs. Consequently, if we eliminate the welfare programs that were created since this time, we will reduce the use of illegal drugs.

7   Weak analogy.

A weak analogy compares two things that have more differences than similarities.

EXAMPLE
Secular humanists argue that creationism should not be taught in the public schools because it is based on religious beliefs and not science. But don't humanists believe in science just like Christians believe in the word of God?

8   Appeal to authority.

An appeal to authority is an argument that uses authoritative testimony fallaciously. The authority's statements also may be biased, misinterpreted, or stated out of context. In some cases, the argument rests only on the authority's name and status and not on any evidence provided by the authority. The argument also can refer to someone who is not an expert in the subject being discussed. In most instances, the authority referred to is merely a popular figure or an expert in another field who is represented as an authority on the issue being addressed. What makes such appeals to authority fallacious as compared to authoritative testimony is that in the latter case, the individual does have expertise on the subject and his or her testimony reflects this expertise. The difference between this fallacy and nominal testimony is that the latter does not represent the individual's testimony as providing direct evidence for an argument, but rather presents only an insightful way to consider the issue (see Section 2.2).

EXAMPLE
Scientology must be a credible way of understanding the world. After all, many famous people, including Tom Cruise and John Travolta, believe in it.

9   Appeal to the people (*ad populum*).

This argument attempts to justify a claim based solely on its popularity. Such arguments may be irrelevant because the claim should be based on factual information, a universally held principle, an authoritative testimony, or some other type of evidence.

EXAMPLE
A January poll showed that seventy percent of the American people believe that UFOs exist. Therefore, we should recognize that they exist.

10   Appeal to tradition.

An appeal to tradition assumes that value, belief, policy, or course of action should continue because it is part of a tradition. The argument does not give any evidence for why the tradition should be maintained, but claims only that because it is a tradition, it should be continued. Often the tradition being supported conflicts with new social values or new information relating to the subject under consideration.

EXAMPLE
One of the most important reasons why the all-male military schools should not admit women is that they have always excluded women. To allow women into these schools would mean ending a long and glorious tradition.

11   Appeal to ignorance.

An appeal to ignorance claims that because something has never been proven false, it is true; or because something has never been proven true, it is false. Such reasoning is faulty because evidence has not been presented that either affirms or denies the argument's conclusion. Although it is true that the only way to prove something is to show evidence for it, lack of evidence does not prove or disprove anything.

EXAMPLE
Because there is no conclusive evidence showing that the images produced in the crop fields of England were made by either extraterrestrials or forces that we cannot explain scientifically, we must assume that they were created by pranksters and are a hoax.

12   Against the person (*ad hominem*).

An *ad hominem* argument is an attack against an individual's character, past actions, or associations. This fallacy usually acts as a diversionary tactic that attempts to disqualify an argument on the basis of an irrelevant affront on the arguer rather than on the merits of his or her argument.

EXAMPLE
I do not agree with Reverend Al Sharpton's boycott of Burger King and his claim that the fast-food restaurant shows no concern for black communities, because he has made many antiwhite statements in the past.

13   False dichotomy.

A false dichotomy is an argument that presupposes only two positions and recognizes no middle ground or alternative positions. Often, when an opponent cannot refute your argument, he or she will resort to simplifying your argument into a false dichotomy. When you recognize that someone is misrepresenting your argument, carefully restate your position by distinguishing it from his or her characterization of the two extreme positions.

EXAMPLE
All leftists do is criticize the free market. If it were up to them, we would have a centralized economy where the government would run all the businesses and industry in the United States.

14   Slippery slope.

A slippery-slope argument rejects a particular action on the ground that once the action is taken, it will lead inevitably to other, less desirable actions. Such an argument overstates the effects of the initial action and does not consider that other actions can be taken to limit any further negative developments.

EXAMPLE
We should not decriminalize marijuana because if we do, the government will decriminalize all illegal drugs. Before you know it, teenagers will be able to buy cocaine, heroine, and LSD at the local convenience store.

15 Straw man.

A straw-man argument misrepresents a claim, thereby making it easier to refute. This fallacy also occurs by attacking a weaker argument while ignoring a stronger one.

EXAMPLE

According to its proponents, affirmative action is a policy that attempts to provide minorities with equal access to employment, education, and government contracts. Backers of this policy always point to the lack of women and African Americans who hold executive positions in Fortune 500 companies. However, they never want to talk about the lack of white males in the National Basketball Association. By their rationale, we should apply affirmative action to the NBA.

16 Red herring.

A red herring is an argument that introduces an issue that is only tangentially related to the issue under discussion. Often, this fallacy attempts to divert attention from the evidence supporting the claim at hand or simply tries to change the subject.

EXAMPLE

Although most people believe that teachers' salaries should be increased so that school administrators can recruit better teachers, these younger teachers have no idea what it was like for teachers just twenty-five years ago. At that time, teachers had forty students in their classes instead of thirty, and there were no reading specialists or teacher's aids to help students who were slow learners. Moreover, the dress code for teachers was much stricter; all the women had to wear dresses, and all the men had to wear ties.

17 Complex question.

A complex question makes an implicit negative statement about the person answering the question. Answering the question condemns the individual to implicate or accept a negative representation of himself or herself. A classic example of a complex question is, "When will you quit beating your spouse?" To defend yourself against a complex question, point out what the question incorrectly presumes, and then characterize yourself or your position in your own terms.

EXAMPLE

Now, after everything that I said, do you still favor weak environmental regulations that allow you to get rich while the local environment and community get sick?

18 Begging the question.

Begging the question is a circular argument that simply restates one of its premises as the conclusion. The argument provides no evidence that would lead you to infer the conclusion; rather, it simply uses the conclusion as proof for itself.

EXAMPLE

The reason that we know God helped to write the Bible is because it says so in the Bible, and we know the Bible is true because God helped to write it.

3

Visual Aids

3.1   *The Purpose of Visual Aids*

3.2   *Two-Dimensional Aids*

3.3   *Three-Dimensional Aids*

3.4   *Media Aids*

3.5   *Designing Visual Aids*

3.6   *Using Visual Aids*

3.1 The Purpose of Visual Aids

Visual aids offer an effective means for representing complex evidence, stressing important information, or demonstrating an activity related to your speech topic. You should use visual aids only when they significantly contribute to your audience's understanding of your speech topic. Although you would probably not need a visual aid for a speech on atheism or Jimmy Carter, you should consider showing examples of Frida Kahlo's paintings when discussing the major themes found in her work, or use a map to indicate where South American rain forests have been depleted. When determining whether you should use a visual aid, ask yourself if it will accomplish one or more of the following goals.

1   Visual aids can clarify complex information.

Often, a visual aid can help you explain an idea and thus make it easier for your audience to understand. For instance, using a visual aid to represent complicated statistical data or the family tree of an animal species will allow your audience to see what they would otherwise have to calculate or diagram in their heads.

2 Use visual aids to illustrate your ideas.

In the same way that an example concretely illustrates a general principle, a visual aid can help you portray an idea more graphically. For instance, a picture can help distinguish between the different shapes of a crocodile's jaw and that of an alligator (see Section 3.2). You can also prove a point about how women are portrayed in music videos by showing examples of rock and roll, country, and rap videos (see Section 3.4). Likewise, consider whether a visual aid would help you explain a point or prove an argument more thoroughly. For example, a line chart can represent the increasing amount of consumer shopping done on the Internet during the holiday season, or a video can help expose how a local industry is dumping waste illegally (see Sections 3.2 and 3.4).

3 Visual aids are integral to demonstrating your ideas.

A demonstrative speech without visual aids is as ineffectual as a persuasive speech without arguments. Demonstrative speeches demand that you actually demonstrate an activity or represent your subject visually and, in some cases, audibly (see Section 5.2). Hence, your visual aids can help your audience see the main steps in a process or characteristics of your subject more clearly. For example, a picture or a model of a piece of technology can help show how its component parts work together (see Section 3.3).

4 Visual aids call attention to important ideas in your speech.

The mere fact that you have produced a visual aid to represent a point will indicate to your audience that the point is an important part of your speech. Such visual aids as a word chart will help your audience recognize the main terms relating to your topic, whereas a cutaway will focus their attention on those parts of an object that pertain to your topic (see Sections 3.2 and 3.3).

5 Visual aids allow your audience to recognize the organization of your ideas.

Displaying a skeletal outline of your speech's main points is one of the best ways to represent the organization of your speech (see Section 3.2). Creating a word chart that shows the chronology of historical events or the steps in a process allows your audience to follow the organization of your speech's main points more easily. For a demonstration speech, placing the main material and equipment you will use in the demonstration on a table from left to right in front of you allows you to explain each component in the order in which it will be used in your demonstration.

6   **Use visual aids to help you speak extemporaneously.**

Displaying and organizing your ideas with visual aids can help you recall your main points more easily and allow you to move away from your outline and speak more directly and extemporaneously to your audience. Regardless of whether you are using a word chart, a series of graphs, or a variety of models, with the right amount of practice, you can use your visual aids to indicate what you need to explain and how you will move from one part of your speech to the next.

3.2 Two-Dimensional Aids

The following is a list of the main types of visual aids that can be either displayed on an easel, distributed to your audience, or reproduced as audiovisual aids. As is the case for most visual aids, these aids can serve a variety of purposes (see Section 3.1). However, they are most often used to clarify complex information, provide a pictorial representation, or diagram relationships between various elements of your topic. When determining what types of aids to use in a speech, consider how each may help you explain your subject more clearly and help your audience understand it better.

1   **Maps.**

A map is a representation of a geographical region. Maps are used most often when you are discussing a historical, political, or environmental subject. However, you can also use a map when discussing other subjects, such as places to travel, economic stratification within a region, trade relations between nations, immigration patterns, or population densities.

When constructing a map, make sure it is large enough for your audience to see easily and that it does not present any irrelevant information. For example, do not use a topographical map when your intent is to show the results of a political election (see Figure 3.1). To represent more clearly the location of the area you are discussing, you may want to use a series of maps that allows you to move from the larger region to your specific area of interest. Thus, when discussing the Florida Everglades you can go from a map of the state, to one of the general region, to a third that shows just the Everglades. To achieve a similar effect, you also could create a map with an enlarged, close-up view of the specific area and have this area jut out from the general area in which it is located.

Your map should represent the different areas and objects that you want to discuss, such as populations or forms of pollution, with various colors or symbols. In addition, use font size and bold letter-

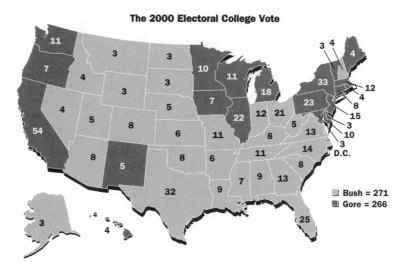

FIGURE 3.1 *Map*

Source: 2000 Election Results http://www.nara.gov./fedreg/elctcoll/2000map.html. Retrieved February 15, 2001.

ing to show the progression of the size or importance of elements on the map. For instance, the name of a state should be larger than the name of a city. Finally, make sure you clearly mark the sites you will discuss and point to them directly when referring to them in your speech.

2   Graphs.

A graph summarizes quantitative information about your subject. You should consider using a graph when discussing a large amount of statistical data or when emphasizing a particularly important set of statistics that supports your thesis (see Section 2.2).

When creating a graph, be sure to designate clearly what you are graphing with different colors, lines, or symbols, and provide a key that indicates what these elements represent. Do not put any needless information on the graph, and avoid any unnecessary shading or graphic designs that may confuse your audience (see Sections 3.4 and 3.5).

Three basic types of graphs are line graphs, bar graphs, and circle graphs.

Line graphs.   A line graph shows quantitative changes in one or more objects over a period of time. A line graph can also show how the amount of something changes when it is affected by another variable.

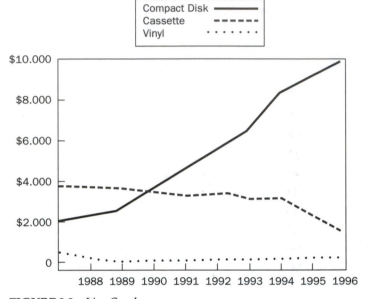

FIGURE 3.2   *Line Graph*

Source: The World Almanac and Book of Facts (Mahwah, NJ: World Almanac Books, 1998) 258.

For instance, a line graph can show the respective increase and decrease in the sales of compact discs, cassettes, and vinyl albums over a period of time (see Figure 3.2).

When you are designing your line graph, the lines representing the graph's data should be thicker than those indicating the graph's axes. In most cases, your vertical axis should represent the quantitative measurement of the subject diagrammed, and your horizontal axis should represent the length of time studied. Because a line graph's main intent is to show change over time, its representation of temporal changes is usually emphasized. Thus, a line graph usually is one and one-half to two times wider than it is high. This horizontal representation of data replicates a standard time-line and our natural eye movement when we are scanning a horizon or reading a text. Make sure your line graph measures change over a suitable period of time. The time period should be neither so short nor so long that the changes appear deceptively large or small.

Finally, remember that graphing temporal changes does not necessarily imply a causal relationship. Hence, you must explain why the data create the line that they do. That is, you must still discuss what

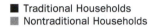

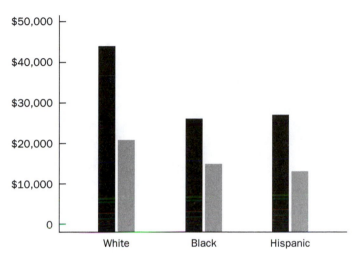

FIGURE 3.3 *Bar Graph*

Source: U.S. Census Bureau, *Statistical Abstract of the United States* (Washington, D.C.: GPO, 1997) 467.

causes the objects graphed to increase or decrease at certain times and what can be deduced by comparing these changes.

Bar graphs. A bar graph allows you to compare various amounts of things at any particular time. The relative size of the bars allows your audience more easily to compare the different amounts of the objects represented. For instance, you can use a bar graph to show the income differences between traditional and nontraditional households according to race (see Figure 3.3).

In a bar graph, one axis should designate the object being measured, and the other axis should represent the units of measurement. Bar graphs can place the units of measurement either on the horizontal or vertical axis, depending on which design is more effective. For example, for a graph on tree growth, you probably will want to place the object being measured (e.g., types of trees) on the horizontal axis, and the unit of measurement (e.g., feet) on the vertical axis to mimic the vertical structure and growth of the trees themselves. Regardless of which axis you use to measure the data, always arrange the bars in

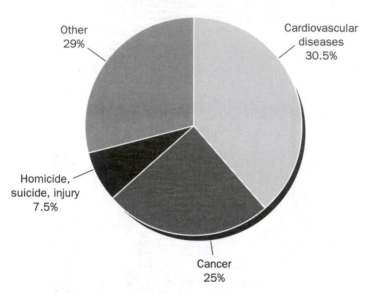

Leading Causes of Death, 1996

FIGURE 3.4   *Circle Graph*

Source: National Center for Health Statistics, *Advance Report of Mortality Statistics,* 1994, Vol. 45, no. 3.

decreasing amounts starting at the top or left side of the graph so that your measurements can be compared easily.

Circle graphs.   A circle graph illustrates the relative amounts of various parts of a whole. Circle graphs are most effective when used to emphasize the proportional relationship between your subject's component parts. For example, you can create a circle graph that shows the leading causes of death in the United States (see Figure 3.4). In a circle graph, the parts diagrammed often resemble pieces of a pie; hence, circle graphs are often referred to as **pie charts.**

     When creating a circle graph, place its largest segment at the top of the graph, and then, moving clockwise, graph its other parts in order of decreasing size until your circle is completed. The circle, as a whole, must always represent one hundred percent of the entity measured and, in general, should portray no more than six different components. If there are many smaller components of the chart that do not represent the main points to be discussed, group them together under the heading "Other," and graph this section last. You may want to highlight one or two of the more important amounts with bright colors. If it is not immediately clear from the graph itself, indicate what percentage of the whole each component part represents.

3 Charts.

A chart provides a convenient visual summary of information that is difficult to communicate orally. It can display relationships between various entities or simply highlight the main points of your speech. A chart may consist of words, statistics, images, or a combination of these elements. When using a chart, focus your audience's attention on no more than three or four main points. You may even want to highlight these points with bright color, bold print, or underlining. Your chart may contain more information than your main points do. When you do include extra information, briefly mention what the audience may want to glean from it, and then give them a brief moment to study the chart. As with graphs, you may want to reproduce your chart as a handout, particularly in the case of recipes or other types of instructions that your audience may want to use in the future.

The most common types of charts are word charts, tables, and flowcharts.

Word charts. A word chart displays the important points, terms, procedures, or principles discussed in your speech. For instance, a word chart can outline the proper and improper ways to gain the attention of the hearing impaired (see Figure 3.5). In a demonstrative speech, a word chart helps your audience follow the procedures you

---

Gaining the Attention of the Hearing Impaired

Tapping	**Waving**
Do:	*Do:*
• Tap on the shoulder	• Wave with one hand
• Shake the shoulder firmly if you need immediate attention	• Continue to wave a few seconds
Don't:	*Don't:*
• Jar abruptly	• Wave close to face
• Hit the person on the head	• Wave too wildly

FIGURE 3.5 *Word Chart*

Source: Amy Fletcher, Speech, Furman University, 1995.

Male vs. Female Earnings and Education Levels			
Education Level	**Female**	**Male**	**Difference**
Some high school, no degree	$16,666	$23,994	$7,328
High school graduate	$21,298	$31,063	$9,765
Some college, no degree	$23,750	$36,546	$12,796
Associate's degree	$28,510	$37,628	$9,118
Bachelor's degree or higher	$37,268	$60,880	$23,612

FIGURE 3.6   *Table*

Source: U.S. Census Bureau, *Statistical Abstract of the United States* (Washington, D.C.: GPO, 1997) 474.

are demonstrating while giving you greater mobility and freedom from your outline. When using a word chart, clearly number your main points or the steps being demonstrated, and use these numbers as signpost transitions (see Section 4.5). Sometimes speakers use peripheral decorations, illustrative designs, and forms of calligraphy to accentuate the information displayed on their word charts. These extra design elements, however, should not interfere or clash with the chart's information or purpose. For instance, do not place an attractive multi-colored border around a chart listing the names of developing countries that have high levels of unemployment and poverty.

Tables.   A table arranges information in an orderly and logical fashion. Most often, tables arrange statistics or list terms in columns and rows so that your audience can compare and contrast measurements or recognize categorical distinctions visually. Again, when discussing your table, focus on no more than three or four main points, although you can suggest ways to interpret or extrapolate other information from the table. For example, you might create a table that shows the difference between male and female earnings based on five different levels of education (see Figure 3.6). Although you may choose to discuss only three levels, afterward allow your audience a moment to study the chart for information that you did not discuss directly.

One of the best media for reproducing a table is an overhead transparency. Overhead transparencies allow you to introduce first certain categories or statistics and then build on them by overlaying your first transparency with others that contain more statistics, categories, or definitions.

Job Routing in an Advertising Agency

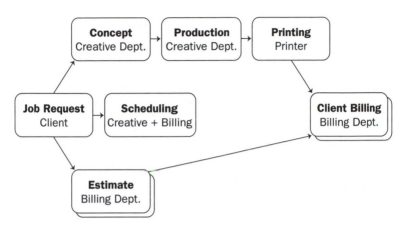

FIGURE 3.7   *Flowchart*

Flowcharts.   A flowchart illustrates the relationships among various parts in a whole and often depicts how each part functions singularly and in combination with the other parts. To create a flowchart, use a series of lines and arrows to represent the relationship between the elements portrayed. In the design of the chart, distinguish those functions, steps, or relationships that occur simultaneously from those that occur sequentially. As with a line graph, the information on a flowchart should be organized from right to left in the same way that you read.

There are two main types of flowcharts. An **organizational chart** shows an organization's structure and the relationships and responsibilities among the departments within the organization. For instance, you can create a chart showing how a work order moves through an advertising agency (see Figure 3.7). A **tree chart** represents the historical chronology or the categorical relationships of a subject. Classic examples of a tree chart are diagrams showing relationships among members within a family genealogy or an animal species. Likewise, a tree chart can show the possible choices in a decision-making process, as in the case of a chart diagramming how a person should decide which investment strategy best suits his or her needs.

4   Pictorial aids.

A pictorial aid is a drawing, diagram, photograph, or poster that displays information relating to your topic. Pictorial aids can also be a series of pictures that show various techniques for performing a

Golf Clubs and Ball Trajectory

| No. 3 Iron | No. 5 Iron | Sand Wedge |

FIGURE 3.8   *Pictorial Aid*

task. For instance, you can create a series of pictures depicting each step in the process of making an arm splint. Additionally, you can create a poster that compares different examples of the same activity. For example, your poster can show the trajectory of a golf ball when the golfer uses three different golf clubs (see Figure 3.8). If a subject is difficult to comprehend, consider using a pictorial aid to represent your information metaphorically. For example, to explain the three main ways that outside elements are obtained by biological cells, you may want to create replicas of a hook, sponge, and syringe that you can place on a diagram of a cell to show how the cell acts like either a hook that grabs the material, a sponge that absorbs the material, or a syringe that pumps material into the cell. Finally, consider using a pictorial aid, such as a picture or poster, to set an aesthetic mood or exemplify particular themes in a speech about art, architecture, or travel.

5   Handouts.

Handouts usually are used to introduce new terms, outline steps in a complex procedure, chart statistics, allow closer inspection of an image, or reproduce information that cannot be presented in any other way. Handouts can also provide information that your audience may like to have in front of them while you speak. Handouts can even include information that you will not discuss in your speech directly, such as telephone numbers and addresses of volunteer organizations that you are persuading your audience to join.

To prevent a handout from distracting your audience, consider when and how best to distribute it. Handing out the material before your speech begins avoids breaking the flow of your delivery; however, you may find that the audience is looking at the handout instead of listening to your speech. If you do pass out your handout before you begin speaking, use the preview summary of your introduction to indicate when you will discuss the handout (see Section 4.1). Then, within the speech itself, use a preview transition to draw your audience's attention to the handout, and then use another transitional statement to direct their attention to your next point (see Section 4.5).

3.3 Three-Dimensional Aids

Technical equipment, sporting gear, a live model, or a replica of an object are all types of three-dimensional aids. Because they are either real objects or represent objects realistically, three-dimensional aids can enhance your audience's sense of the object you are describing or the process you are demonstrating.

Before using a three-dimensional aid, practice holding it, handling its moving parts, performing your demonstration with it, and pointing directly to the part of the aid you will discuss. Also, if you are demonstrating various stages in a process, such as adding layers of dye to a batik, make samples of each stage so that your audience can gain a better sense of how the object evolves into its final form. If the object is too small, make a larger replica of it.

Finally, consider ways to supplement your three-dimensional aid with other aids, especially if a three-dimensional object is too large to present. For instance, when speaking on a piece of architecture, use a model to display its design, a chart to document its dimensions, a map to identify its location, and a series of pictures to show what it looks like from various perspectives.

1   Models.

A model is either a real object or a replica of a real object. Because a model may be difficult to create on your own, check local institutions associated with your subject to see if they can provide you with a model for your speech. For example, call your local Red Cross to see if they will lend you a Resuscitative Annie for a speech on cardiopulmonary resuscitation (CPR). You can also use another person as a model in your speech. In speeches dealing with such subjects as exercise programs, massage techniques, or dance routines, consider using models to perform your demonstration while you explain what the models are doing. This technique will allow you to concentrate on your explanation and prevent you from breathing heavily while trying to speak and demonstrate a strenuous activity simultaneously.

2   **Mock-ups.**

A mock-up enlarges all or just part of a real object. By represent-ing a particular part of a real object, a mock-up enables you to focus on the specific part of the object being discussed while removing those parts that are irrelevant to your point. Another advantage of a mock-up is that it is usually larger than the actual object and thus can be seen and handled more easily. Hence, if you are trying to demon-strate something very small, like body piercing, draw a diagram of the body part on a piece of poster board, cut a hole into the poster board where the piercing will be, and then use a pencil as your nee-dle and a large replica of the jewelry to show how the body part is pierced.

3   **Cutaways.**

A cutaway is a model in which the outer covering of the object is removed in order to show its inner parts. Like mock-ups, cutaways en-able you to show and explain only those parts of the object pertinent to your speech. A model of the human anatomy that exhibits the epi-dermal, respiratory, circulatory, and skeletal systems in distinct layers is a classic example of a cutaway model. As with all other visual aids, be sure to point directly to the component of the cutaway that you are discussing; otherwise, your audience may not recognize what part of the model you are referring to.

3.4 **Media Aids**

Media aids use various types of technical equipment to commu-nicate sounds and images to your audience. Consequently, these aids can help you present information while enhancing your audience's vi-sual and auditory experience of your topic. Although employing me-dia aids can be very effective, limit their use to no more than one-third to one-half of your speech. When giving a demonstrative speech, for instance, demonstrate as much of your subject as possible directly in front of your audience (see Section 5.2). Then use media equipment to recreate what is too large or complex to demonstrate or what must be recreated electronically for the audience to view in its natural envi-ronment. For example, consider using media aids to demonstrate any-thing from conducting an orchestra to learning how to wind surf. Finally, always practice ahead of time to see how much time it will take to present your media aids, what lighting and volume levels are ap-propriate, and what technical accessories such as light bulbs or pro-jection screens are needed.

1   Projectors and video aids.

Slide projectors, overhead projectors, video presenters, and video cassette recorders (VCRs) are all types of visual aids that can reproduce images and information on your subject.

Slide projectors are used to show slides of artwork or photographs, although they also can be used for maps, charts, graphs, and other documents. You should always try to present a slide of an image rather than holding up or passing around an image you found in a book. Handling a book can be awkward, and passing it around may distract your audience from your oral presentation. To obtain slides of copyrighted images, contact libraries, academic departments, museums, and businesses that may sell or lend you slides. You can also have slides made by a photography store. If you do have slides made, find out how much time it will take to get them back.

Overhead projectors use transparencies to display charts, graphs, or images. One advantage of using an overhead projector is that it can present information in a sequential order. However, avoid the common mistake of covering the transparency with another piece of paper to conceal information that will be introduced later. This technique projects a large, black image that looks unprofessional. To keep information hidden until you introduce it, create a second transparency with the additional information, and place the second one over the first. For instance, begin with a transparency whose left column lists important terms, and then overlay it with another containing the definitions of each term in the right column. Use the same technique of overlaying transparencies to represent each of the progressive steps in a process. You may also want to turn off the overhead projector when you are between transparencies to eliminate projecting a distracting light onto the screen.

Like overhead projectors, **video presenters** project images onto a screen. However, unlike overheads that use only transparencies, a video presenter can project either a transparency or a paper document. They also allow you to magnify slide images, and, because they have a movable arm, you can use a video presenter to highlight various parts of a three-dimensional object. In this way, video presenters allow you to display information more easily and eliminate the need for other technologies such as slide projectors.

In general, you should use a **video cassette recorder (VCR)** only when presenting something that cannot be demonstrated in the classroom. Moreover, when you do use a VCR, use it sparingly. Often, speakers rely too heavily on a videocassette to explore their topic and do not fulfill their role as a speaker. As a result, they lose their credibility as well as their audience's interest. When using a VCR, always have the video cued to exactly where it should begin. Then, when working with the videocassette, point directly to what you are discussing and explain it. If the videocassette is being narrated, turn off the sound and explain in your own words what is taking place on the tape. Another way to use a video effectively is as a visual summary of your main points. For example, when giving a speech on mountain climbing, first explain the climbing equipment and demonstrate as much of the process as possible in front of your audience. Then show a video of someone actually climbing while you re-explain what he or she is doing.

2   Audio aids.

Audio aids either amplify your voice or reproduce music and other audio tracks such as selections from a speech, a poetry reading, or the sounds of nature. The main types of audio aids used in speeches are microphones, compact disc (CD) players and audio cassette decks.

You probably will not use a **microphone** in your speech class. However, if you do use one, you must first practice using it so that you can adjust your volume, pitch, speed, and so on to the microphone's amplification. Most importantly, determine how far you should stand from the microphone so that your pronunciation is clear and your voice does not sound too loud or too soft. As a general rule, the appropriate distance to stand away from a microphone is twelve inches. Also, by breathing properly and speaking slowly you can avoid blowing air into the microphone. Improperly pronouncing consonants such as *c, h, k, p,* and *t* will often cause you to blow excess air into the microphone, so be careful.

Compact disc players and **audiocassette decks** reproduce musical scores and other auditory sounds. If you are using an audio aid to exemplify a piece of music, state what you want your audience to listen for in the piece. Consider either previewing first what they will hear and then playing the piece, or explaining the piece while you play it. In the latter case, it is very important to check the volume level to be sure that your audience is able to hear the aid while listening to you speak. After playing your selection, remember to review its most significant parts.

When preparing your speech, always practice how you will operate these aids. Make sure to cue the piece properly, and if you are playing it back, use the tracking device to cue the piece again. When using the pause button, turn down the volume to avoid static. You should always try to use a high-quality compact disc or cassette player that is easy to set up and operate.

3   Computer aids.

Computer graphic presentations use software programs, such as Microsoft PowerPoint or Lotus Freelance Graphics, to present high-quality graphic aids in your speech. Such software programs provide **templates** (predesigned outlines, graphs, and graphic aids) into which you place information. The **slides** you create from these templates can then be projected onto a computer monitor or translucent screen and used as a speaking aid. These programs also allow you to incorporate audio and video material into your slides, thereby eliminating the need for a VCR or cassette player. However, you will need the proper software, computer, and projection devices to show your slides on a screen if you are speaking to a large audience.

If you have a basic knowledge of word processing programs, you should have little problem learning how to use these programs. Most graphic programs offer tutorials that provide step-by-step instructions on how to create presentation material. Because these programs are so easy to use, often the issue is not whether you can produce the slides, but whether you will use too many of them in your speech.

Computer aids are best used when you are presenting new material or when you want to offer an overview and then some specific points about your subject. Each slide should have a title and a list of three to five bulleted points. The layout should remain consistent throughout all of your slides; keeping your titles, points, font style, and graphics consistent brings uniformity to your presentation.

In general, do not rely on your slides entirely. Rather, determine which points can be explained more effectively with a slide and which cannot. Elaborate and detailed forms of evidence do not lend themselves well to this graphic format and thus should be presented orally. Moreover, you should not add graphic elements to your speech just because you have the technology to do so.

It also is very important to practice your graphic presentation. When you are practicing your speech, make sure that you are in control of the technology and that the technology is not in control of your speech. Often, speakers allow the use of technology to shape their presentations. The usual result is that their ideas become disjointed, their delivery sounds choppy, and their movements appear awkward. In addition, they spend too much time looking at the screen rather than at their audience. To avoid these problems, practice using your mouse, maintaining a smooth delivery, and making eye contact with your audience when you move from one slide to the next. Remember to stand on one side of your screen or monitor so you do not block your audience's view.

Always arrive early so that you can determine whether your software and equipment are in working order. Also, try to run through your presentation quickly to catch any software incompatibilities or glitches that can occur. Finally, always have a hard copy of your slides in case the equipment is malfunctioning and you have to use the print-outs as visual aids or handouts.[1]

3.5 Designing Visual Aids

A well-designed visual aid can help your audience understand and remember a point and may even increase their agreement with it. Although Section 3.4 discussed some aspects of designing visual aids, the following guidelines offer additional prescriptions for creating two-dimensional aids such as maps, graphs, charts, and overhead transparencies (see Sections 3.2, 3.3, and 3.4).[2]

1   Design your own visual aid.

The information you place on your visual aid can come from one or more sources, including your own experience. When you do use in-formation from a source or copy its design, use an oral citation to ac-knowledge where the aid's content came from, or place a reference to the source on the aid (see Section 6.4). Because your aid should present only information directly relevant to your speech, you will most likely not want to reproduce every aspect of a chart or graph from a source, but modify it to fit your needs. Thus, although you should never fal-sify the information you obtain from a source, you can design it dif-ferently or eliminate unnecessary information. For instance, you can create a bar chart that compares illegal drug use among three different populations in one year by taking information from a line chart that diagrams the changing rate of drug consumption among these popu-lations over a longer period of time.

When designing your aid, remember that its main intent is to help your audience understand your topic more easily. Thus, you should al-ways keep in mind how your aid's design will help your audience process information more quickly and fully.

2   Be sure your aid is visible to all audience members.

The standard size for any map, graph, or chart displayed on a posterboard in an average-size classroom is twenty-four by thirty-six inches with two-inch margins. If you cannot find or create an aid that it is large enough for your audience to see, display the information on a handout, or decide whether the information is suitable for visual pre-sentation (see Section 3.2).

3   **Make any writing short, simple, and easy to read.**

Present information on an aid in the clearest, most concise way possible. Do not use unnecessary words, provide needless information, or overdecorate your aid. In general, do not add anything to your aid that will obscure its essential point.

Always print with block letters or use calligraphy or a stencil to create readable letters. Make sure that all your lettering is large enough for your audience to see. To differentiate between types of information, make your most important points at least three inches tall, your subpoints at least two inches tall, and any other writings at least one inch tall. To avoid an overcrowded design, limit your use of different font styles, and do not print everything in capital letters. Pay close attention to your line spacing and word spacing; placing your lines and words together too closely can be confusing.

For transparencies, slides, or a computer aid, use a thirty-six to twenty-four point font for titles, a twenty-four to sixteen-point font for subtitles, and a sixteen to fourteen-point font for any other writings (see Section 3.4). For handouts, use a range of font sizes from twenty-four points to twelve points (see Section 3.2).

4   **When creating a graph or chart to display on an easel, use a strong paper that will support itself.**

Use a strong, thick paper, such as posterboard, so that your aid will not fall off your easel. Always number your aids on the back so that you can keep them in their appropriate order. Furthermore, do not roll up your posters prior to your speech. Rolled posters are difficult to handle and frequently fall from the easel, thus distracting your audience.

5   **Keep colors vivid and simple.**

To ensure clarity, use dark-colored letters (e.g, black or dark blue) on light-colored paper (e.g., white or yellow), and use no more than two or three colors.

Use colors and lines to reinforce mood, impressions, and values. Colors adjacent on the color wheel (e.g., red-orange, yellow-green) suggest compatibility, change, or progress, whereas opposite colors (e.g., black-white, yellow-blue) can suggest contrast and opposition. Represent your most important information with bold colors, bold print, or underlining, and less important information with lighter colors.

Always use the same design elements throughout a group of visual aids. For instance, use the same color or icon to represent the same thing on different aids, and use the same outline format on a series of word charts (see Section 3.2).

6   To help your audience recognize the most significant
     points, place your most important information in the center
     of your aid.

Divide your aid into thirds both vertically and horizontally, and
place your most important information at the four places where the
lines intersect. Do not crowd this information with peripheral information or design elements. Instead, use the open space to direct your
audience's attention to your main points. In some cases, such as with
maps or line graphs, you may not be able to arrange your information
this way (see Section 3.2). However, try to follow these guidelines on
most of the aids you create.

7   Create design elements that have multiple functions.

Because an aid offers a limited amount of space, use design elements such as color, space, and lines in combinations that will produce
multiple meanings at once. For example, plot population densities on
a map by using a series of light to dark colors to designate the size and
location of the population (see Section 3.2). Similarly, when constructing a bar graph, use a group of bars that show the aggregate and subto-
tals of the item represented. For instance, use four sets of bars to
compare the crime rates of four different locales. Then divide each bar
into two with the first representing violent crimes and the second representing property crimes. Added together, the number of crimes
charted by the two bars would constitute the total number of crimes
per city.

8   Be sure that all maps, charts, and graphs contain a title
     and key that denote the information contained in the aid.

Create a short title that explains the contents of your two-dimensional aid (see Section 3.2). Do not, however, use the title to express a
claim about the information contained in your aid. Rather, your explanation of the aid's content should provide the basis for making such
a claim. For example, entitle a graph on the population growth of various Southern states, "Population Growth Rates in the United States,
by Region, 1980–2000," and then show how the graph illustrates where
population rates are growing the fastest.

Your aid also must include a key that shows what aspects of your
subject (e.g., regions, populations, budgets, resources) are being portrayed and how these elements are depicted on the visual aid (e.g., by
color, complete or broken line). You do not have to create a key when
you can designate what each figure (e.g., line, bar, slice) of your circle
graph represents right next to the figure itself. Make sure the unit of
measurement (e.g., miles, dollars, pounds) used to measure your sub-

ject is represented somewhere on the aid, and indicate whether large numbers have been abbreviated (e.g., "in millions of dollars").

9   Do not use misleading symbols on your aid.

Use icons or symbols that accurately reflect the proportional relationships among the variables diagrammed on your aid. That is, the size of the icons should match the relative size of the entity they represent. For example, if the military budget was reduced by one-third this year, make the tank representing this year's budget two-thirds the size of the tank representing last year's budget. Do not attempt to influence your audience by exaggerating the size of your icon. Audience members easily recognize such attempts at manipulation and interpret them as being intentionally deceptive.

Finally, do not place unnecessary data, measurements, or graphics on your aid. For instance, do not represent grid lines on a graph. Instead, allow the information charted to create its own points of reference. If too many points require plotting, consider representing only the averages or eliminating the extremes.

3.6 Using Visual Aids

The following guidelines suggest how to present visual aids in your speech. (Some of these suggestions have already been given in the previous sections of this chapter, but their importance warrants that they be repeated here.) Remember to keep your audience's attention focused on your speech's oral text rather than on your aid so that your aid supplements, rather than overshadows, your speech.

1   Focus each aid on no more than three or four major points.

Placing too much information on one aid may confuse your audience. In most cases, you should use a visual aid to display information relating to no more than three or four specific points, unless you are using a word chart to outline your main points. If your aid provides additional information, give your audience an indication of what they can deduce from it, and then allow them to study it on their own.

2   Limit your use of visual aids to no more than one-third to one-half of your speech.

Do not overuse visual aids, especially audiovisual aids (see Section 3.4). Although you can use slides, overhead projectors, and video presenters for up to one-half of your speech, use a strong oral delivery to keep your audience's attention focused on you and your speech's text.

Never play a VCR for more than two minutes at a time, and always provide your own narrative with the video. Do not let the video's narrator speak for you: Informing your audience is your responsibility. Hence, if the video is narrated, turn off the volume and explain the video yourself. Most importantly, do not create a long, awkward moment of silence by letting your video play without your saying anything.

The standard approach to using visual aids is to introduce, explain, and summarize one aid at a time and then move on to the next. However, you can use multiple aids at once, such as in the case of having a map to represent the area being discussed and a statistical chart containing information about the area represented.

3   **Never use a visual aid that adds little new information, illustrates a minor point, or disrupts the flow of your speech.**

Such visual aids will distract your audience from the main points of your speech. They may also cause you to lose credibility because they can make your speech appear uninformative and unprepared.

4   **Determine exactly when you will use your aid and how much time you need to discuss it.**

Practice speaking with your aid so that you know what you will say about the aid, how you will handle it, and when you will move to your next point. Also practice any writing or drawing you will make so that it is easy to read or recognize. You may even want to write or draw anything before you begin your speech to eliminate potential problems.

In addition, realize that being nervous may cause you to forget or rush through what you want to say or do with your aid. Here again, the only way to avoid these potential problems is to practice until you are fully comfortable working with your aids.

5   **Be sure that you have all of your aids ready at the time of the presentation.**

Before choosing your speaking aids, find out what equipment, such as an easel, table, or screen, will be available to you so that you can determine the best way to display your aid. You also should set up and test all your speaking aids before your presentation to ensure that your speech will flow smoothly.

When you arrive at the classroom, make necessary adjustments to the room, the podium, and your equipment. Also make sure that all your equipment is running properly: Set the volume of audio equipment, cue your audio or videotape, check your microphone for distortion, or try to use the slide carousel. In general, try to prepare everything well before you begin your speech (see Section 3.4).

6   Practice working with an assistant.

Have your assistant's movements choreographed so he or she feels comfortable and knows when to enter and exit, where to go, and exactly what to do in the presentation (see Section 3.3). For instance, if your assistant is going to demonstrate an exercise, make sure that he or she wears the appropriate clothing and stretches beforehand. Also, prepare verbal or nonverbal cues for your assistant's entrance and exit.

Be careful when asking for a volunteer from your audience to help you demonstrate something in your speech. This person may feel awkward, lack enthusiasm, or act foolishly and disrupt your speech. Either choose volunteers who are less likely to respond in these ways, or be prepared to respond to their behavior.

7   Prepare transitions that will move you to and from your aid and introduce the purpose of the aid.

Use a transitional statement to tie your oral text to your aid (see Section 4.5). Before explaining your aid, pause briefly so that your audience can study it. Then, after explaining the aid, summarize your main point(s), give your audience a brief moment to consider the aid, and then use a transitional statement to introduce your next point.

8   Remember to maintain eye contact with your audience.

You should maintain good eye contact with your audience rather than look at your aid continuously (see Section 7.3). To help you maintain eye contact, practice speaking with the aid, use cues on the aid to remind you of what you need to say, and, if necessary, memorize important information (see Section 7.4).

9   Explain how the information on your aid is organized.

After introducing your aid and explaining its main intent, briefly show how the information is organized. However, do not belabor this point. For instance, when using a chart, explain what its rows and columns represent, but avoid any overly technical or scientific explanation of how its data were compiled (see Section 3.2). In addition, clarify any flaws in the data, such as its potential margin of error (see Section 2.2).

10 Always point directly to the item on the aid that you are discussing.

When explaining the design of your aid, point to axes, columns, and so on that organize your information directly (see Section 3.2). Likewise, point to the place on a map or the number on a chart that you are discussing so that your audience clearly recognizes what specific part of the aid you are discussing.

Be careful not to obscure part of your aid with your arm or body. To prevent this problem, consider using a pointer or pencil. When using a slide, overhead projector, or video presenter, use a pointer to avoid creating a shadow with your hand or finger (see Section 3.4). When not using the pointer, place it out of range so that you do not pick it up and play with it to expend nervous energy.

Instead of reaching across your aid to point to items, begin on one side of your aid and then move to the other to point out specific information. When crossing in front of your aid, do not turn your back toward your audience. Rather, continue facing them while sidestepping to the other side of your aid. Then, from your new position, point to the information being discussed.

11 Consider covering and then removing your aid before and after you use it.

You should reveal your aid only when the information displayed by the aid becomes pertinent to your speech. Therefore, consider covering any aid until you introduce it so that it does not distract your audience. Also, do not apologize for the size of an aid. You are responsible for making sure that it is easy to see and read.

4

Organization

4.1   *General Speech Structure*

4.2   *Introductory and Concluding Statements*

4.3   *Thesis Statement and Preview Summary*

4.4   *Patterns of Organization*

4.5   *Types of Transitions*

4.6   *Principles of Outlining*

4.1 General Speech Structure

The following outline provides the general framework for organizing most informative or persuasive speeches. [Ceremonial speeches often follow different organizational guidelines (see Chapter 5).] This general structure should be understood as a basic model that you can adopt completely or modify to satisfy the needs of your particular speech. Consider how you can combine, omit, or alter elements of the general speech structure to present your particular topic, thesis statement, evidence, and appeals in the most effective manner possible. For instance, by beginning your speech with a personal narrative, you can simultaneously perform the first two functions of an introduction (see Section 4.2). You also can combine the audience response step in your conclusion with your closing remarks (see Sections 2.1, 5.4, and 7.2).

1   Introduction[1]

Gain and maintain your audience's attention.   The function of your opening statement is to stimulate your audience's interest in your topic. There are many different techniques for sparking your audience's interest (see Section 4.2). You can begin by describing an important historical or current event affected by your topic or by defining a particular aspect of your topic that you will return to later in your speech. You also can clarify a popular misunderstanding about your topic or illustrate it with an insightful statistic, fact, or authoritative statement. If you want to take a more indirect approach, begin with a series of questions alluding to your topic, or employ a pun on your speech's title or subject matter. However, never begin by apologizing for being unprepared, ridiculing your topic, telling your audience you are nervous, or denouncing your speaking abilities. Trying to decrease you audience's expectations may cause you to lose credibility.

Relate your topic to your audience.   After sparking your audience's interest in your topic, show its significance. By establishing your topic's significance early in your speech, you supply your audience with good reasons to listen attentively to the whole speech. One of the best ways to characterize your topic's importance is to relate it to your audience's immediate or future concerns. For example, you can describe how your topic affects society or how it influences the way your audience thinks and acts. You also can state how your speech will add to your audience's general understanding of your topic.

Relate your topic and audience to yourself.   It is often important to begin building your *ethos,* or credibility as a speaker, in your introduction. There are three main ways to build your credibility (see Section 2.1). You can verify your knowledge of your topic by referring to personal experiences or training you have with respect to your topic, or by describing your research and citing your main research sources. You can also build your credibility by tying your views on your topic to a value that your audience holds. Establishing an ethical basis for how you will treat your topic will help you gain your audience's trust and support. Last, consider expressing empathy with your audience's perception of and concerns about your topic so that they will see you as someone who understands their needs and interests and can help fulfill them.

State your thesis, and forecast the organization of your speech.   After stimulating your audience's interest and relating yourself and your topic to your audience, explain the intent of your speech and outline its general structure. That is, state your thesis and give a brief summary of your main points (see Section 4.3). Together, your thesis and preview summary should clarify your speech's purpose, preview its overall structure, and show how each main point will explicate your thesis statement. Moreover, consider using your thesis statement and preview summary to reinforce your topic's significance or the mutual values you and your audience hold with respect to your topic.

2   Body

Divide your topic into your main points.   Your main points consist of the central ideas, issues, processes, arguments, and so on, that you will explore in your speech. All of your main points must provide information that will fulfill the intent of your thesis statement. Your speech should consist of three to five main points that you want to elucidate or prove. Each main point should be a distinct idea that can stand on its own. At the same time, each main point should relate clearly to your thesis and to every other main point. Your main points should have relatively the same degree of significance and the same number of subpoints, and should be allotted approximately the same amount of time within your speech (see Section 4.6). When organizing your main points, consider adopting one (or a combination) of the organizational patterns or types of speeches that best suits your topic, thesis statement, and main points (see Sections 4.4, 5.2, and 5.4).

Provide evidence for your main points.   A **subpoint** is a piece of evidence that supports your main points. Similarly, a **sub-subpoint** provides evidence in support of a subpoint. In general, use explanations, descriptions, statistics, examples, analogies, narratives, and testimonies, as well as the other types of evidence and arguments, to explain, define, or prove each of your main points and subpoints (see Sections 2.2 and 2.3).

Use transitions to unify your speech.   Transitions are statements or phrases that relate the various parts of your speech to one another and thus help to unify your speech. There are many different types of transitions, each of which performs a distinct function (see Section 4.5). The three main types of transitions are preview transitions, which foreshadow what is to come in your speech; review transitions, which summarize what you have already said; and signpost transitions, which enumerate various points in your speech.

3   Conclusion

Forewarn your audience that you are about to conclude.   Indicate that you are going to conclude by saying something such as "In conclusion," or simply suggest that you are concluding by using a long pause and then raising your tone (see Section 7.2). Along with signaling that you are concluding, you may want to begin developing your concluding statement at this point by returning to a theme or motif used earlier in your speech or introducing a new theme that embodies the functions and sentiment of your conclusion (see Section 6.1).

Review the main parts of your speech.   Review your speech by summarizing your thesis statement and main points. When summarizing, do not refer vaguely to the general content of your speech. Rather, succinctly reexplain how your main points and subpoints provided evidence for your thesis statement. To provoke your audience's memory, you may want to restate specifically your most important pieces of evidence. Alternatively, try summarizing your speech by providing new evidence that is consistent with the evidence you already have given in your speech. When used appropriately, this technique will allow your audience to see your subject from a new perspective while simultaneously reminding them of your main points.

Strengthen your audience's positive response to your speech.   Highlight the shared ethical grounds you have established between you, your topic, and your audience to build on the ethical and emotional bond you have established with them in order to ensure their favorable response to your speech. You also can explain how your speech allows your audience to understand your topic more completely or differently than before, or suggest ways they can explore your topic further or interpret another, similar subject in light of the information you have provided.

End your speech.   End your speech with a concluding statement that brings closure to your speech and captures your speech's purpose (see Section 4.2). Some of the main ways to conclude a speech are to offer a quotation that captures your thesis, ask a rhetorical question that highlights the problem you have addressed, employ a figure of speech that captures your convictions, or give an optimistic statement about the future. Regardless of the technique you choose, do not end your speech by stating, apathetically, that you are finished speaking. Rather, offer a concluding statement that captures at least one of the main ideas, aims, or sentiments of your speech.

4.2 Introductory and Concluding Statements

How you begin and end your speech can greatly influence the way your audience receives your speech and how they will remember it. Thus, your speech's introduction and conclusion are as important as its body. Because your introduction and conclusion are so integral to your speech, they should be consistent with the general tone and content of the main points in your speech's body. Together, all three parts of your speech should create a unified whole.

One way to unify your speech is to seek **closure** by weaving the evidence or appeals from your introduction into your speech's body and conclusion. By referring back to a piece of evidence, an appeal, or a motif used earlier in your speech, the technique of closure not only unifies your speech, but also gives the evidence or appeal greater meaning and significance at your speech's end (see Sections 2.1, 2.2, and 6.1). Although the examples presented in this section all show how to achieve closure, you do not always have to use the same type of statement to begin and end your speech. Rather, you can use any of these types of statements as long as each fulfills the main purpose of an introductory or concluding statement.

The main functions of your introductory statement are to gain your audience's attention and to make them more receptive to your speech and thesis. The main functions of your concluding statement are to capture the purpose of your speech and to evoke those sentiments you want your audience to feel as a result of your speech. In many instances, you will want to end your speech with an optimistic statement about the future. Thus, your concluding statement could stress how your speech provides your audience with a better understanding of your subject or how your proposed solution will make their lives better. However, you do not always have to end on an optimistic note; rather, leave your audience with a sense of how they should view your subject regardless of whether it is a feeling of optimism or pessimism, harmony or conflict, hope or despair.

When constructing your introductory or concluding statements, consider using one of these techniques, many of which are types of evidence that have been explained in more depth earlier (see Section 2.2).[2]

1 Shock

Use a startling statement, story, or other piece of evidence to spark your audience's interest and stir their emotions. This technique is best used when you are facing an inattentive or reluctant audience, when you want to create a confrontational atmosphere, or when your topic, on its surface, appears unoriginal or uninteresting. As a concluding technique, shocking your audience may create a strong and lasting impact.

INTRODUCTION

Every one of you in this room deserves to be in jail! Why? Because unless you are doing everything possible to control government spending, you are stealing money from your children and your grandchildren!

CONCLUSION

Let me end by telling you the good news. You have all been granted a pardon. But you must promise to work together to limit uncontrolled government spending. If you do not, your children have every right to take away your social security and leave you desperate on the streets. Given the way you are allowing this government to destroy their future, don't think they won't do it!

2   Statistics.

Presenting statistics frames your subject in a clear and rational way. Thus, beginning or ending your speech with statistical evidence may add to your credibility. The two main ways to use statistics in an introductory statement are to show the scope of your subject, or to surprise, even shock, your audience with data they are unaware of.

INTRODUCTION

Most people accept alcohol consumption as a normal part of daily life. But recently, the Department of Justice announced that four out of every ten fatal car crashes in America involve alcohol. Similarly, the *Christian Science Monitor* reports that eighty to ninety percent of all crimes involve alcohol. In Maine, half of adults surveyed said that someone in their family has a serious alcohol problem. Perhaps the time has come to rethink our attitudes toward alcohol.

CONCLUSION

When you put all the facts together, alcohol consumption should be treated as a public health problem, not as a normal part of our lives. Prohibition clearly is not the answer. But when half the families in Maine have to watch their loved ones slowly destroy themselves, we must recognize that we are dealing with a public health emergency. Perhaps we can all learn from the state of Minnesota. According to a 1996 issue of the *Harvard Mental Health Letter,* the state of Minnesota found alcohol treatment reduced crime rates by sixty-six percent and alcohol use by forty percent. Such numbers show us that an effective solution is close at hand.

3   Testimony.

Whether it is from an authority or someone who has direct experience with your subject, begin and end your speech with a testimony. By quoting someone with expertise in your topic, you implicitly transfer his or her credibility to you. Testimony also can lend authenticity to your speech when you provide statements from individuals who have real-life experiences with your subject. When offering testimony, try to find quotations that offer either vivid descriptions of the person's experience, or direct and forceful declarations of the authority's position.

INTRODUCTION

"It happened fast," reports Joe McBride, president of the Montauk Boatmen and Captains Association. "We used to fish for brown or sandbar sharks in the summertime. Now, we are lucky to see one of them because they are so overfished down south." According to the December 23, 1997, issue of *Newsday*, Mr. McBride's comments are consistent with the conclusions of scientific experts, who have found an alarming decline of sharks around the world. "The best available data says we are fishing sharks twice as fast as they can reproduce," says Sonja Fordham, fisheries specialist for the Center for Marine Conservation.

CONCLUSION

In this speech I have tried to show just how threatened these beautiful and mysterious animals are. You should also know that even our best efforts to solve this problem might not be enough. As Jack Musick of the Virginia Institute of Marine Science says, "Even in the rosiest scenario, it is going to take at least a decade to make progress in restoring stocks."

4   Narrative.

Whether you use a report, anecdote, or story, a narrative can create concrete, evocative images through which your audience may experience your subject. Your narrative should be long enough that your audience recognizes it is a story, but short enough that their minds do not begin to wander.

INTRODUCTION

The story is frightening. "It was twilight in Sudan when U.S. missiles tore across the horizon and then three explosions lit up the darkening sky," recounts the *New York Daily News*. "At that instant, other American cruise missiles screaming through the Hindu Kush mountain range were striking a rugged corner of Afghanistan. The simultaneous cruise missile attacks came without warning and were so swift their targets didn't know what hit them. State-run Sudan television interrupted its programming to announce that the country was 'subjected to an aerial strike by American warplanes that aimed at strategic targets.' Sudanese television aired graphic footage of the factory in flames and rescuers wearing surgical masks over their faces as they pulled the wounded from the twisted metal. It was not clear if there were any dead."

CONCLUSION

I began this speech with a story of the ugly reality of the war against terrorism. But let's step back eleven days before those U.S. cruise missiles struck. "She already knew that her son was dead," reported the *New York Times*. "But as Sue Bartley and one-hundred fifty other mourners left a memorial service . . . for the American victims of Friday's terrorist bombing, they were hoping against hope that Mrs. Bartley's husband, Consul General Julian Bartley, was still alive. They listened to a reading from Ecclesiastes, heard a mournful taps, then went home to wait, grasping red roses in trembling hands. Within hours, their wisp of hope was gone. Using torn clothing, strands of hair and a ring, doctors positively identified Mr. Bartley's badly disfigured body this evening, adding his name to a list of eleven dead Americans that included the Bartley's twenty year-old son, Jay." This dramatic account of Sue Bartley's pain should provide reason enough to explain why President Clinton's actions were necessary.

5   Current event.

Relating your topic to a current event helps establish your topic's significance by associating it with events that most likely are on your audience's mind. This technique also provides you with an effective way to take your audience from the outside world into your speech and back out again.

INTRODUCTION
If you have been following the news lately, you probably watched the progress of Steve Fosset as he attempted to become the first person to fly a hot air balloon around the world. Of course, Fosset did not make it. He crashed into the cold, stormy sea and was lucky to be rescued. But Fosset knew the enormous risks he faced, and still he persevered. He did not let his fear get the better of him. Fosset was not afraid to risk it all because he believed the reward is worth it. Similarly, Tom Roberts believed that building a family business was worth the effort, and so he spent his life working to achieve his dream.

CONCLUSION
Hot air ballooning is not for everybody. Some of you may even think that Steve Fosset's goal was ridiculous. But it meant a great deal to him, and that's the point. He refused to surrender to fear. He believed that he had not yet achieved his dream, and so he gave it his best. Tom, you gave it your best, and now your dream is your family's future.

6   Analogy.

Analogies allow you to put complex ideas in terms that your audience can more easily understand. Using an analogy to introduce a complicated subject may allow your audience to become more comfortable with your speech. Whether introducing or concluding your speech, use descriptive language to build your analogy.

INTRODUCTION
Ronald Reagan once compared the Soviet Union to an octopus whose powerful tentacles were poised to stretch out around the world to devour freedom-loving nations. But today, the red octopus has washed

ashore and finds itself helpless and desperately seeking to survive in the new-world economy.

CONCLUSION
By all accounts, Russia is no longer the powerful octopus it was during the Soviet era. But some of you may recall walking along the beach and finding a stranded creature of some kind or another. Maybe you even poked it with a stick to see if it was still alive. If you did, you probably jumped six feet in the air when it suddenly moved. The same principle holds true for Russia. It may be sleeping, but its tentacles are still powerful.

7   Humor.

Using humor is an effective way of capturing your audience's attention and putting them at ease. A concluding remark, joke, anecdote, or pun can leave your audience with an amiable feeling. Whichever you choose, always tie your humor directly to your point, avoid telling elaborate and offensive jokes, and use humor sparingly so that you are not perceived as lacking seriousness (see Section 5.3).

INTRODUCTION
"There's no time like the present." You've all heard this familiar saying a thousand times. However, you have probably never heard the next line, which is, "Especially if it's for me!" Yes, time really is a valuable gift, but we should never be selfish about it. So today I want to urge you to spend your time productively by volunteering to help others.

CONCLUSION
They say, "big things come in small packages." I learned that well when I told my mother I wanted a Mustang for my high school graduation, and she gave me the Hotwheels version of the car. Still, the greatest gift she gave me was her time, attention, and love; and there was nothing small about that. By volunteering a little bit of your time, you can mean something big to someone who needs your help.

8   Rhetorical question.

A rhetorical question is a question whose answer is often readily apparent (see Section 6.5). Beginning your speech with a rhetorical question entices your audience into thinking about the purpose of your speech without stating it directly. Closing your speech with a rhetorical question is an effective way to keep your audience thinking about your speech's purpose long after you conclude.

INTRODUCTION
Who was more loyal to the Cleveland Browns, the owner, who moved the team to Baltimore for a better stadium deal, or the people of

Cleveland? Unfortunately, in professional sports today, both owners as well as athletes are loyal to only one thing: money. Pursuing the almighty dollar may be good for players and owners, but it hurts the team, their fans, the league, and ultimately, the game, no matter what professional sport it is.

CONCLUSION

If Michael Jordan had left the Bulls before retiring, would anyone have remembered what team he played for in his last years? Probably not. In the minds of his fans, Michael Jordan will always be a Chicago Bull. However, many of today's sport's superstars think of themselves as temp workers, and many team owners think of themselves as corporate raiders. Their lack of commitment hurts not only the teams' host cities and their fans, but also the games we all love to watch.

9 Affirming a value.

Introducing or concluding your speech with a value supported by your audience increases the likelihood that they will accept your thesis. Tying your claims to a commonly held value may also build your credibility. Affirming a value you share with a receptive audience allows you to solidify their agreement with your thesis quickly and may allow you to move them to act on it. Moreover, beginning your speech by affirming a value can effectively and quickly win over a potentially unreceptive audience. In a similar way, ending your speech by affirming a shared value may leave your audience with a lasting positive image of you and your topic.

INTRODUCTION

The Judeo-Christian tradition is clear in saying that one of our greatest moral duties is to love our neighbors as ourselves. People of all faiths and no faith alike can agree that this moral principle indeed should be "the golden rule." If we do not treat others with tolerance and respect, how can we expect anything but intolerance and disrespect from them? That is why today I want to convince you that we should affirm the rights of homosexuals to marry.

CONCLUSION

In conclusion, if you are not willing to give homosexuals the right to marry, then you are necessarily supporting a system that would allow homosexuals to deny heterosexuals the right to marry if they were in the majority. Christ was right: We should love our neighbors as ourselves. That does not mean we have to do what they do or believe what they believe, but it does mean we have to respect their values as we would want them to respect ours.

10 Stating your thesis.

In most instances, you do not want to begin or end your speech with your thesis statement. On rare occasions, however, you should consider beginning and ending your speech with your thesis statement. Some such occasions are when you want to create a sense of candor and directness, when you want to stress your position, or when the amount of evidence you want to discuss leaves little time for an introductory or concluding statement.

INTRODUCTION
The number of unplanned teenage pregnancies has reached such epidemic proportions that we must do everything we can to combat this grave social problem. Today I want to propose a policy that integrates the services of government agencies and schools with those of nongovernmental agencies, such as churches and women's groups, to solve the problem of teenage pregnancy.

CONCLUSION
Unplanned teenage pregnancies in America must be reduced. To reduce teen pregnancies, we must combine the funding, staffing, and services of government agencies with those provided by schools, churches, and women's groups. The only way we can solve the problem of teenage pregnancy is to pull together the resources of all these public and private institutions. I hope you agree and will support my plan.

4.3 Thesis Statement and Preview Summary

Your thesis statement declares the intent of your speech. It should state the main subject, purpose, and ideas you will discuss. Your preview summary shows how each of your main points will develop your thesis. Together, your thesis and preview summary establish the purpose of your speech and show how you will fulfill that purpose. The guidelines offered here suggest how to develop an effective thesis statement and preview summary.

1 When creating your thesis statement, ask yourself questions about your speech's topic and intent.

Begin by asking yourself what topic you want to discuss and why you want to discuss it (see Section 1.3). Next, ask yourself how your audience might react to your thesis. In this sense, ask yourself why your audience would find your topic significant and why your speech is worth hearing. Likewise, ask yourself whether your potential thesis will allow you to address those issues relating to your topic that your audience will find informative, persuasive, and entertaining. Also ask how you could word your thesis so that your speech appears interesting, inviting, and morally acceptable. Finally, consider the relationship between your potential thesis and your speaking situation. Ask whether your thesis is appropriate given the setting for your speech, the time allotted to you, the audience you will speak to, and the general social conditions of the moment in which you will speak.

2   Consider the rhetorical purpose of your speech.

In general, the rhetorical purpose of a speech consists of what you want to accomplish with your speech, the impression you want to give about you and your topic, and the reaction you want to receive from your audience. The main goals of a speech are to inform, persuade, or entertain your audience—or some combination of the three. If your intent is to inform, decide what general and specific ideas, issues, and information you want your audience to know and understand about your topic as a result of your speech (see Section 5.1). When seeking to persuade, consider how you want your audience to act or think differently about your topic. Also think about what type of thesis statement, evidence, arguments, and appeals will incline them to change their perception of your topic, their personal behavior, or their public actions (see Section 5.3). If your purpose is to entertain your audience or have them commemorate a person or occasion, determine what themes, appeals, and language your audience would enjoy hearing, or which of these would bring them together in celebration (see Section 5.5).

3   Determine the specific purpose of your speech.

The specific purpose of your speech identifies the exact goals you want to achieve with your speech. In many ways, your specific purpose simply restates your rhetorical purpose in terms of the particular claim you want to pursue, ideas and evidence you want to discuss, and audience response you want to achieve. Thus, it narrowly defines your intent in terms of main issues you want your audience to consider, the precise information you want them to know, the distinct arguments you want them to agree with, and the specific response or actions you want to elicit as a result of your speech.

When determining which goals you will pursue in your speech, consider what immediate or short-term results you could accomplish and what long-term and sustained results are possible. Most of time, you will want to focus on achieving direct results, such as providing your audience with a greater understanding of your topic or persuading them to pursue some immediate action. Because changing life habits and deep-seated values takes a great deal of convincing and effort, speakers rarely hope to accomplish long-term goals and drastic results through a speech. However, you can use your speech to show your audience how they can take both immediate and future steps to reach a larger goal.

4   **Create a working thesis that reflects your rhetorical purpose, your specific purpose, the areas of the topic you want to discuss, and your potential conclusion.**

To help guide your research and develop your outline, create a working thesis that captures the specific intent of your speech and previews the areas of your topic you need to address to fulfill your purpose. Be prepared to modify this tentative thesis as you continue to collect and analyze your information. After you have a sufficient grasp of your research material, begin formulating your final thesis statement.

5   **State your thesis in a simple, declarative sentence that makes clear what you will discuss and how you will discuss it.**

Your thesis should consist of a statement that specifically addresses what you will explore or prove in your speech.[3] It should also directly reflect the relationship you want to establish with your audience. That is, it should assert the main intention of your speech. Thus, you should directly state that you intend to inform your audience about a topic, demonstrate a set of procedures, defend or refute an argument, justify a policy, or influence your audience to act or think differently (see Chapter 5). Your thesis should then specifically state the main ideas, procedures, arguments, and so on that you will discuss. By combining these two functions, your thesis statement not only will make clear precisely what your speech is about, but will also define the role you play as a speaker and the response you hope to gain from your audience.

6   **Make sure the wording of your thesis presents your speech's intent in the clearest, most effective way possible.**

Consider how the words you use will affect your audience's reception of your thesis and speech. Do not use overly technical language that may intimidate or put off your audience. Moreover, be sure your phrasing captures your main intentions and sentiments as well as appeals to your audience. For this reason, do not exaggerate the character of your proposal when you intend to offer only a modest change in a policy, and do not use vitriolic rhetoric that may offend some members of your audience (see Section 6.1).

7   **Directly follow your thesis statement with a preview summary of the organization of your speech.**

Your thesis statement and preview summary can be combined into one sentence or can consist of several sentences. Regardless of their structure, use your thesis statement to articulate your speech's main purpose and your preview summary to indicate how each of your main points will develop your thesis. Together, your thesis and preview summary should clarify your speech's purpose and main ideas so that your audience can establish the appropriate expectations about your speech and feel satisfied once these expectations are fulfilled.

8   **Repeat or rephrase your thesis statement throughout your speech.**

Working your thesis statement into your speech in various ways will continually remind your audience of how your thesis relates to your main points. Repeating your thesis may also increase the probability that your audience will accept your thesis. Along with stating your thesis in your introduction, you may want to rephrase it when introducing a main point, use it in a transition, and restate it when summarizing your speech in your conclusion (see Sections 4.2 and 4.5).

EXAMPLES

Although most of you have heard of Salvador Dali and surrealism, I would like to explore further the man and this artistic movement by discussing the man, the movement, and the surrealist themes and motifs found in Dali's most famous paintings.[4]

My intent today is to inform you about the potential dangers of exercising in the extreme heat and explain how to prevent and treat heat stroke.[5]

In this speech, I will argue that single-sex schools and classes offer women substantial educational, social, and personal benefits that cannot be gained in a traditional, coeducational setting.[6]

After examining the limits of the voucher system, I will show that the crisis in public education can be solved only through state initiatives that provide equal funding for all public schools.[7]

4.4 Patterns of Organization

Although the general speech structure presented in Section 4.1 provides the basic design for most speeches, the following organizational patterns present various ways to arrange evidence in the body of your speech. These patterns can be used in a variety of ways: You can adopt one of these patterns wholly, combine several different patterns, or use one in combination with a type of informative, persuasive, or ceremonial speech (see Sections 5.2, 5.4, and 5.6). For instance, when presenting an informative speech on jazz music, you may first want to give a chronology of jazz's history and then move to a topical organization to discuss three popular types of jazz: swing, bebop, and fusion. When choosing which pattern of organization to use, consider which one best coheres with your topic, thesis, evidence, and speaking situation (see Sections 1.3, 2.2, and 4.3).[8]

1 Chronological.

A chronological pattern highlights how your topic has developed over time. It is typically used to discuss the evolution of a historical event, the chronology of a person's life, or the succession of steps in a process. When constructing a chronology of your topic, consider using your speech's introduction to provide some background information on your topic. Then build your speech's body around a narrative that depicts the main events in your topic's chronology (see Section 2.2). Within this narrative, employ a variety of explanations, examples, and testimonial statements to represent your topic more fully. Similarly, use descriptive language that will allow your audience to visualize and experience vicariously the evolution of your topic.

2 Spatial.

A spatial pattern provides you with an effective means for describing the arrangement of your topic's physical properties and their functions. When your main intent is to describe the empirical properties of your topic, use this organizational pattern. For example, use a spatial pattern to explain the functions of various parts of an ecosystem, a mechanical object, or a piece of architecture. When describing your topic spatially, begin at its designated point of entry, and then describe how a person would move through it; or explain where its vital resource (e.g., water, blood, electricity) originates, and then describe how this resource functions as it flows through the object you are discussing.

3 Topical.

The topical pattern is most often used to divide your topic into standard categories or establish artificial groupings that reflect how your thesis approaches your topic. You can use a topical organizational pattern to compare anything from different weather or pollution patterns, to different types of parliamentary government or Protestant churches, to different genres of literature or mondo films. As with any comparative explanation, you should divide and explain each major division of your topic separately while weaving appropriate comparisons into your speech.

4   Deductive.

Like the deductive reasoning process, the deductive pattern allows you to move from general to more specific information about your topic (see Section 2.3). Thus, one effective way to organize your speech is to begin with a general definition of your topic, and then discuss some specific elements or illustrations of your topic. For example, when giving an informative speech about extrasensory perception, you could begin with a general definition of extrasensory perception, then explain some common characteristics of extrasensory perception, and finally describe an extrasensory experience through the testimony of a psychic (see Section 2.2).

5   Inductive.

Here again, like the inductive reasoning process, the inductive pattern allows you to move from specific to more general information about your topic (see Section 2.3). It is often used to build an argument by describing a series of specific examples of your topic and then summarizing what is generally true about them all. For instance, you can use this pattern first to describe several murders committed by different serial killers and then explain the general pattern of criminal behavior of most serial killers.

6   Parallel.

The parallel pattern allows you to focus on one particular element of your topic by repeating the same idea in different ways. This organizational pattern is best used when you want to offer several examples that illustrate the same point, to rephrase an explanation in slightly different yet illustrative ways, or to use a variety of metaphors and analogies to represent your topic (see Sections 2.2 and 6.5). When adopting this pattern, consider introducing each main point by using a parallel sentence structure and organizing each point in a similar way. For example, in a speech on African American inventors, focus each of your main points on a single inventor, introduce each inventor with a similarly constructed statement, give a short biography of each, explain each inventor's most significant contribution, and close with a personal quotation from each inventor.

7 Climactic.

The climactic pattern places your weaker points or arguments first, and your strongest and most effective points last. So that you do not loose your audience immediately, you should present one of your stronger arguments first, then your weaker ones, and finally, your strongest argument.[9] In some cases, you can use a climactic pattern to present your evidence incrementally and then combine each point into a more comprehensive claim. Consider using this organizational pattern for any type of persuasive speech (see Section 5.4).

8 Anticlimactic.

An anticlimactic pattern reverses the sequence of the climactic pattern and places your stronger points or arguments before your weaker ones. This pattern is not often used for two reasons: Convincing an audience, especially a hostile one, usually requires that you build on your evidence incrementally and thereby slowly move your audience toward your position; and after giving your strongest argument, your audience may think that the rest of speech contributes little to your claim. One instance when you should use this pattern is when you want to respond immediately to a previous speaker's arguments.[10]

9 Cause and effect.

The main function of the cause-effect pattern is to help you explain the cause-effect relationships pertaining to your topic (see Section 2.3). Although you may want to introduce your topic by stating some notable effects associated with it, organize the speech's body more chronologically by explaining its causes first (in increasing degrees of significance) and then its effects. In general, use this pattern to organize speeches dealing with the causes and effects of medical conditions, psychological illnesses, political developments, or social problems.

10 Problem and solution.

This is the general pattern used when you are discussing a problem and its solution. You can begin your speech by describing some symptoms of the problem or by giving a positive account of your solution before explaining the problem. Because of its focus on the temporal development of a problem and its solution, however, you should explain the problem first and then the solution in your speech's body. Although almost all persuasive speeches address a problem and its solution, several specific types of persuasive speeches, such as the stock issue speech and the policy speech, deal directly with problems and solutions (see Section 5.4).

4.5 Types of Transitions

Transitions are words, phrases, or statements that help establish a relationship between the parts or points of your speech (see Section 4.1). The eight types of transitions listed in this section perform a variety of functions: They provide information about your speech's structure, they signal what you have said or are about to say, and they identify the significance of a point. Transitions tell your audience something about your speech and what you, as the speaker, are going to discuss, so try to make eye contact with your audience when using a transition (see Section 7.3). Adopt a similar vocal technique when delivering your transitions, such as first pausing and then raising your tone and increasing your speed (see Section 7.2).

1   Preview transition.

A preview transition announces what you will be discussing next. Preview transitions often are used after your initial summary, to introduce your first main point, and after your last main point, to cue your conclusion (see Section 4.1). You can also use one to introduce each of your main points.

EXAMPLES

Let us begin by

Initially,

This brings us to the point of

It is important to recognize that

Let us now move to

I want to end by

To conclude,

2   Review transition.

A review transition brings logical coherence and clarity to your speech by summarizing what you have just said. Moreover, to provide a further indication of where you are going in your speech, you can tie your review transition to a preview transition that indicates what you will discuss next. Some good times to use a review transition are when you want to review a point before introducing a visual aid, tie together the main elements of a cause-effect relationship, or summarize the premises of an argument before stating its conclusion (see Sections 2.3 and 3.6).

EXAMPLES

As previously noted,

In summary,

We recall that

Up to this point we have seen that

Now if . . . , then

Having shown that . . . , let us now see how

3   Signpost transition.

Like the numbers in an outline, signpost transitions simply enumerate the various points of your speech. They can number items on a list, the order of steps in a process, or information displayed on a chart (see Sections 3.2 and 5.2).

EXAMPLES

My first point is

The second step is

Third,

4   Chronological transition.

A chronological transition indicates the temporal characteristic of a point or the temporal relationship between two points. By using a series of chronological transitions, you can convey the historical development of your topic or the time between steps in a process.

EXAMPLES

Before

Meanwhile,

Presently,

Following this event,

In the next few years,

After several minutes,

Early in her career,

Later in her life,

5   Spatial transition.

A spatial transition conveys the spatial relationship between elements in your speech. Use a series of spatial transitions when explaining the parts of an object or the elements of a visual aid. You can also combine spatial with chronological transitions when outlining the steps in a process.

EXAMPLES

Next to

To the right of

Adjacent to

On the opposite side of

6   Qualifying transition.

To clarify the significance of a point or characterize the relationship between points, use a qualifying transition (see Section 6.1). You can also use an argument qualifier to express the strength of the logical relationship between the premises and conclusion of an argument (see Section 2.4).

EXAMPLES

Unless

Although

Based upon the condition that

Only if

However,

It is likely that

This is only true if

Consequently,

Hence,

Therefore,

Thus, it follows that,

In all probability,

7   Relational transition.

A relational transition provides a link between points having the same or a similar significance, function, or meaning. Use a relational transition to show the relationship between your main points or to show how evidence supporting one point is similar to evidence supporting another. To emphasize the congruity between each main point, consider introducing each with the same transition, such as, "Another argument against the proposal is. . . ."

EXAMPLES

In addition,

Similarly,

Likewise,

So, just like

Another example of this is

Comparatively speaking,

This is very similar to

8   Oppositional transition.

Rather than linking similar ideas, an oppositional transition relates two points having a different meaning or significance. Consider using an oppositional transition when showing different perspectives on the same point, distinguishing between opposing arguments, or discussing the strengths and weaknesses of a point.

EXAMPLES

This is different from

Conversely,

Whereas

Unlike what I have just said,

On the one hand,

On the other hand,

4.6 Principles of Outlining

The main function of an outline is to represent the organization of your speech. Thus, your outline should clearly depict your speech's introduction, body, and conclusion and the main points, subpoints, and transitions that support and tie together each of its main parts (see Section 4.1). For the same reasons that you develop a preliminary thesis statement, you should create a working outline to help you collect and organize your research material (see Section 4.3). This working outline should contain potential main points, supporting evidence, and introductory, transitional, and concluding statements. Once you have collected and analyzed your evidence, you should begin formulating your thesis statement and organizing your ideas into an outline, and then, if necessary, into a manuscript. When developing your outline, continually verify that its parts remain consistent with your thesis statement, that each part relates clearly to the part before and after it, and that the whole speech is moving toward your intended conclusion (see Sections 4.1 and 4.3). Use the following principles to help you construct your outline or prepare your manuscript. For examples of both speech outlines and manuscripts, consult the Appendix.

1   Design your outline or manuscript so that it is easy to read when you are delivering your speech.

To avoid any problems that may occur with shuffling note cards, type your outline on a standard 8.5-by-11 inch sheet of paper.

To help you read your outline more easily, use an enlarged and bold font, and add extra line spacing. Similarly, when constructing a manuscript, you may want to use a fourteen-point font and double- or triple-space your pages. These design techniques make it easier for you to find your place in your speech's text after making eye contact with your audience. You also may want to use capital letters, different font types and sizes, and underlining to help you recognize the important elements in your text.

You also should consider creating large margins on either side of your text so that you can make any necessary last-minute changes or add notes to remind you of important delivery techniques. For example, if you talk too quickly, write "slow down" and "pause" in the margins to remind you to speak more slowly (see Section 7.2).

Finally, be sure to number each page so that you can easily rearrange your pages if they become disorganized. Place your title page and bibliography on separate pages so that you can set them aside when speaking.

2 Clearly distinguish between the main parts of your speech and between your main points, subpoints, and sub-subpoints.

The primary function of an outline is to demarcate the main parts of your speech and show the relationship among your points (see Section 4.1). Making these distinctions clear will help you write and deliver your speech. To help you distinguish between the main parts of your speech, follow these standard rules of outlining:

- Use Roman numerals to indicate the main parts of your speech, and designate them by name (e.g., "I. Introduction," "II. Body," and "III. Conclusion").

- Represent any transitions by separating them with an extra line, by indenting or italicizing them, or by naming them (e.g., "Transition:").

- Indicate main points with capital letters (e.g., "A.," "B.," "C.").

- Identify subpoints by indenting and using Arabic numbers (e.g., "1.," "2.," "3.").

- Designate sub-subpoints by indenting twice and using lower-case letters (e.g., "a.," "b.," "c.").

If your approach to a topic does not lend itself to this traditional style of outlining, create your own outline format. However, remember to use various symbols consistently when representing the different elements of your speech.

3   **Use your outline to reflect a clear symmetrical relationship among your speech's various parts.**

In general, each of your main points should have approximately the same number of subpoints, and each subpoint should have relatively the same number of sub-subpoints (see Section 4.1). By following this rule, you place the same emphasis and allot the same amount of time to congruent points. This technique enhances your speech's organizational structure and helps your audience differentiate your main points from your subpoints.

In general, when outlining a main point, make sure it has at least two subpoints. If a main point has fewer than two subpoints, consider making it into a subpoint of another main point, or eliminate it altogether. An exception to this rule is when you want to restate quickly some standard historical facts or operational procedures.

Subpoints should have no more than four sub-subpoints. If a subpoint has more than four sub-subpoints, consider making it into a main point. A possible exception to this rule is when your sub-subpoints consist of a list of items that you will discuss briefly.

4   **Use each main point to discuss a different issue relating to your topic.**

Your main points should not repeat one another; that is, they should be mutually exclusive. However, to make your speech coherent, you will need to establish some relationship between successive points. This coherence can be maintained effectively with strong transitional statements (see Section 4.5).

5   **Use a combination of complete sentences, short phrases, and separate words in your outline.**

Although a general rule of outlining holds that you should use a consistent grammatical form throughout your outline, it is often more effective to use different grammatical forms to represent different components of your speech. Since the content and organization of your speech are important, consider writing your main points and transitional statements as complete sentences (see Sections 4.1, 4.4, and 4.5). You may even want to use parallel sentences for all of your main points and transitions (see Section 6.1). This technique serves a variety of functions: it helps you recall your ideas more quickly; it provides a logical symmetry to your speech; and it allows you to identify the main parts of your speech more easily.

When outlining your subpoints, consider when you should use full sentences (as in the case of quotations), and when you should use short phrases for explanations, descriptions, and narratives so that you are forced to discuss them more extemporaneously (see Section 2.2). In addition, consider when you should represent your sub-subpoints with a single word. A single-word reference will help you recall the idea while reminding you to limit your discussion of it.

6   Place your oral citations within your outline, and place a bibliography of your sources at the end of your outline.

To make sure you use oral citations when necessary, place the reference next to the evidence drawn from the source (see Section 6.4 and the Appendix). You must also provide a bibliography of your sources at the end of your outline. If your instructor does not designate what particular notational system to use for either your citations or bibliography, find one that best suits your needs, and follow it throughout your speech. Two widely used styles of documentation are the Chicago style (see *The Chicago Manual of Style,* Fourteenth Edition) and the Modern Language Association (MLA) style (see the *MLA Handbook for Writers of Research Papers,* Fifth Edition). Examples of these two styles follow.

Chicago Style

Books

Book by one author
Loewen, James M. 1996. <u>Lies my teacher told me: Everything your American history textbook got wrong</u>. New York: Simon & Schuster.

Book by two or more authors
Shulman, James L., and William G. Brown. 2000. <u>The game of life: College sports and educational values</u>. Princeton, NJ: Princeton University Press.

Edited book
Sora, Joseph, ed. 1998. <u>Corporate power in the United States</u>. New York: H.W. Wilson.

Chapter or article in an anthology
Anderson, Christopher. 2000. Disneyland. In <u>Television: The critical view</u>. 6th ed. edited by Horace Newcomb. New York: Oxford University Press.

Periodicals

Newspaper article by one author
Rogers, Terry. 1997. "Taking a stand against pollu-
    tion." <u>San-Diego Union-Tribune</u>, 17 October, A1,
    A27.

Anonymous newspaper article
"The public school emergency." <u>New York Times</u>, 14
    November 2000, A30.

Article from a news periodical by one author
Check, Erika. 2000. "Monkeying around with the
    brain." <u>Newsweek</u> 136(27 November) 76.

Journal article
Craig, Richard. 2000. "Expectations and elections:
    How television defines campaign news." <u>Critical
    Studies in Mass Communication</u> 17, no. 1: 28-44.

Other Sources

Government document
U.S. Department of Commerce. 1992. <u>Workers with Low
    Earnings, 1964 to 1990</u>. Washington, D.C.: GPO.

Published interview
Jagger, Bianca. "Bianca Jagger: Eyewitness to Mur-
    der." Interview by Nancy Collins. In <u>George</u>
    5(November 2000): 86-89, 96-100.

Interview that you conducted
Brown, Wendy. Interview by author. Atlanta, Ga, 1
    September 2000.

Article from web site
Ritter, Bill. 2000. "Sniffing Out a Mate," in
    <u>ABCNEWS.com</u> [web site], 27 March 1998. [cited 15
    September 2000]. http://204.202.137.110/sections/
    living/DailyNews/pulse_sexsmells0328.html.

MLA Style

Books

Book by one author
Loewen, James M. <u>Lies My Teacher Told Me: Every-</u>
    <u>thing Your American History Textbook Got Wrong</u>.
    New York: Simon & Schuster, 1996.

Book by two or more authors
Shulman, James L., and William G. Brown. <u>The Game</u>
    <u>of Life: College Sports and Educational Values</u>.
    Princeton: Princeton University Press, 2000.

Edited book
Sora, Joseph, ed. <u>Corporate Power in the United</u>
    <u>States</u>. New York: H.W. Wilson, 1998.

Chapter or article in an anthology
Anderson, Christopher. "Disneyland." <u>Television:</u>
    <u>The Critical View</u>. 6th ed. Ed. Horace Newcomb.
    New York: Oxford University Press, 2000. 17–33.

Periodicals

Newspaper article by one author
Rogers, Terry. "Taking a Stand Against Pollution."
    <u>San-Diego Union-Tribune</u> 17 Oct. 1997, late ed.:
    A1+.

Anonymous newspaper article
"The Public School Emergency." <u>New York Times</u> 14
    November 2000: A30.

Article from a news periodical by one author
Check, Erika. "Monkeying Around with the Brain."
    <u>Newsweek</u> 27 November 2000: 76.

Journal article
Craig, Richard. "Expectations and Elections: How
    Television Defines Campaign News." <u>Critical</u>
    <u>Studies in Mass Communication</u> 17 (2000): 28–44.

Other sources

Government document
United States. Dept. of Commerce. <u>Workers with Low
    Earnings, 1964 to 1990</u>. Washington: GPO, 1992.

Published interview
Jagger, Bianca. "Bianca Jagger: Eyewitness to Mur-
    der." Interview with Nancy Collins. <u>George</u> (No-
    vember, 2000): 86–89, 96–100.

Interview that you conducted
Brown, Wendy. Personal interview. 1 September 2000.

Article from web site
Ritter, Bill. "Sniffing Out a Mate." <u>ABCNEWS.com</u> 27
    Mar. 1998. 15 Sept. 2000 <http://204.202.137.110/
    sections/living/DailyNews/pulse_sexsmells0328.html>.

5

Types of
Speeches

5.1   *Principles of Informative Speaking*
5.2   *Types of Informative Speeches*
5.3   *Principles of Persuasive Speaking*
5.4   *Types of Persuasive Speeches*
5.5   *Principles of Ceremonial Speaking*
5.6   *Types of Ceremonial Speeches*

5.1 Principles of Informative Speaking

All speeches, regardless of their topic, have an informative dimension. In an informative speech, your main intent is to either inform your audience about an unknown topic, elaborate on a topic they know little about, clarify a misunderstood topic, or present a well-known topic in a new light (see Section 5.2). In a persuasive speech, you will provide background on your topic as well as offer new information that will support your main claim (see Section 5.4). In a ceremonial speech, you must relay information that highlights the honoree's achievements and the reasons for the celebration or other event (see Section 5.6). Thus, the way you use evidence, make appeals, and present yourself in your speech play an important role in informative speaking and how well your audience receives your speech (see Sections 2.1, 2.2, 7.1, and 7.2). Thus, consider the principles of informative speaking given in this section when you are preparing your speech.

1   **Arouse and maintain your audience's interest in your topic and speech.**

Get your audience to listen attentively to your speech by first stirring their interest in your topic (see Sections 4.1 and 4.2). Often, you can arouse your audience's interest by showing your topic's significance. For instance, you can relate your topic to current events or to your audience's everyday concerns and experiences. To maintain their interest, explain how your speech adds to your audience's general understanding of your topic or how the information presented will be of value to them. To establish a more personal relationship between your audience and topic, relate your topic to a prior speech given in your class, a person that most of the audience knows, or the community in which they live.

You should also consider three techniques that will increase your audience's curiosity about your topic. First, consider asking a series of questions whose answers seem to be unrelated. Then tie your answers to these questions together by showing how each relates to your topic. A second technique suspensefully narrates a sequence of events involving your topic (see Section 2.2). If you can build a strong sense of anticipation for the story's ending, you may be able carry that excitement through the rest of your speech. Finally, set high expectations for your speech so that your audience is skeptical about your ability to accomplish your task but is then pleasantly surprised when you fulfill your goals. For instance, tell your audience that at the end of your demonstration speech on fishing, you will cast your lure into the garbage can sitting at the other end of the classroom.

2   Consider ways to employ the four modes of proof—logical, ethical, emotional, and normative—to inform your audience about your subject.

Although each form of proof is based on a different type of appeal, all can help inform your audience about your topic (see Section 2.1). Increase your speech's logical appeal by offering clear and engaging evidence to support your thesis and main points. In a speech on new medicines, present the results of an experiment on a new drug and then give concrete evidence of how it helps the body fight a disease. Likewise, when discussing the politics of a social movement, present a succinct chronology of the main events that led to legislative, social, and cultural changes.

Along with making logical appeals, you will need to build your credibility as a speaker (see Section 2.1). One common way to build your credibility is to present research from qualified sources or to describe a personal experience relating to your subject. You can also increase your credibility by appealing to your audience's values. For example, you can stress the value your audience places on education by telling them how a professional athlete went back to school to complete his or her college degree after signing a multimillion dollar contract.

Next, balance your logical and ethical appeals with emotional appeals (see Section 2.1). For example, when discussing the civil rights movement, explain how your research gave you a greater appreciation for the personal fortitude of those who practiced nonviolent civil disobedience. Finally, integrate normative appeals into your speech by discussing common experiences, narratives, and values that your audience identifies with (see Sections 2.1 and 2.2). In a speech on the Louisiana bayou country, capture the flavor of the region and the character of its people by narrating a local folktale. In addition, appeal to your audience's sense of the mythical in a speech on the American West by comparing the historical evidence on the West to how it is portrayed in Hollywood films.

3   Less is more.

Always speak in greater detail about a smaller number of points rather than trying to discuss multiple points briefly. By focusing on fewer points, you can show a greater understanding of your topic and relay more insightful information about it. Conversely, when attempting to discuss too many points, you may simply skim the surface of your topic. This superficial treatment usually makes your speech sound disorganized or as if it is just a series of commonsense explanations strung together. Because you can never discuss all the issues related to your speech, tell your audience what you are *not* going to discuss and why. This shows that you are aware of other issues relating to your topic and briefly explains the reasons why you chose not to discuss them.

4   Strike a balance between the old and the new.

Reassure your audience by starting with what they already know about your topic, and then provide new ideas and information. Novelty is essential to effective informative speaking. When discussing new developments relating to your topic, begin with ideas or issues that are well known or simple, and then move to new or more complex matters. Likewise, make your audience comfortable with a new topic by comparing it to other topics with which they are already familiar. Last, after citing familiar statistics, examples, and quotations, introduce unknown, yet insightful information that shows your topic in a new light (see Section 2.2). For instance, in a speech on the Olympics, discuss how the ancient games held oratory and dramatic competitions alongside athletic events.

5   Be consistent, yet use variety.

By organizing your speech's body in a coherent way, returning to a particular theme throughout the speech, and repeating certain forms of evidence in each of your main points, your audience will be able to recognize the structure of your speech more easily (see Sections 2.2, 4.4, and 6.1).

Once you have built your speech on a coherent and consistent structure, look for ways to add variety to your speech so that it does not become monotonous. First, find ways to combine different forms of evidence that will balance each other's strengths and weaknesses and allow you to appeal to the logical, moral, and emotional sides of your audience. Second, consider how you can rephrase complex ideas so that your audience hears them explained in different ways. Third, find ways to add an element of surprise to your speech. For instance, compare two seemingly unrelated statistics, or use an analogy or metaphor to tell a story with an unusual ending.

Finally, balance your audience's desire for consistency and variety by combining similar and different stylistic and speaking techniques (see Sections 6.1, 6.2, 7.1, and 7.2). One such technique is to start each of your main points with a similarly constructed topic sentence, but then end each point with a different figure of speech (see Section 6.5). You also could repeat similar speaking techniques to help represent similar aspects of your speech. Thus, lower your tone and slow your pace every time you give a definition, but raise your voice and speed up your delivery when offering an example. You also should vary your delivery to represent the different parts of your speech as well as the different logical and emotional qualities of your evidence. Varying your vocal and gesturing techniques will also prevent you from sounding monotone and appearing stiff.

6   Use evidence and language that is specific and concrete.

Always try to provide a concrete description, example, or statistic; and use clear, concise language when discussing each of your major points (see Sections 6.1 and 6.2). At the same time, avoid introducing too many abstract principles and technical terms by stating your point in more common ways that are readily apparent to your audience. Thus, rework a complex explanation into an analogy based on something from nature or everyday life, or tie any abstract idea or principle to a clear fact, tangible description, revealing statistic, or specific example that represents your point more explicitly (see Section 2.2).

7   Use transitions, qualifiers, and your vocal delivery to represent your speech's organization and content.

Transitional phrases that move you from one part of your speech to another such as, "My first point is" and, "This brings us to the point of" help your audience follow your speech's organization (see Section 4.5). Qualifying statements such as, "One of the study's most crucial findings was" or, "A minor effect of the problem" help them recognize the weight you place on your evidence (see Section 6.1). In a similar way, extending a pause and changing your tone, speed, and volume can help your audience recognize when you are moving from one part of your speech to another (see Section 7.2).

8   Be energetic and enthusiastic.

Part of your credibility as a speaker rests with the spirited manner in which you discuss your topic. If you are not enthusiastic about your speech or show no personal interest in your topic, you will lose your audience's interest and attention. Thus, always deliver a strong piece of evidence with conviction, show that you enjoy the story you are telling, and display confidence in your ability to speak.

5.2 Types of Informative Speeches

The subject of most informative speeches is a person, place, or event that you want to help your audience better understand. However, you can create an informative speech on most any topic (see Section 1.3). The main intent of any informative speech is to explain, describe, define, or demonstrate a topic; hence, each of the main types of informative speeches listed in this section are named according to your speech's purpose and the primary form of evidence you will use to fulfill that purpose. When preparing an informative speech, first determine its main intent, and then choose which of the various types of informative speeches will accomplish your purpose best. Also, remember to use the general speech structure for organizing your whole speech, and, if necessary, one or more of the patterns for organizing the speech's body (see Section 4.1 and 4.4).

1   Speech of Explanation.

The main intent of this speech is to explain a person, place, event, process, idea, or issue whose main characteristics, components, causes and effects, or history is either unknown to or not fully understood by your audience.[1] Usually, a speech of explanation breaks down your topic into its main parts or subject areas. For example, you can explain the Palestinian Intifada by discussing its main political groups, or define Hinduism by addressing its most sacred beliefs. A speech of explanation can also offer a series of explanations, descriptions, and analogies that clarify a technical subject, such as how a compact disc player works (see Section 2.2). Or you can explain a new topic by comparing and contrasting it to an old topic (see Section 4.1). For example, you can explain how digital communication is changing the nature of interpersonal relationships by showing the differences between everyday communication and communication in cyberspace. A speech of explanation may also address a complex subject that, on its surface, appears rather simple. For instance, you could explain the various physiological processes that occur when someone falls asleep. To see a good example of a speech of explanation, consult the Appendix.

Use a chronological, spatial, or topical pattern of organization.   Depending on your topic, use one or several of the organizational patterns outlined in Chapter 4 to formulate your speech (see Section 4.4). For instance, you could combine chronological and topical patterns to organize a speech on the history of AIDS and its possible causes and cures.

Go beyond merely stating the facts about your topic, and use evidence that will analyze and explain it in more detail.   Explain what your topic's main components are and how they function, how its major causes produce their effects, and what possible future developments are likely to occur. When offering a chronology leading up to a major historical event, do not just state when each prior event occurred, but describe what actually happened, explain why the event is significant, and discuss the role of important individuals related to the event. Likewise, do not simply state the major episodes in a person's life, but analyze how these events affected his or her behavior, beliefs, and accomplishments.

Use examples, narratives, testimony, and other forms of evidence to explore your subject further.   Supplement your explanation of a subject by citing a specific example that illustrates your explanation, telling a story that represents your explanation's main idea, or offering testimony that further clarifies your explanation (see Section 2.2).

2   Speech of definition.

Topics for a speech of definition usually include a term, idea, person, place, event, or object that is not well defined or is defined improperly. Your speech of definition will help your audience to understand your topic and distinguish it from other similar subjects.[2] For instance, use a speech of definition to discuss a group of people that your audience knows very little about, like a dangerous paramilitary group. In addition, you could introduce your audience to a new term such as *postmodernism,* or clarify a controversial one such as *feminism.* You may also want to define something in a way that differs from its conventional definition so that you can pursue a unique interpretation of your topic. For example, when defining *addiction,* you may want to concentrate on psychological addictions to exercise or sex, rather than physical addictions to alcohol or drugs.

Create a thesis statement that defines the term and states what implications your definition has for your subject.   Make clear in your thesis statement why defining the term differently from its more common definition is important (see Section 4.3). Then, in the body and conclusion of your speech, explain how the new definition provides your audience with a new and richer understanding of an issue, event, or controversy related to your topic (see Section 4.1).

Before offering a new definition, clarify the term's standard definition. Begin with a standard definition so that you can compare it to your new definition. When constructing your standard definition, refer to the dictionary. Then create a new definition by showing how professional lexicons and dictionaries define the term. You also should research critical essays found in periodicals and scholarly journals that discuss the term. Use these various definitions to develop the term's etymology; break the term down into different categories; or show its usage in various historical, geographical, or professional settings (see Section 2.2). Finally, explain the advantages of your new definition, such as its clarity or applicability to a set of issues, while showing the disadvantages of the standard definition, such as its ambiguity or impractical usage.

Define the term by explaining its similarities and differences to other terms with which it is often associated.   Another way to define your term is to compare it to its synonyms. Conversely, use an oppositional definition to explain what the term is not (see Section 2.2). You also can compare the term's denotative and connotative meanings, or contrast the term to other terms with which it is often associated or confused. For instance, differentiate a *liberal* from a *libertarian, impressionism* from *expressionism,* or a *fraction* from a *fractal.*

Illustrate your definition through an analogy, example, or other forms of evidence.   Use an analogy to represent how your term is used based on how another, similar term is used. You can also illustrate your term with an example or explore its usage in a famous literary or historical quotation (see Section 2.2).

Do not confuse your audience with too many definitions.   Rather than baffling your audience with a vast array of possible definitions, focus on a small set of definitions so that they recognize its most important elements. Remember that "less is more" (see Section 5.1). For similar reasons, draw the implications of your definition from a limited set of issues.

3   Speech of description.

This speech describes the various characteristics of a person, place, thing, or activity. Use this speech to create a clear picture of your subject by vividly describing its properties, qualities, appearance, actions, or behavior. When organizing a speech of description, consider using one or a combination of the chronological, spatial, or topical patterns of organization (see Section 4.4). For instance, when giving a descriptive speech on London, you may want to first give its history, then describe the layout of its streets and neighborhoods, and finally, explain the character of street life.

Focus your speech on describing your topic.   The primary purpose of a speech of description is to help your audience visualize your topic. Hence, you can limit your purpose simply to informing and delighting your audience with a rich description of your topic (see Section 2.2).

Complement your description with other forms of evidence, such as explanations, examples, testimony, and narratives.   As with any description, concentrate on giving a detailed account of specific attributes of your topic, rather than stating vague generalities about its well-known characteristics. For example, describe the motifs found in a piece of architecture, and then explain how these motifs reflect a certain set of religious or social values. Consider presenting narratives and examples that will embellish your description (see Section 2.2). For instance, describe an event in a politician's early life that reflects his or her political ambition, tell an anecdotal story that highlights a peculiar incident relating to a major historical event, or cite a series of examples that show the various ways different animals have evolved in order to adapt to a changing ecosystem.

4   Speech of demonstration.

A speech of demonstration usually shows how to do something or how something works. Classic topics for demonstration speeches include different first aid techniques, exercise routines, and hobbies, but also consider alternative topics such as new computer technologies or alternative energy sources. When choosing a demonstrative speech topic, consider whether it will keep your audience's attention because it is a new, unfamiliar, or complicated process. Do not choose a mundane topic such as making a peanut butter and jelly sandwich or applying cosmetics. Instead, present a demonstrative speech on making peanut butter or putting on clown makeup.

Choose a topic that you can demonstrate in the allotted time, and practice the speech so you know what to concentrate on and what to omit. As a general rule, you should consider your audience as novices and focus your speech on introducing the main steps in the procedure you are demonstrating. If time allows, you can show them one or two more sophisticated or intricate techniques or aspects of your topic. For instance, after showing them the fundamental techniques of riding and stopping a skateboard, you might have time to show them one basic trick.

Remember that the most important part of a demonstrative speech is the demonstration itself. Thus, if your demonstration does not add anything new to your topic, find another topic to demonstrate. Likewise, do not just explain your topic while displaying your visual aids, but actually demonstrate something in your speech.

When performing a demonstrative speech, divide your subject into separate steps, clearly explain each step's primary function, and then relate each step to the next until you show how to complete the whole task or how your subject works as a whole. If necessary, explain the criteria used to determine whether the task was accomplished correctly.

Use both the chronological and spatial patterns of organization. Demonstrate each step of a process in its proper sequence and spatial order (see Section 4.4). Start with either the subject's designated beginning, entrance point, or source of energy. Then follow its most common path of development. Next, explain each of the subject's major components, its purpose, and the procedures for its proper employment. Do not skip a step, even if you think your audience is familiar with it; instead, briefly summarize the step and then continue to the next. If a step takes too long, explain what would occur in the step, and then show a sample of the results you previously prepared.

Present interesting and helpful background information pertaining to your subject.   Present this background material early in your speech, perhaps in your introduction or first point. For example, give a brief history of your subject, categorize its main types, or introduce the equipment that you will use in the demonstration. In the case of such equipment as sporting gear, work tools, or hobby supplies, you may want to discuss the range of styles, costs, and uses for this equipment and suggest what someone who wants to take up the activity should pay for this equipment.

In some instances, consider presenting a broad overview of the process or activity you are demonstrating before breaking it down into its individual steps.   This overview serves several important functions. First, it shows what the activity looks like when actually performed.

Second, it shows the process as a whole before you artificially break it down into steps. Third, it allows the audience to see the goal of the activity demonstrated. Fourth, it builds your credibility by showing that you can perform the task well.

Use visual aids to help demonstrate your subject. Because the main intent of a demonstration speech is actually to demonstrate your subject, you will need to use visual aids that will help your audience see the steps you are demonstrating or the object you are explaining and describing (see Chapter 3). Remember, a speech without visual aids usually is not considered a demonstration speech. Determine when, how, and with what types of visual aids you can help your audience better understand what you are demonstrating.

Use appeals to authorities. Integrate into your speech examples and testimonials of authorities or professionals who use the procedures being demonstrated (see Section 2.2). Compare and contrast their different techniques, and offer expert opinion on the best and worst ways to perform the activity being described.

Connect each step of your demonstration with appropriate transitions, and use a word or phrase to represent each step. Use transitional phrases such as "Begin by," "After having . . . , proceed to," and "Remember to" to indicate where you are in the process being demonstrated and to relate important pieces of information about each step (see Section 4.5). Use signpost transitions to number each step, and repeat the number each time you refer to the step, rather than referring ambiguously to each step by repeating the word *Next*.

You also should consider using a mnemonic device to help your audience follow the process you are demonstrating. Such a device also will allow you to recall the steps more easily, thus giving you freedom from your outline when you are demonstrating (see Section 7.4). For instance, use the phrase "Stop, Drop, Roll" when demonstrating what to do when caught in a fire and the phase "Look, Listen, Feel" when determining the need for CPR. Also consider creating a word chart to represent the steps being demonstrated (see Section 3.2).

Repeat the main steps in the procedure you are demonstrating. As you break down and build up each step being demonstrated, restate each step in similar ways so that the audience begins to recognize and remember the sequence of steps more easily.

Talk through your demonstration. Always try to explain an activity while you are demonstrating it. However, if explaining and demonstrating your subject at the same time is too difficult, have an assistant demonstrate the procedure while you explain what he or she is doing (see Section 3.3). Alternatively, you could explain the procedure first and then give some helpful hints, such as do's and don'ts, or tell a story that deals with your topic while you are demonstrating the procedure. These techniques prevent you from having long, awkward moments of silence while performing your demonstration.

5.3 Principles of Persuasive Speaking

The general intent of persuasive speaking is to convince your audience to accept the idea, adopt the value, or engage in the action advocated in your speech. You can also induce your audience to question their previous beliefs, change their attitudes about your topic, or view your topic from an alternative perspective. Persuasive speaking highlights the evidence, arguments, and strategies of persuasion that will accomplish one or more of these tasks (see Sections 2.2, 2.3, and 2.4). Because different subjects necessitate different strategies of persuasion, consider which of the principles listed in this section will help you persuade your audience to accept your thesis statement (see Section 4.3).

1 Consider your audience's attitude toward your subject and your thesis statement.

Although several different ways to assess an audience have already been discussed, persuasive speaking also demands that you evaluate your audience's prior attitude to your subject and thesis so that you can present the most convincing speech based on your audience's particular character (see Section 1.2). To this extent, you can define your audience's attitude in terms of how receptive they may be to your thesis statement (see Section 4.3).[3] A **receptive audience** is one who already agrees with your main claim. Because they already hold the same convictions you do, you can state your thesis directly and strongly. This directness allows you to build on the common beliefs you share early in your speech. Then, because your audience is familiar with your arguments and agrees with them already, you can give succinct arguments and concentrate more on using effective language and emotional appeals, rather than presenting hard evidence and rigorous arguments throughout your speech's body (see Sections 2.1 and 6.1). Such vivid language and strong emotional appeals will increase their agreement with your thesis and move them to act upon their convictions.

An **unreceptive audience** generally disagrees with your claim. Before facing an unreceptive audience, determine why they disagree with you. Consider, for instance, what values, beliefs, and attitudes they have that oppose yours, and then try to construct arguments and appeals based on values and evidence they agree with in order to lessen their opposition to your claim (see Section 1.2). With an unreceptive audience, you may not want to state your thesis directly because your audience's immediate reaction may be very negative (see Section 4.3). Hence, do not state your main claim directly, but briefly outline the main points you will discuss.[4] To be convinced, these audience members will need to hear strong evidence and arguments in support of your thesis before you state it (see Sections 2.2 and 2.3). You also should seek to accomplish only a moderate goal with your speech and use neutral language that will not antagonize your audience. The only exception to these rules is when you intentionally want to provoke your audience with a thesis statement that asks them to change their thinking or actions dramatically.

Speaking to an unreceptive audience also demands that you begin your speech by building your credibility and establishing those beliefs and values relating to your topic that you and your audience hold in common (see Section 2.1). First, clearly yet respectfully refute the best arguments against your claim, and then present the strongest evidence and arguments supporting your claim (see Sections 2.2 and 2.3). Then, when making your arguments, always tie your claim to principles, values, and concrete evidence that your audience already accepts or would have difficulty refuting. Finally, use expert testimony and cite your sources extensively so that your audience immediately recognizes the authoritative support for your evidence and arguments.

Finally, you may have a **neutral audience**—one who has not previously considered your topic or does not hold any strong beliefs about it—or a **mixed audience**—one whose members agree and disagree with your claim to varying degrees. When you have either type of audience, try to appeal to everyone. Begin by stressing how your topic affects everyone. Point out how your topic may affect individuals or groups differently, but how everyone shares some of its common effects. Then identify the values and beliefs about your topic that they all may share with you (see Sections 1.2 and 2.1). Then apply those values and beliefs to your topic and show how these values underlie your thesis or one of your claims. Next, summarize important background information about your topic so that your audience members all start with the same knowledge base and thus will be inclined to view your topic similarly. Move then to presenting clear and convincing evidence as to why they should accept your claims (see Section 2.2). Last, use strong language and emotional appeals to increase their agreement with your claim or to motivate them to act on it (see Section 2.1).

2   Present strong evidence and rational, sound, and clear arguments.

Of the four modes of proof, logical proofs provide your audience with the most effective arguments based on strong evidence and clear reasoning (see Section 2.1). If members of your audience believe you are manipulating them with weak evidence and faulty reasoning, they may reject everything you say.

In general, place your strongest evidence and logical arguments in your speech's body. However, placing such evidence in your introduction can win over audience members early as well as set a rational tone. The best types of evidence to use when making logical appeals are factual explanations, irrefutable statistics, and testimony from renowned authorities (see Section 2.2). Also, remember that a well-constructed deductive, inductive, causal, or two-sided argument can have great logical appeal (see Section 2.3).

3   Increase your persuasiveness by showing your audience that you are trustworthy and hold the same values as they do with respect to your subject.

Explore ways you can build your credibility as a speaker (see Section 2.1). For instance, you can show empathy for your audience's views and concerns about your topic. Specifically, you can explain how you hold to the same moral, ethical, or political principles as they do and then show how to apply these principles to the issue at hand.

One of the best methods for establishing an ethical bond with your audience in a persuasive speech is to appeal to your audience's hierarchy of values (see Section 1.2). For example, you can show how your claim places more importance on human life or the environment than on profits, or how your claim tries to bring people together based on their commonly held values and needs rather than trying to split them apart based on their differences. By establishing this bond, you present yourself as someone who seeks consensus and is considerate of everyone's views.

You can also enhance your trustworthiness by honestly stating the limits of your claims. You can point out the flaws in an argument you support, assert how a rational person could hold an opinion different from yours, or present evidence in a neutral manner so that your audience formulates their own judgment about an issue. Finally, you can gain credibility implicitly by referring to credible authorities and clearly stating your sources in oral citations (see Section 6.4). Both of these techniques will show that your evidence and claims are based on reliable sources.

4 Appeal to your audience's values and emotional needs.[5]

By using such appeals, you can represent yourself as sharing the same emotional ties to your topic as your audience holds (see Section 2.1). You also can appeal to your audience's emotions by explaining how your claim benefits their families or community. Similarly, you can construct proofs that appeal to your audience's sense of equality, fairness, and justice.

Other ways of making a valuative appeal are to show the personal and social benefits resulting from your speech's claim. Here, you can use an unlimited array of evidence and arguments. For example, you could use a hypothetical example to show how an individual or group of people will gain more self-esteem, save money, or achieve greater success by adopting the ideas or actions you advocate (see Section 2.2). You could tell a story about how someone following your suggestions was able to advance his or her political rights or personal welfare. Moreover, you could give a legal argument that shows how the law you advocate will help your audience overcome illegal or immoral forms of power, social control, or individual manipulation (see Section 2.3). Similarly, you can present a causal argument explaining how a policy caused a group of people harm and how your policy will treat them more fairly.

When appealing to your audience's emotions, understand the legitimate reasons why your audience may have such emotions, and direct your appeals accordingly. In other words, determine how to arouse their emotions in justifiable ways. And never fake your emotions; a false expression of sentiment will cause your audience to suspect your motives. One of the best ways to express your emotions sincerely is first to visualize the event or action that stimulates the emotional response in you, and then attempt to describe the event, action, or the response to your audience.

You should determine what level of the emotion you want your audience to experience. Be careful when appealing to emotions such as fear and anxiety or sympathy and pity. In general, your audience will react to a point in the way that you present it. Appeals to fear and anxiety may prevent your audience from dealing with a problem sensibly, and thus may cause them to think about or react to the issue impulsively rather than rationally. Even worse, by overstating your emotional appeal, you may make your audience so uncomfortable that they stop listening or turn against you because they see you as the "bearer of bad news." Consequently, appeal to fear only when you can show that there are legitimate reasons why your audience should be fearful; that is, clearly explain how the ideas or actions you are criticizing will negatively affect them. Thus, limit and direct your appeals to fear and anger to those people and actions that pose a grave threat to your audience and that clearly represent a view or action you vehemently oppose. Also, avoid trying to invoke pity on behalf of greedy, mean, or lawless people. When necessary, however, argue that regardless of their negative personal traits, such people should be treated fairly and decently, for this expression of fairness will build your credibility (see Section 2.1). Finally, remember that, in most cases, the closer in space and time your audience is to your topic, the stronger their emotional tie to your topic will be.

When invoking sympathy and pity, vividly describe the events, people, actions, and emotions so that your audience lives vicariously through your description. Always emphasize the ways in which your audience can change these emotions into activities that will improve a situation; this emphasis allows your audience to experience a full range of emotions and convictions, from empathy for others, to anger directed at the injustice you describe, to a sense of personal integrity for taking up the cause you are advocating.

5   **Relate commonly held beliefs, norms, and narratives to your claim.**

Offer narratives, examples, and arguments based on myths, legends, stories, proverbs, and commonsense beliefs shared by your audience (see Sections 2.1 and 2.2). Consider telling a story about someone who gave his or her life for the cause you are advocating. Or create an argument from signs that explain how the election of a political candidate in a foreign country can be interpreted as a sign of the country's movement toward greater democracy or freedom (see Section 2.3). These strategies reflect values, traditions, and principles that may increase your audience's agreement with your claim or stimulate them to act on it.

6   **Support your claims by stating both general moral or political principles and specific evidence and arguments.**

Because of time limits, you will be unable to give detailed explanations and arguments about every aspect of your topic. Consequently, first provide a general analysis of the moral principles, philosophical ideals, or general policy guidelines that pertain to your topic and claim, and then offer specific examples, explanations, statistics, and arguments that support your general statements (see Section 2.2). For instance, explain how a new discovery is causing us to redefine a past event, show how a political ideal is put into practice by a policy, or refute a common belief about a government program by offering statistics that show the program in a different light.

7   Apply principles and values consistently.

Your audience is more likely to change their thinking or action if the suggested change is consistent with their present thinking about a related subject. Thus, use analogies that show how your position is consistent with their thinking on similar matters (see Section 2.2). For instance, show how a voucher system that allows parents to choose which private or public school their children will attend is similar to the G.I. bill, which allows military personnel to use government money to attend the private or public university, college, or trade school of their choice.

8   Ask your audience to make small and gradual changes in their thinking or actions.

Unless you are speaking to a very receptive audience, ask your audience to make small and incremental changes rather than drastic ones. Be realistic about what you can expect from a mostly unreceptive or neutral audience, and stress moderate changes in their thinking or actions. However, if your solution mandates an extensive plan, stress what needs to be done in the immediate future, but tie these actions to your long-term goals. This strategy is often necessary when you have to convince an unreceptive audience that you are not offering a quick fix to the problem.

9   Use a cost–benefit analysis to weigh the disadvantages of your claim against its advantages.

Show that the changes you are recommending will produce benefits that outweigh their costs. You can give this analysis in purely quantitative terms by contrasting the initial costs of your plan with its future savings, or qualitatively, by comparing the principles upheld in your speech to those forfeited. For instance, you could contrast the cost of special education programs for disabled students with the money saved in welfare services that the government otherwise would incur if such programs did not exist. In a speech on art and freedom of expression, you could weigh the feelings of a community who want to ban an unpatriotic work of art against the artist's right of free expression. You can also conduct a cost–benefit analysis by clearly stating why it is to your audience's advantage to adopt your position or engage in the action you advocate and why it is to their disadvantage not to do so.

10 **Make detailed comparisons between things your audience accepts (or opposes) and other things they view positively (or negatively).**

Such associations may incline your audience to view your claims more favorably while weakening their support for opposing ones. For example, use an analogy to compare something you favor to something they favor, or show how the value or principle you are arguing against has some clear negative implications for something they are familiar with. When making such comparisons, always use strong, positive or negative terms.

11 **Qualify your claims clearly so you do not overstate them.**

Because it may be difficult to explain all the factors contributing to a complex problem, you should not overstate your case by wording your statements too definitively, such as, "One's genetic makeup is *the* cause of alcoholism," or "The *only* solution to racism is. . . ." Rather, make it clear that you are discussing the primary factors relating to the problem or solution; hence, qualify your statements by saying, "Although environmental influences play some role in one's propensity to alcoholism, for the most part, it is determined by . . . ," or "Although racism must be fought on a variety of fronts, our main efforts should be directed in three areas. . . ."

12 **Limit the potential criticisms against your claim by addressing these criticisms directly.**

Point out any potential problems that may undermine your claim, and try to explain them away. Moreover, always qualify a proposed program or policy by stating the circumstances under which your program's goal would not be reached, such as a lack of funding or staffing or because of an economic downturn. Likewise, if you base your claim on an existing program or policy that has had some problems, explain how to modify the program to avoid such problems. Moreover, show how, despite its failures, the program was largely successful.

13 **Use humor sparingly and always as a means to address your issue.**[6]

The intent of a humorous statement is to make light of an issue related to your subject to ease the tension of dealing with a difficult subject. In most instances, your humor should lead back to the issue at hand. The only exception to this rule is when you want to gain your audience's favor by poking fun at yourself, your audience, or the setting. Try to create humor that reflects a lighter side of your topic or shows that you or the people you are discussing have a sense of humor about themselves and their agenda. In addition, use evidence humorously by playing on a word, presenting contradictory statistics, restating an outrageous quotation, or relating a current event to your speech in an unexpected way. When using hyperbole or understatement, show through your wording, tone, and gesturing that your exaggeration is meant to humor and not mislead. Then, if possible, apply the general sentiment of your hyperbole to an example or idea in a more feasible or realistic way.

Do not try to tell jokes for big laughs, because if the jokes are not well received, your audience may resist further attempts to be informed, persuaded, or amused. Likewise, do not offend your audience's sense of decency with a mean-spirited attack on an opponent. Finally, never make a stereotypical comment about a group of people.

14 When motivating your audience to act or when arguing for a program or policy, offer a clear plan for implementing your suggestions.

Once you have established the evidence and arguments supporting your claim, give your audience a clear, concise plan explaining how the program or policy can be put into effect, or show how they can change their actions in the easiest manner possible. Here again, you should stress short-term rather than long-term goals, although you may have to explain the advanced stages of your plan.

Be as specific as possible about your recommendations, unless the information you need to assess, such as the cost of your proposal, is not available. If you are advocating a policy or program, determine and discuss what funds, staff, equipment, and time are required to make improvements. If you are suggesting a course of action, such as how to train for a triathlon, explain the specific exercises, diet program, and timetable one should use or follow to accomplish the goal (see Section 5.4). You also should provide any material that will allow your audience to act on your suggestions. For instance, distribute handouts, pamphlets, letters, or petitions that your audience can keep or sign.

Finally, make clear who the main agents are for solving the problem or changing the policy. If the main agent is a government administration, private company, or civic association, explain why one of these groups is the best candidate for solving the problem or enacting a different policy because it has the responsibility, means, or record for doing so. If the main agents are individuals acting on their own behalf, direct your appeals to your audience as people who can change their present situation by adopting your proposal. However, do not limit your appeal only to individual audience members by saying that they should further educate themselves about the issue or call their political representatives on behalf of your proposal, when in fact the balance of power to resolve the problem lies with other persons or institutions.

5.4 Types of Persuasive Speeches

Each of the following types of persuasive speech uses different strategies of persuasion: the first is the basic organizational structure used in the classical age; the second is used to move your audience to act on a proposed solution to a problem; the third, to argue issues of fact; the fourth, to argue issues of values; and the fifth, to advocate a policy. As with the organizational patterns and types of speeches previously discussed, you can combine two or more of these types of persuasive speeches or alter their organization to fit the needs of your particular topic, thesis statement, and evidence (see Sections 2.2, 4.4, and 5.2). Moreover, you should consider how to modify these persuasive speech types to achieve more specific goals. For instance, you could integrate elements of Monroe's Motivated Sequence with the policy speech to develop a more effective speech on how to solve a problem with a policy, or you could use the refutation step of the classical speech to focus your speech on offering criticisms against an argument.

1   Classical speech.

The classical speech follows one variation of the organizational structure typically used in classical oratory, particularly for legal speeches.[7] Although that organizational structure has been simplified here, this format can still present arguments on almost any subject effectively, especially those subjects in which it is important to clarify the facts about some event, indicate how these facts should be interpreted, or refute counterarguments that your audience holds. For instance, consider using this speech design when making such claims as, "Neither Bush nor Gore won the 2000 presidential election in Florida," or "Bill Clinton committed perjury," or "Terrorism is a form of global warfare."

Introduction.   Use your introduction to begin building support for yourself and your claim and to familiarize your audience with the issues you will address (see Sections 4.1 and 4.2). One way to win your audience's favor is to establish your credibility by showing knowledge of your topic, citing common moral values, and extending goodwill to your audience (see Section 2.1). To reflect your moral convictions, you can refer to a maxim, value, or principle that you will later use as a basis of an argument, appeal to an expert authority or person with high moral standing that agrees with your claim, or make appeals on behalf of people who have been treated unfairly. You also can show the significance of your topic, indicate the new approach you take to your topic, or begin painting your opponent and his or her claim in a negative light. To make your audience more receptive to your speech, use common terms, metaphors, and analogies that are easy to understand (see Section 6.1).

Narration.　The narration step provides a description of the facts relating to your topic. You should present the necessary background information relating to your topic, such as the people involved in the issue, their actions and motives, the main events surrounding your topic, and any eyewitness accounts or documentation of what occurred. Once the facts are stated, you should indicate the basis of the dispute regarding the facts. Some effective rhetorical strategies for highlighting the dispute are to attack your opponent's claims or credibility or to imply how the facts contradict his or her claim by offering an amusing anecdote, curious paradox, or (rhetorical) question (see Sections 2.2 and 6.5).

　　If your audience and the facts of the case are strongly predisposed against your claim, be very brief, offer a neutral description of the facts, and insinuate how extenuating circumstances, or other possible ways to look at the evidence, must be considered. If your audience and the facts favor your claim, then develop the chronology of events more fully and vividly, but do not belabor your point. Either way, your presentation of the facts should be brief, clear, descriptive, and well-ordered.

Partition.　Like a thesis statement and preview summary, your partition states what elements of your subject you will discuss (see Section 4.1). Here, you can state what facts you accept and then outline those that are in dispute, or you can indicate the rationale of the main arguments you will use to reinterpret the events or actions in question.

Confirmation.　A confirmation uses evidence to construct arguments in favor of your position (see Sections 2.2, 2.3, and 2.4). Thus, your confirmation should demonstrate how the facts related to events or actions under question lead to your claim. You also can show how the events or actions do not violate the principles of a definition, code, or law by which they are being judged; or you could indicate how the facts should be judged by a different set of criteria. Another way to confirm your claim is to paint the events and actions under scrutiny in a positive light by showing how they lead to beneficial results.

Your confirmation should be limited to three or four main proofs. When possible, use clear transitions to tie your arguments together and move your audience from one argument to the next in a manner that shows the logical consistency of your arguments (see Section 4.5).

If an opponent has spoken first or if your audience strongly disagrees with your claim, begin with your strongest arguments and move to your weaker ones. You may even want to switch the order of your arguments and refutation. To create both a strong initial and final impression, conceal your weakest arguments between your stronger ones.

Refutation.   The refutation presents arguments against counterclaims that either endorse another position or attempt to disprove your claim. You should spend the majority of your time refuting your opponent's strongest arguments and quickly dismiss his or her weaker ones with direct and specific counterarguments. Here again, concentrate on refuting no more than three or four main arguments.

When refuting an argument, first, clearly state the arguments you will refute and show their relevance in terms of how they affect your audience's perception of your topic or position. Then refute your opponent's arguments by attacking his or her argument's faulty or insufficient evidence. In addition, point out how the argument misrepresents evidence or does not consider evidence that would contradict its claim. You might also show how your opponent's arguments use illogical reasoning or commit a logical fallacy, such as a straw man fallacy or an attack on the person (see Sections 2.3 and 2.5). Finally, explain the significance of your refutation by indicating how your audience should understand your topic differently. You should also show how the combined strengths of your argument outweigh those of your opponent.

Conclusion.   As in most persuasive speeches, your conclusion should summarize your arguments and your criticisms of opposing arguments. To summarize effectively, briefly recall your main arguments and reiterate how they outweigh your opponent's. In addition, consider using an authoritative testimony, example, or analogy to point out either the positive implications of your argument or the negative implications of your opponent's (see Section 2.2). You also should end your speech with an emotional and ethical appeal on behalf of yourself and your claim, and against your opponent and his or her position. These appeals should use strong language and moving figures of speech (see Sections 2.1, 6.1, and 6.5). Two ways to make such appeals are to arouse sympathy for those negatively affected by the opposing arguments, or to express outrage against those whose arguments or actions violate a commonly held value or norm.

2   Monroe's motivated sequence.

This speech is organized in a sequence of steps that follow the same reflective thinking process we usually use when trying to solve a problem.[8] This organizational pattern may help you to first make your audience aware of a problem, then persuade them to accept your solution, and finally, motivate them to act on your solution. Persuasive speeches that induce your audience to adopt a diet plan, quit smoking, work for a nonprofit organization, recycle, or start an Individual Retirement Account (IRA) can be based on this organizational structure.

Bring attention to the problem.   Begin by focusing your audience's attention on the problem. Use a rhetorical technique such as a thought-provoking statement, quotation, or statistic that makes your audience aware of the problem (see Section 4.2). Next, clearly state what the problem is and its origins, causes, effects, and scope. Explain how the problem may be caused by social, economic, environmental or other factors. To make the problem more apparent, describe some of the negative consequences of the problem, offer statistics showing the extent of its negative effects, or present authoritative testimony that boldly asserts the severity of the problem (see Section 2.2). When necessary, show how others have not understood the problem clearly and thus have failed to solve it.

Show there is a need to solve the problem.   Show how the problem affects your audience. Describe the problem's significance for particular individuals (or communities) and for society in general. Relate the problem to your audience's personal concerns or their sense of fairness, justice, and equality. Also explain how others are harmed by the problem or how the problem affects society in general. At this point, consider offering an example, lay testimony, or analogy to a similar issue to characterize the problem's effects in a more specific or personal way (see Section 2.2). Next, explain why the present conditions are unacceptable, and point out that if nothing is done, the problem will persist and may cause more detrimental effects in the future.

Show how your solution will satisfy the problem.   Present your solution to the problem. First, support your solution by referring to the accepted values or principles on which your solution is based. Then clearly state the main elements of your solution, and explain how it will work and what is needed to make it work. Also, give evidence showing its potential effectiveness. Present evidence such as authoritative testimony, examples, and statistics that proves the merits of your solution (see Section 2.2). When possible, offer a case study that shows how your solution has resolved the problem elsewhere. If no such example or evidence exists, make the rationale or warrant underlying your solution as strong and clear as possible so your audience can recognize the reasoning behind your solution (see Section 2.3). To strengthen your audience's acceptance of your solution, address any potential objections that could be raised against your solution. If necessary, qualify your solution by pointing to its limitations. Nevertheless, show how your solution is the best means for solving the problem and that its advantages outweigh its disadvantages.

Help your audience visualize the positive results of your solution. Vividly describe the advantages of your solution. Clearly explain how your solution will rectify the problem, describe the concrete benefits that will result from it, and cite specific examples showing how your solution improves the present situation. Consider appealing to commonly held values by showing how your solution will allow individuals to live more productive and healthy lives, or how it will allow an institution to fulfill its goals. You can also describe how your solution will treat people more fairly, provide them more opportunities, or rectify past injustices. Specifically, you can state how your solution will save money, eliminate waste, better serve a population, or solve a problem more quickly than other solutions. Conversely, you could also paint a negative yet realistic picture of what will occur if the problem is not resolved. Explain the continuing negative effects it has on individuals, describe the deplorable conditions it causes, and project what subsequent problems may occur if nothing is done.

Motivate your audience to act on your solution.   Encourage your audience to take action to solve the problem. Solicit their help by appealing to their ethical convictions, by citing examples of others who have helped solve a similar problem, or by challenging them to help you reach a goal. Stress the positive role they can play in resolving the problem or ways in which the problem will persist if they do not take the action you advocate. Then present them a plan for taking action. Make sure the plan is concrete and feasible and does not entail great effort. Again, if the real agents of change are larger institutions, such as a government agency, corporation, university, or nonprofit organization, explain what these institutions must do to solve the problem, and encourage your audience to petition the institutions on behalf of your solution. Finally, provide any material that will facilitate your audience's participation in resolving the problem. For instance, distribute pamphlets, letters, petitions, or telephone numbers that your audience can read, sign, or call to support your solution.

3   Speech of fact.

The speech of fact as well as the following value and policy speeches are all variations of the traditional **stock issue speech.** The stock issue speech provides a standard or "stock" organizational structure you can use to persuade your audience to accept or reject a claim of fact, value, or policy (see Section 2.3). The speech of fact offers strategies and a general organizational structure for proving or disproving a claim based on a fact or an interpretation of a fact. Your claim or thesis statement can state that a fact existed in the past, exists in the present, or will exist in the future. Likewise, a speech of fact may be based on a thesis statement that makes a claim about what was factually true in the past, is true in the present, or will be true in the future (see Section 4.3).[9] Your speech's claim can concern all types of facts such as scientific, historical, legal, and social facts that you either will prove or disprove. For example, thesis statements such as "Human beings evolved from animals," "Shakespeare was not the author of his plays," "Lee Harvey Oswald did not kill President Kennedy," "Microsoft is an illegal monopoly," "Media violence causes violence in society," or "There will never be peace in the Middle East" are all factual claims. Although some of these factual claims imply policy issues, your intent in a speech of fact is to prove only the matters of fact. However, as shown in the following subsections, you can indicate in the closing part of your speech how your factual claim would affect a related policy.

Provide general background information on your subject.[10]   How you present this background information will depend on your topic, intent, and audience's attitude and knowledge about your topic. If your audience is unfamiliar with your topic, you may want to establish the basic facts, issues, and interpretations related to it. If the fact or an interpretation of the fact is generally accepted as true, present the fact or interpretation as clearly and fairly as possible so that you can refute it later. Finally, if your topic is highly controversial and your audience is familiar with a variety of conflicting factual evidence and interpretations, offer them clear and succinct explanations of these various facts and interpretations, including those you will support.

Establish the criteria on which a factual claim about your topic can be proved or disproved.   State such criteria as what is the best definition of a term in your claim, what kind of statistical evidence would be needed to prove your claim, who should be considered as an authority on your topic, what kinds of cause-and-effect relationships must be shown to accept a claim about your subject, or what legal statutes must be used to judge the factual basis of a claim (see Sections 2.2 and 2.3).

Refute the facts and interpretations that argue against your claim. Show how any opposing claim of fact does not adhere to the standard criteria you have just stated: Indicate how the opposing claim rests on faulty or insufficient evidence such as overly simplistic explanation, a misleading statistic, or an improper definition; or show how it does not consider certain pieces of evidence or new information that would refute the claim (see Section 2.2). In addition, address any fallacious arguments such as those based on invalid logic, a hasty generalization, an erroneous cause-and-effect relationship, an incorrect application of a legal statute, or an appeal to a nonauthority (see Sections 2.3 and 2.5). If a counterclaim offers any legitimate evidence, you may want to acknowledge its merits, but then indicate how such evidence is limited and does not outweigh the overall problems with the claim.

Provide evidence and arguments that show how your claim fits the criteria you have established, and offer a factual understanding of your topic.   Present evidence that offers a more thorough explanation or description of your topic, and state why and how this evidence is more sufficient than any counterclaims that read the facts differently. Also, create arguments based on the facts you have proven that are more logically coherent and rigorous than the arguments you previously refuted (see Section 2.3).

When necessary, show the important implications or applications of your factual claim.   In some speeches of fact, the claim you have proven should cause your audience to reassess their understanding of your topic. In such instances, clearly indicate how they should see or understand your topic differently. In other speeches, the facts you have proven or refuted may have implications for a value they hold or a policy they endorse. If your factual claim does have such implications, offer some suggestions about how your audience should reconsider the value or policy in light of the facts you have presented. Also, realize that because you may need to prove or disprove a fact on which a value or policy is based, you should consider incorporating elements of the speech of fact into a value or policy speech (see the following section).

4   Value speech.

The value speech asserts a thesis statement or claim that either a particular value should be accepted or rejected, an entity should be judged as possessing a certain value, or one value or entity possessing a value should be preferred over another (see Section 4.3).[11] Hence, rather than attempting to persuade your audience whether something is true according to the standards of truth set in a speech of fact, you use the value speech to make a qualitative claim about a value or an entity's character based on the criteria you establish that define that value. Value speeches often consider the merits of a moral claim based on the criteria of right and wrong or good and bad, such as, "A bad means never justifies a good end," "Mercy killing is acceptable in certain situations," or "Teenagers should practice abstinence and not engage in premarital sex." However, a value speech also may consider other values such as what is better or worse, more or less advantageous, or more or less pleasing. For example, claims such as, "Picasso was the greatest artist of the twentieth century," "Children should study music and not computers," "You should not invest in Internet companies," or "Beauty is in the eyes of the beholder" also are valuative claims.

Provide general background information on your topic.[12]   Familiarize your audience with any of the terms, issues, or controversies related to your claim. Define any unfamiliar terms, clarify those that are often misunderstood, or offer a new yet suitable definition of a common term. In each case, establish a definition that will allow you to imply your claim once your audience accepts the definition. You also may want to inform your audience about any events, issues, or controversies surrounding your topic to begin to see its implications and significance. Some effective ways to have your audience think about your claim are to offer an example or narrative that illustrates how people are affected by the issues you raise, provide testimony that endorses your claim, or present an analogy that helps your audience understand your claim (see Section 2.2).

Identify the value on which your claim is based.   Clarify the moral principal, religious doctrine, political ideology, social norm, belief system, practical rule, or aesthetic ideal that supports the value inherent in your claim. Your goal here is to show how your value is consistent with a set of beliefs that your audience finds credible. Thus, once you have provided the backing that establishes the general ideals and merits of the value system, you then can explain how the value you advocate provides a warrant for your claim (see Section 2.3). At this point, you will want to explore how the value supports such ideals as moral goodness and decency, social equality and fairness, individual liberty and independence, cultural awareness and tolerance, practicality and efficiency, or uncommon valor, beauty, or achievement. In some instances, you may need to explain how your value is a particular means to a greater end. For instance, you may want to show how adopting your value will cause your audience to become more moral persons overall, or how accepting your value is best for both individuals and society as a whole. Conversely, you can explain how embracing a moral principle will cause your audience to act more ethically in a variety of specific situations.

Offer criteria for judging the merits of the value your claim endorses. Explain and justify the standards of the value endorsed by your claim. Standards for judging a moral, religious, or other principled act can be explained in terms of those qualities that define the value. Thus, you will want to define and describe, in detail, those qualities such as goodness, equality, fairness, tolerance, and so on that exemplify the value your claim endorses. Other standards, such as what or who is the best, most efficient, or most influential can use a combination of qualitative (e.g., highest combined skill level, greatest leadership qualities, grandest achievements) and quantitative (e.g., most awards, best average, largest sum) criteria to establish your claim. Consider judging the value according to whether it achieves the most significant results, whether it achieved its ends by the best or most appropriate means, or whether it established an important precedent or displays qualities unmatched by others of its kind. To help you establish these criteria, refer to those authorities, social values, or personal convictions or standards of measurement that provide the basis for your criteria.

Apply these criteria to your claim.   Show how your claim adheres to the criteria you have just established. Provide evidence such as explanations, examples, statistics, and analogies that illustrate how your value fits the criteria you just presented or how the subject of your claim can be measured favorably against these criteria (see Section 2.2). Create arguments that show how the characteristics of your value or topic fit the criteria you established and thus lead logically to your claim (see Section 2.3)

Contrast the merits of the value inherent in your claim to the limits of other values.   Present evidence and arguments that show why your values are better than other values. Similarly, show why applying your values to your topic offers more benefits than applying alternative values. When comparing and contrasting values, explain how your val-

ues give priority to the criteria you have established as a basis for judging your claim. In some instances, you may want to argue that the resulting criteria or goal of personal integrity, moral goodness, just
means, social cohesiveness, or greater quantity should be the basis of
judging your value as better than another. At other times, you might
what to hold that more personal autonomy, social freedom, technical
efficiency, or higher quality should be the standard of comparison.

Show the relevance of your value by addressing its implications or by
applying the value to similar issues.   Explain the implications of your
value claim by exploring what other positive consequences may result
from your claim. To establish a contrast, show how an alternative value
does not yield such positive results. Consider offering analogies, examples, and narratives that illustrate how you can apply your value to
other similar subjects (see Section 2.2). Finally, if your moral claim has
some policy implications, briefly state how your audience should view
the policy differently or endorse a change in the policy (see the following section).

5   Policy speech.

A policy is a set of prescriptions, procedures, or statutes that an institution adopts to achieve a goal, solve a problem, or administer
services. The institution whose policies you are discussing can be anything from a government agency to a private corporation to a nonprofit
organization. The main intent of a policy speech is to make a case for
rejecting the **status quo,** or present policy, and adopting an alternative
policy in its place. Some of the main reasons you can give for a change
in policy are that the new policy solves the problem more effectively,
treats people more equally and fairly, is more efficient in its administration of services, or achieves some other benefit. (If you like, you can
do the reverse and support a present policy and argue against any or
all of the alternative policies.)

As a general rule, you should place equal emphasis on each step
in a policy speech, although the amount of time you spend on each
step ultimately will depend on your audience's familiarity with the
problem, the status quo policy, the alternative policies, and the policy
you are advocating. In some cases, you may want quickly to review a
well-known problem and policy and spend more time explaining your
proposal. In cases where the policy makers failed to understand the
problem correctly, you may want to give a more detailed critique of
their misreading of the problem and their policy's consequential failure to solve it. Although the policy speech adapts the general speech
structure, you can integrate elements from the other persuasive speech
types presented in this section (see also Section 4.1). For instance, to

justify the policy claim that "Marijuana should be legalized for medical purposes," you may first have to prove both the factual claim that marijuana offers effective therapeutic relief that no other medicine offers, and the valuative claim that using marijuana for medical purposes is no more immoral than using other controlled substances, like morphine, for the same reasons. Similarly, after proving that openly gay men and women do not negatively affect military effectiveness, you can indicate how this factual evidence should cause the military to reassess its "Don't ask, don't tell" policy.

Introduce the problems and the policies you will discuss.[13]   Begin by describing the problem, citing some of the negative effects of the present policy, or stating how your proposed policy is working elsewhere. Next, explain why your audience should be concerned with the problem and the present policy by showing how the problem and policy affect them and others. You may also want to suggest what benefits they can expect from your proposal. Then, to help build your credibility, state how you became interested in the problem and what personal experiences or training you have in dealing with the problem, institution, or policy being discussed. You can also cite the main sources and authorities that you have consulted to construct your speech. Finally, give your thesis and initial summary. Briefly outline the problem, the present policy and its inadequacies, and your proposed policy and its advantages (see Section 4.1).

Argue against the present policy and for your proposed policy.   Critically analyze the inadequacies of the present policy. Explain the problem the present policy attempts to solve. Show the problem's scope and characterize its main negative effects. When possible, discuss the moral principle, economic tenet, legal statute, or social belief that the present policy is based on or the original policy it was modeled after (see Section 2.3). In addition, state the primary goals the policy set out to achieve. Give credit to the policy if it has achieved some successes. Most importantly, give evidence showing that the policy does not address the problem effectively or efficiently, or that there are problems inherent in the policy itself that do not allow it to accomplish its own goals. Also, show why minor modifications of the present policy will not solve the problem. When applicable, you should point to other problems that the present policy causes and predict what will occur if the present policy is not changed.

Briefly review and consider various alternative policies.   Explain the main components, strengths, and weaknesses of the major alternative policies. Compare these policies to the present policy and the one you advocate. Explain the limits of these alternative policies, and indicate why your policy is better.

Propose and defend your policy.   Your policy can modify the present policy, adopt one outlined by an authority, or offer a new solution grounded in evidence. Explain the principle or previous policy on which your proposal is based, and state its primary goals (see Section 2.3). Show how your policy deals with the problem more clearly and solves it more effectively. Use evidence to support your proposal: For example, cite examples and case studies showing where it has worked, quote experts who endorse your proposal, and offer statistics showing its effectiveness (see Section 2.2). You can also explain how the proposed policy achieves certain values and goals, such as to advance justice, increase security, expand opportunity, decrease waste, or prevent corruption.

Outline how your policy will be implemented.   Show that your policy is possible to implement and is a feasible solution to the problem. Explain its main guidelines, costs, staffing, and technical needs, and give a timetable for reaching its goals whenever possible. Give evidence that shows where a similar policy has been implemented effectively.

Subject your policy to possible criticisms, and show how its benefits outweigh its limitations.   Refute potential arguments that may be raised against your policy. Qualify your arguments by citing those circumstances that may prevent your policy from working effectively, and stress what must be done to prevent these circumstances from occurring. Additionally, state what, if any, potential disadvantages may result from the policy, but show how these do not outweigh the advantages that will be gained. Finally, consider describing the worst- and best-case scenarios that could result from your policy (see Section 2.4). This strategy gives your audience the chance to visualize the minimal and maximal advantages of your proposal.

Conclude your speech.   After using a statement or phrase indicating that you are about to finish your speech, summarize your main points. Restate the depth of the problem, the disadvantages of the present policy, the evidence that supports your policy, and the procedures for implementing your policy. Then end your speech by recalling the advantages of the proposed policy, cite evidence of its potential success, or have your audience visualize the problems that will persist if the present policy is not changed (see Section 4.1).

5.5 Principles of Ceremonial Speaking

Unlike informative and persuasive speaking in which you present evidence to clarify your topic or support a claim, ceremonial speaking mainly uses evidence and appeals to praise a person, place, or event and to arouse and entertain your audience. The following principles of ceremonial speaking will help you prepare and deliver an inspiring speech (see Section 5.6). You should also consider adopting these principles when you need to positively characterize a person, place, or event in an informative or persuasive speech (see Sections 5.2 and 5.4).

1   Create a ceremonial speech that is short and eloquent.

Except for those times when you are the primary speaker, keep your ceremonial speech short, that is, from one to five minutes long. Such brevity demands that you choose ideas and words that will have a dramatic effect and that you practice your delivery so that you can convey the appropriate meaning and feeling of your speech in the short time you have. Use a climactic organizational pattern and intonation, particularly when concluding the speech (see Sections 4.4 and 7.2).

2   Adapt your speech to the occasion and to the person, place, or event you are celebrating.

Base the content, language, and delivery of your speech on the character of the person or event being celebrated. Your speech should also try to capture your audience's sentiments toward the honored person or event. For instance, if you are presenting a prestigious award at a formal awards ceremony or commemorating a solemn occasion, use a formal style of language and a serious tone of voice (see Sections 6.1, 6.2, and 7.2). However, if you are giving an anniversary speech to close friends at a small dinner party or a testimonial on behalf of a gregarious friend, use informal language and a more sentimental or whimsical tone.

3   Establish your personal relationship with the honoree.

One of the main ways to build your credibility in a ceremonial speech is to tell the audience about your personal relationship with the honoree (see Section 2.1). Do not spend too much time talking about yourself; rather, briefly explain why you were chosen to deliver the address. At a more professional occasion, focus on your professional association with the honoree. At an informal occasion, describe your personal or familial relationship to him or her.

4 Consider the emotional needs of your audience, and attempt to fulfill these needs with your speech.

Determine what mood your speech should set. In some cases, you may want your speech to create a festive mood, whereas in other speeches, you may need to convey respect for the honoree's accomplishments or allow your audience to grieve. In each of these situations, use the right appeals, language, and delivery to fulfill these needs (see Sections 2.1, 6.1, 6.2, 7.2, and 7.3).

When giving a ceremonial speech, focus more on conveying your emotions, respect, and sincerity than on providing a great deal of information about the honoree. Most of your audience will already be familiar with the honoree, so your main intent is not to inform or persuade, but to inspire and celebrate. Consequently, ceremonial speeches focus more on emotional appeals than they do on logical ones.[14] However, you will still want to reacquaint your audience with the achievements of the celebrated person so that you can strengthen their respect and admiration for him or her. Hence, to inspire your audience, be creative with your explanations and descriptions rather than simply informative (see Section 2.2).

5 Unify your audience through shared emotions and sentiments.

For instance, narrate a personal experience involving the honoree, quote an expression he or she always uses, or describe one of his or her everyday activities that reflect a value or characteristic that everyone who knows the honoree will recognize. Similarly, when celebrating a group's achievement, describe the enthusiasm and camaraderie felt by people who have worked together on behalf of a cause, organization, or event so that they and others can reexperience these feelings through your speech.[15]

6 Amplify the virtues of the honoree by specifically referring to his or her personal qualities, actions, and contributions.

Expound upon the honoree's wisdom, honesty, courage, diligence, and other virtues held in high regard.[16] Do not generally state that the honoree has a good character and has accomplished many things; rather, cite specific examples of the honoree's virtues and accomplishments so that your audience recognizes his or her unique qualities and contributions. Acknowledge how the honoree accomplished a feat first or better than others, turned a bad situation into a positive one, or unselfishly helped those in need. To provide greater insight into the character of the honoree, describe a relatively unknown achievement or offer an original interpretation of one of his or her attributes. You can also compare the honoree's actions and character to a famous person known for those same actions or qualities, or relate a story about the honoree that exemplifies these qualities.

7   **Balance your adulation of the honoree's professional accomplishments with praise for his or her personal achievements.**

Although your speech should concentrate on the honoree's professional work, you also should mention those activities related to the honoree's personal life that he or she deems important. For instance, describe his or her family life, community activities, or work with nonprofit organizations. Never, however, praise the honoree's wealth and power as accomplishments in themselves, but only as means through which the honoree pursued other, more honorable ends.

8   **Do not understate or exaggerate your emotions or praise for the honoree.**

Use descriptive words and figures of speech that allow you to express yourself in an honest yet moving way (see Sections 6.1, 6.2, and 6.5). Do not use complex words and sentences that make you sound overly formal or pompous. You should also avoid falling back on overused clichés or trite statements that characterize the honoree in a nondescript way. Rather, try to express your feelings with innovative statements that capture the honoree's particular qualities.

Never attempt to give a speech if you will be unable to control your emotions. This lack of control only creates an awkward situation for both you and your audience and diverts attention from the person commemorated. Also, do not exaggerate your praise for the honoree or use tasteless humor that may embarrass the honoree or make your audience uncomfortable.

5.6 Types of Ceremonial Speeches

The main intent of most ceremonial speeches is to commemorate an individual, institution, or occasion. There are many different types of ceremonial speeches. Some, such as an inaugural address, are given at a major political or cultural event. Other ceremonial speeches, like the ones described in this section, are performed at more common celebrations and events. Ceremonial speeches usually are shorter than informative and persuasive speeches, and their intent is more to celebrate and entertain than to inform or persuade. Thus, ceremonial speeches do not follow rigidly the general speech structure but require you to organize your speech, present information, and make appeals based on the specific type of ceremonial speech you will give and on the needs of the occasion or person celebrated (see Section 4.1). However, because many of these speeches celebrate similar accomplishments, you can adopt the strategies and techniques of one ceremonial speech in another as you see fit.

1 Speech of introduction.

This speech is performed when you are asked to introduce a speaker to an audience. As the person giving the introduction, your main functions are to welcome the speaker, build the speaker's credibility, state the speaker's topic, create a welcoming atmosphere for everyone, and arouse the audience's interest in the speaker and his or her topic. Keep your speech brief—around one to three minutes.

Research the speaker's background. Try to obtain the speaker's resume beforehand so that you can become familiar with his or her professional accomplishments. Sometime before your presentation, ask the speaker to clarify any questions regarding his or her work. If you do not know how to pronounce the speaker's name, ask him or her to pronounce it for you; do not risk embarrassing the speaker and yourself. Practice pronouncing the speaker's name until you can deliver it fluently.

Welcome the audience and tell them who is sponsoring the speaker. Begin by warmly greeting your audience. Then introduce the event, speaker, and sponsor, and show the connection among them. For instance, if the speaker is part of an ongoing lecture series, state its purpose and the ways in which the speaker's topic relates to the series' main theme. You also should briefly describe what, if any, professional relationship the speaker has with the sponsoring institution or any personal relationship you may have with him or her.

Present the speaker's main accomplishments. Discuss the speaker's previous accomplishments, but focus mainly on those relating to his or her present topic. Provide some general background information on his or her professional training, refer to his or her major accomplishments and awards, and then discuss how his or her present work relates to the speech being presented. As in any ceremonial speech, briefly acknowledge some of the speaker's nonprofessional achievements (see Section 5.5).

Introduce the speaker's topic. Do not attempt to summarize the speaker's speech. Rather, simply state what his or her main topic is by tying it to a current event, a professional issue, or the speaker's previous work on the topic. Do not include any statements or anecdotes that the speaker has made to you before the speech. Such statements and stories may be a standard part of the speech that he or she is planning to give. Also, do not overstate your praise for the speaker's oratory skills; doing so may inflate your audience's expectations.

Arouse your audience with a dramatic conclusion. After first announcing the speaker's name, begin building on the audience's anticipation of the speaker by using both moving language and an emphatic delivery style as your introduction draws to a close (see Sections 6.1 and 7.2). Finally, conclude your introduction by repeating the speaker's name and the speech's title or topic.

2 Speech of presentation.

The intent of this kind of speech is to present someone with an award. As the award's presenter, you will need briefly to explain the award's purpose, describe the selection process, and state the honoree's accomplishments. Here again, your speech should be brief, perhaps one to three minutes long, depending on the number of awards being given and the prestige of the award relative to that of the other awards being presented.

Begin by acknowledging the significance of the award and discussing its intent. Describe the award, explain how and why it was created, whom it was named for, and how long it has been given. You also should specify the meaning of the award. Explain what it honors, the criteria used to select the winner, and the significance of the award for the audience and its recipient. If possible, let the award describe itself by restating the inscription on the plaque, certificate, or diploma that the honoree receives. Acknowledge past recipients, and praise all the nominees for their general accomplishments.

Acknowledge the recipient's achievements. Show how the recipient's achievements, character, and deeds exemplify what the award is intended to represent. Most importantly, specifically state those achievements that are being acknowledged by the award.

Use a climactic delivery when presenting the award. Regardless of whether the audience knows who has won the award, try to build a feeling of suspense and enthusiasm for the recipient when you are presenting the award. Build enthusiasm by using an emphatic language and delivery style when stating the recipient's accomplishments, the award's title, and then the speaker's name immediately before presenting the award (see Sections 6.1 and 7.2).

3   Speech of acceptance.

A speech of acceptance is given on those occasions when you are receiving an award. When accepting the award, be sure to thank the institution, association, or people who are giving you the award, recognize those who have contributed to your work, and try to express what receiving the award means to you. Here again, if you are the main honoree, you can speak for a longer period of time, but if your award is one of many being presented, limit your remarks to one to three minutes.

Thank the association, institution, or people who are giving the award.   Thank the institution for acknowledging your work, and express your appreciation for the way in which the award brings attention to the work that you, your colleagues, and others do.

Acknowledge the work of others who have helped you in a significant way.   Name and briefly describe the role of the main people who have helped you accomplish the activities being honored. Keep this list to a maximum of three or four people. Then, if necessary, recognize the contributions of others by grouping them according to their function: for instance, thank your funding agency or assistants. Finally, express your gratitude for the one or two people who have inspired you or supported you throughout your work. Remember to be courteous to your audience and the other honorees by keeping your list of acknowledgments short. Do not belabor your acknowledgments by randomly identifying too many people.

End your speech with a final statement of gratitude and thanks.   Express what receiving the award means to you now and what it will mean in the future. For instance, state that receiving the award represents a lifelong goal and that you appreciate its recognition of your work and the social cause you are working for.

4   Toast.

A toast is a salute or short speech celebrating the accomplishments of a person, group, institution, or event. When offering a toast, you should praise and offer fond wishes to the celebrated. If you are asked to give a salute, memorize a few brief, moving statements. If your toast is meant to be a short speech, make it one to three minutes long. Either way, a toast should be eloquent yet concise. Thus, choose your thoughts, words, and phrases carefully.

Focus on the prominent attributes or accomplishments of the person or occasion being toasted.   Refer specifically to the accomplishments you are toasting. For example, if you are making a toast at a wedding, briefly describe the specific attributes of the newlyweds that will allow them to have a successful marriage.

Reflect both your personal sentiments and those of your audience. You most likely are giving the toast because you have a long, personal relationship with the person, institution, or event being commemorated. Thus, indicate what your relationship is with the commemorated, and express your feelings of respect and joy toward the accomplishment you are toasting. You should also arouse your audience's feelings for the commemorated. Consider telling a short story or offering a quotation that represents the character of the celebrated or captures your audience's sentiments toward the celebrated. Again, use these statements to bring everyone together based on their mutual feelings of admiration, respect, and happiness.

If you are giving a toast to commemorate an anniversary, describe the original event being celebrated and the virtues it represents.   First, describe some of the activities and events leading up to the original event. Next, explain how the original event and its subsequent developments, such as a couple's children, the growth of a business, or the accomplishments of a volunteer group, represent certain virtues that your audience reveres. You should also acknowledge and praise those individuals and groups who contributed to the accomplishments being toasted. Finally, encourage your audience to preserve the memory of the original event and celebrate its success by promising to maintain its ideals and pursue similar goals.

Use a climactic delivery style and offer a concluding statement that looks to the future.   Close your speech with a statement wishing the celebrated continued success, happiness, and good luck. If you are giving a salute, keep your glass raised to approximately shoulder height throughout the salute, and then raise it even higher when you are about to finish. If you are giving a short speech, keep your glass at your side as a nonverbal cue that you are not ready to give the actual toast. Then give your audience a verbal cue such as, "So let us toast," so they know when to raise their glasses. Finally, practice your delivery for a strong, climactic ending (see Section 7.2).

5 Testimonial.

A testimonial honors and praises a person for his or her accomplishments. Testimonials are usually given at an awards banquet, a hall-of-fame induction ceremony, or a retirement party. As the speaker, your two main goals are to praise the honoree's accomplishments and express your audience's admiration for the honoree. Testimonials are approximately five to ten minutes long.

Praise the honoree's professional accomplishments.   Although you will want to state and praise the honoree's professional activities, do not belabor this point by discussing each one specifically. Instead, state some of the honoree's major achievements, and then focus on one accomplishment that he or she was most proud of or that you can offer a unique insight into. Then, as with most ceremonial speeches, pay tribute to his or her personal endeavors related to his or her family or community.

Praise the honoree's personal characteristics and virtues.   Consider explaining the honoree's positive impact on his colleagues, place of employment, and profession. For instance, describe the honoree's role in maintaining high morale in the workplace or his or her part in reaching a common goal. Similarly, tell a story of a relatively unknown event that reflects his or her uncompromising principles, personal fortitude, or compassion for others.

Express sentiments that reflect your audience's admiration for the honoree.   Illustrate how the honoree should be remembered by describing, for instance, the easy way he or she related to others or supported his or her colleagues or friends. You may even want to tell a humorous story about an amusing event or describe an odd personal idiosyncrasy that reflects an admirable characteristic of the honoree.

End by recalling favorable memories of the honoree and wishing him or her continued success in future endeavors.   For instance, close your testimonial by describing a memorable event shared by members of the audience, yourself, and the honoree. Finally, end by wishing the honoree a healthy and rewarding future. If the honoree will still be active professionally, wish him or her the best of luck in all future endeavors. If the honoree is retiring, wish him or her a long, enjoyable retirement during which he or she can pursue lifelong interests.

6 Eulogy.

The intent of a eulogy is to honor a deceased person or persons. As the eulogist, you will want to praise the person's personal attributes and virtues and move your audience from their feelings of grief to a celebration of the person's life. Eulogies can be from five to ten minutes long, depending on the prestige of the deceased, the significance of the memorial event, and the number of speakers.

Focus on the personal character and virtues of the commemorated. Praise the individual's attributes rather than his or her professional accomplishments, although you should mention the latter, particularly when they reflect the deceased's most salient virtues. Again, do not rely on general platitudes and empty clichés; rather, cite specific activities or statements that reflect the deceased's personal character (see Section 5.5).

Discuss the effect the person has had on others and on you. Describe how a particular individual, group, or community was influenced by the deceased. Moreover, acknowledge those closest to the deceased, and express your and your audience's condolences and support for them during this time of misfortune.

Present a quotation, describe a personal quality, or narrate a story that portrays a virtue, value, or personality trait that characterizes the person being eulogized. Quote an expression the deceased always used, describe one of his or her everyday activities, or recall an event or personal experience involving the deceased that shows how the deceased thought about life, acted unselfishly, or cared about others (see Section 2.2).

Move your audience from feelings of grief and pain to feelings of respect for the deceased and happiness from having known the deceased. Construct a series of poignant statements that allows your audience to grieve collectively, and then celebrate the personal attributes and accomplishments of the deceased. Consider, for instance, creating a narrative that moves your audience through the psychological stages of disbelief, denial, resentment, and, finally, their acceptance of the person's death.[17] You may want to conclude your eulogy with uplifting statements that bring your audience together through their positive memories of the deceased. Furthermore, state how the deceased would want the audience to remember him or her and how the deceased would want his or her memory to be kept alive through their deeds. Finally, consider consoling your audience by explaining how the deceased's passing and their grief is part of a natural human process.

6

Style

6.1   *Principles of Style*

6.2   *Grammar, Composition, and Word Choice*

6.3   *Revising Your Style*

6.4   *Oral Citations*

6.5   *Figures of Speech*

6.1 Principles of Style

Your writing and speaking style are not simply the way you embellish your ideas with words and phrases. Rather, your language and style are the means through which you express your ideas and construct the picture of the world and yourself that you want to convey to your audience. Your style can play a fundamental part in showing your audience that what they once thought was insignificant is interesting, what was complex is comprehensible, what was dubious is definite, and what was improbable is possible. Moreover, a clear, genuine, and expressive style will enhance your credibility, whereas a dull, insincere, and uninspiring style can diminish it (see Section 2.1).

Developing an effective style is one of the most demanding yet beneficial aspects of becoming a good speaker. You can improve your style in several different ways. (1) Read and listen to a variety of authors and speakers, and study their stylistic techniques (i.e., word choice, sentence composition, organization, figures of speech, etc.). (2) Practice writing speeches by imitating the style of great authors and speakers and by rewriting your own speeches; take a whole text or a passage and rewrite it using alternative words and figures of speech, varying the sentence structures, and rearranging the main points (see

Chapter 4 and Section 6.5).[1] (3) Familiarize yourself with the basic principles of style presented here and in Sections 6.2 and 6.3.

1   The two most important elements of a good style are clarity and appropriateness.[2]

A clear style demands that you choose words, present evidence, and organize your main points so that your audience understands your speech in the way you intend. Hence, avoid ambiguous terms that may cause your audience to misinterpret what you say. Instead, select words that accurately convey what you mean. Use a new, uncommon, or technical term only when it best represents your point; otherwise, use a familiar term that your audience understands immediately (see Section 6.2). You also can achieve clarity by enunciating your words properly (see Section 7.2). When providing evidence, make sure your information is easy to comprehend and its relationship to your point is readily apparent. Arrange your main points so that they develop your thesis statement in a logical and consistent manner (see Section 4.4).

2   Use a speaking style consistent with the type of speech you are giving.

In an informative speech, use descriptive and explanatory words and phrases that allow you to bring new insight to your topic (see Sections 2.2 and 5.1). Also, choose a pattern of organization that allows you to explore various facets of your topic yet is well-ordered and easy to follow (see Section 4.4). In a persuasive speech, use words and statements that allow you to articulate clearly an abstract principle and then apply it directly to the issue at hand (see Section 5.3). You will also need to select words and statements that allow you to scrutinize closely a faulty piece of evidence or argument and construct a coherent, logical argument supporting your thesis statement (see Section 2.3). Finally, because expressing admiration and emotions is very important in ceremonial speaking, you should use descriptive narratives, heartfelt appeals, and eloquent phrasing that allow your audience to relive events, reexperience emotions, and increase their adulation for the person or event being celebrated (see Sections 5.5 and 5.6).

3   Depending on your abilities, choose either the plain style or a combination of the plain, middle, and grand style of speaking.[3]

If you have limited writing and speaking skills, create a style that adheres to the basic standards of formal writing yet is conversational in its overall tone. More generally, all speakers should use this **plain**

style when their intent is to convey simple ideas in the most direct way possible. Thus, the plain style is used to inform an audience about basic facts, make simple and concise arguments, or quickly summarize background information that is commonly known. The plain style consists of short, simply structured sentences, familiar words, common metaphors and analogies, easy-to-follow narratives, and uncomplicated arguments (see Section 2.2). Likewise, both your verbal and nonverbal delivery are more subdued than the more expressive delivery techniques used in the other two styles (see Sections 7.2 and 7.3).

If you have more advanced writing and speaking skills, consider combining the plain style with the two other styles of classical rhetoric. Use the **middle style** when you want to please your audience with more sophisticated analogies and metaphors, arguments based on common beliefs, and sympathetic appeals (see Sections 2.1, 2.2, and 2.4). You will want to use the middle style most often because it allows you to deliver your speech with an appropriate combination of formal and conversational stylistic elements and effective verbal and nonverbal delivery techniques (see Sections 6.2, 7.2, and 7.3). When striving for the middle style, use multiple sentence structures, descriptive words, rich narratives, and more highly developed arguments.

Finally, use the **grand style** when you want to move your audience to action. Because moving your audience to act on your proposal takes a great deal of persuasion and encouragement, the grand style calls for colorful and rigorous language, emphatic delivery techniques, and strong ethical and emotional appeals (see Sections 2.1, 7.2, and 7.3). Thus, it consists of eloquent figures of speech, complex sentences, distinctive definitions and explanations, and elaborate and logically precise arguments. However, remember you should not attempt to sustain the grand style throughout your speech. Rather, concentrate your use of ornate language, complex arguments, and spirited delivery techniques where they are most effective.

4   Create a title that represents your speech's topic and thesis statement in a clear and inviting way.

Your speech's title should arouse your audience's interest in your topic while communicating your speech's main idea. You can achieve these goals in a variety of ways: You can express succinctly the main idea of your thesis statement or turn it into a question, you can refer to your strongest evidence, or you can employ a figure of speech that highlights your speech's topic and intent (see Sections 4.3 and 6.5). Whichever form you choose, try to make your title as concise as possible—between three and seven words.

5   **To help your audience remember your speech's main ideas, repeat your main points and key evidence more often than you normally would in written composition.**

Restate and rephrase your thesis statement and main ideas throughout your speech so that your audience easily recognizes the relationship between your thesis and main points (see Section 4.3). You also may want to word and construct each of your main points in a similar way so your audience recognizes their similar function and weight. These techniques will help emphasize your main points and make your speech more coherent and easier to remember. To build on earlier points, rephrase what you have already said, and then either add new information or discuss your topic from a new perspective.

6   **Make suggestions and ask questions to extend goodwill to your audience.**

Rather than always stating your opinion in a declarative sentence, consider when you could rephrase your point in the form of a suggestion, question, or rhetorical question (see Section 6.5). Asking a question or offering a suggestion may incline your audience to become more actively involved in listening to your speech, which may increase the likelihood that they will accept its claims. Such techniques also have the ethical appeal of showing that you believe your audience, given their own free will, will agree with your statements (see Section 2.1). You can also build a good rapport with your audience by saying something like, "As you already know," before presenting information they already are familiar with. However, make sure that what you will discuss is common knowledge; otherwise, you risk making your audience feel inadequate or slighted.

You can also employ the rhetorical strategy of asking and briefly answering a series of questions. For instance, you might say, "Will my proposal prevent all animal testing? No. Will some researchers try to circumvent these restrictions? Probably. But will my policy prevent most of the abuses related to animal testing? Yes." This technique shows your audience that you have weighed the potential limits and benefits of your ideas.

7   **Develop a secondary theme or motif or repeat an engaging phrase throughout your speech to embellish your thesis statement and add a literary flair to your speech.**

The theme, motif, or phrase that you employ can highlight or characterize a particular aspect of your topic or simply reconfirm your thesis statement (see Section 4.3). For instance, because it may be difficult for your audience to accept cultural differences, you may ask them to "see with a native eye" each time you introduce a new aspect of the medical practices of Native American shamans. Another technique is to repeat a quote such as, "I am not a crook" each time you present more evidence against the ethical character of Richard Nixon.

8 To maintain your audience's attention, add some uncertainty to your speech.

Your thesis statement, preview summary, transitions, and organization should provide your audience with a clear sense of where you are going in your speech (see Sections 4.3, 4.4, and 4.5). This sense of predictability reassures an audience who are receiving information orally. However, do not make your speech so predictable that your audience becomes bored with simply listening to information about your topic. Rather, develop innovative ways to compose and deliver various elements of your speech—such as your introductory and concluding statements, examples, or narratives—so that your audience is kept wondering how these elements fit into your overall design (see Sections 2.2, 4.2, and 6.2).

9 When speaking, never start discussing one idea and then begin another, tangential idea before completing the first idea.

Though such jumping from one thought to another often occurs in conversation, in a speech, it shows a lack of preparation. Instead, finish your first thought and then use an effective transition such as, "Before I go any further, let me say that. . . ." This will allow you to introduce what should have been the preceding point (see Section 4.5).

10 Create a unified, coherent, and emphatic speech.

Write, organize, and deliver your speech so that your audience is always clear about where you are in your speech, what you are discussing presently, and how your present point relates to your thesis and the rest of your speech. One way to maintain such clarity is to use transitions that rephrase your thesis, main points, and evidence while indicating where you are in your speech (see Section 4.5).

You should also try to maintain some symmetry in the size and importance of your main points, evidence, and arguments. This symmetry can be created in a variety of ways: (1) by using the same number of subpoints to support each of your main points; (2) by using parallel paragraph forms, sentence structures, or transitional phrases; and (3) by establishing similar patterns in your vocal delivery to reflect similar parts of your speech, main topics, and types of evidence (see Sections 4.6 and 6.2). At the same time, avoid a monotonous speech by varying the type, length, and style of your words, sentences, ideas, and figures of speech (see Section 6.5). Use single-syllable words, short sentences, and multiple pauses when stating something evident or representing a long, tedious process, and use multisyllable words, longer sentences, and a rapid speed when discussing a rushed activity or sequence of events (see Section 6.2).[4] Finally, use words that sound pleasant, rough, silly, and intelligent—such as *heavenly, gutsy, goofy,* and *profound*—to help capture those qualities of the person or object you are describing.

6.2 Grammar, Composition, and Word Choice

Whereas Section 6.1 offers some general principles of style, this section describes more specific principles and techniques that will help you adopt your word choice, verb tense, grammar, and other stylistic elements to an oral medium.

1   Although you should speak in a conversational manner, follow the basic rules of grammar and composition when writing and delivering your speech.

In general, try to use complete sentences to express complete thoughts. Make sure that your sentences' subjects and verbs agree and you are using the proper forms of pronouns, adjectives, and adverbs. To sound more conversational, you can begin more of your sentences with a conjunction such as *and, or,* or *but* than you would in written composition. You should also use conjunctive adverbs such as *moreover, however,* and *therefore* to represent more clearly the relationships among your ideas.

You can also use sentence fragments more often when speaking than when writing. However, limit their use to when you want to sound conversational or when you want to emphasize the fragment's effect. On the other hand, steer clear of such conversational habits as searching out loud for the right term or phrase and using filler words. Likewise, avoid using run-on sentences, technical jargon, and euphemisms. While run-ons make you sound uneducated, jargon and euphemisms can make you sound verbose or pompous.

In addition, do not use slang expressions that make you appear unprepared or faddish. For instance, when recalling a conversation with a friend, do not say, "So, I'm like . . . and she's like. . . ." Rather, use more formal and correct phrasing such as, "When I asked her . . . , she replied. . . ." Use slang only on those selective occasions when you want to establish a personal relationship with your audience or emphasize the regional or cultural character of an expression or idea.

Although you should adhere to the rules of grammar, do not construct sentences and use words that make you sound impersonal or overly formal. To establish a more conversational and personal rapport with your audience, use such personal pronouns as *I* and *you* instead of indefinite pronouns such as *one* or *everyone*. Use the latter only when you want to create distance between you and your audience or when you want to create a sense of objectivity with your statement, as in the case of "Everyone would agree that. . . ."

Also, do not vary the words you use to refer to the same thing as often as you do in written composition. Too many variations of the same word may make it difficult for the audience to follow your ideas. For the same reason, use proper nouns and names more often than you use personal pronouns (e.g., *he, she, them*) and demonstrative adjectives (e.g., *this, that, those*).[5] Use either a personal pronoun or a demonstrative adjective only once before returning to the proper noun or name so your audience can follow your reference more easily.

Making your pronoun reference clear and avoiding dangling modifiers are extremely important in speech. Violating these rules can cause confusion in your audience's mind about what (i.e., grammatical antecedent) you are referring to. For instance, consider the statement, "Dog owners must be very consistent when training dogs or they will be very frustrated in the years to come." The statement does not make clear whether the pronoun "they" refers to the dogs or owners and thus whether the lack of consistency will frustrate the dog owner (because the dog is not trained) or the dog (because he does not understand the commands). Likewise, the statement, "Leaving a trail to the stolen money in off-shore bank accounts, the government began to get suspicious" implies that the government was both hiding the money and investigating the fraud. To correct this dangling modifier, you would need to state the name of the person who had stolen the money: "Because Johnson left a trail to the stolen money in off-shore bank accounts, the government began to get suspicious."

2   Use terms that present your ideas clearly and effectively.[6]

Express your ideas in vivid, illuminating terms that are nevertheless familiar. Try to use terms that mean exactly what you intend, and do not imply meanings that will cause your audience to misinterpret your point. For instance, do not use the term *psychotic*, which connotes a severe psychological ailment, when you mean to say that someone's actions appeared *frantic*. Similarly, do not define an action as *illegal* when it was *unethical* but still legal. However, when trying to convey a value or elicit a particular response from your audience, use a term that will produce the effect you seek. Saying, "The court ruling *stripped* citizens of their constitutional rights" will have greater impact than stating, "The court ruling *disregarded* their rights."

Use an uncommon or technical term only when it is integral to your subject and will allow the rest of your speech to be less wordy (see Section 6.1). When introducing such terms, define them clearly, and use examples and analogies to expand your definition (see Section 2.2). On occasion, refer to an old term and give its etymology to bring some historical character to your speech, or create a new term, such as *Oprah-fied*, to capture your idea forcefully and focus attention on your point.[7]

3   Try to use evidence in the most direct and concise way.

Keep your explanations, examples, narratives, and anecdotes as short as possible (see Section 2.2). This is not to say that you can never offer an extended analysis or story, but their length should be correlated to their significance and effectiveness. That is, you should never add needless details to a piece of evidence when such details add little to the point you are making. In this same vein, you should avoid stringing together redundant adjective and adverb phrases.

As for statistics, round off very complex numbers, and summarize your data in the most succinct manner. Limit your discussion of the methods used to collect or analyze research data. To help show the research's legitimacy, however, explain concisely how the data were collected, and give an example of the research results, perhaps by quoting a response from a questionnaire. Finally, do not use long quotations that add little to your point. Instead, summarize any important information before the quotation, and use only those parts of the quotation that provide additional evidence or further refine your point.

4   Use active and passive voice and the imperative mood to emphasize ideas in your speech.

Construct the majority of your sentences in the active voice. Using the active voice, as in "Abraham Lincoln issued the Emancipation Proclamation to end slavery," highlights the individual performing the action and allows your audience to experience the event more directly. Using the passive voice, as in "The Emancipation Proclamation was issued by Lincoln to end slavery," stresses the act itself and not the agent of the action and thus allows you to sound objective. To convey an idea forcefully or reflect a sense of urgency, use the imperative mood. For instance, you could say, "Always take your shoes off before entering a

Japanese home" to underscore the significance of this social norm. You can selectively employ imperative sentences when stressing an important procedure in a demonstration speech, and raise your volume to make your command more emphatic (see Section 7.2).

5   Although you may use contractions, do not overuse them.

Using contractions is more permissible in public speaking than in some forms of academic writing. However, using too many contractions makes you sound overly informal and unprepared. Moreover, contractions can sometimes be difficult for your audience to discern clearly and may cause your audience to misunderstand your point, as in the case of mistaking the word *should* for the contraction *shouldn't*. Thus, either avoid using certain contractions, or slow down, raise your volume, and make a conscious effort to pronounce them clearly (see Section 7.2).

6   Use gender-neutral and inoffensive terms.

Be careful not to offend anyone with the language you use. To avoid gender bias when using pronouns, use the phrase *he or she,* or refer to people in the plural. For this same reason, use gender-neutral nouns, such as *chairperson* or *chair* instead of *chairman*. Also, be sure that your ethnic and racial references are free of prejudice, stereotypes, or negative connotations.

Do not use language that may demean a group of people unintentionally. For instance, do not refer to the physically disabled as *invalids*. Similarly, do not inadvertently stigmatize those you are trying to help by, on the one hand, overstating their plight, or on the other hand, unconsciously belittling their condition by using terms such as *helpless* or *hopeless* that have condescending connotations.

Finally, never belittle other people, even if you disagree with them. Demeaning language often is seen as offensive regardless of whether your audience agrees with you or whether your opponent is being unreasonable. Use language that shows respect for other people even though you disagree with their position.

7   Always qualify your terms and statements to reflect their size, strength, and importance.

For instance, do not use the word *all* when referring to *most* or *some* members of a group. Likewise, use the term *some* instead of *many,* or the phrase "an important factor," instead of "the only factor," to limit the scope of your claim.

You also should clarify the relative importance of a statement whenever necessary. To be clear, use phrases such as, "What is critical here . . . " or, "The most important step is. . . ." When summarizing a source or quoting testimony, use terms that clearly reflect how fully or narrowly the individual discussed the issue, or how strongly or weakly he or she endorsed a claim. There is a great deal of difference, for example, between saying "Johnson states" and "Johnson passionately argues." Making the weight of such statements clear to your audience helps them gain a better understanding of the individual's viewpoint. You also can use descriptive phrases such as "Now imagine that . . . " or, "Try to feel . . . " that indicate how your audience should perceive your point.

8   **Avoid using phrases such as *I think, In my opinion,* or *I believe.***

Such phrases either repeat what is already implicit or make it appear that you are the only one holding the stated position. Use these phrases only when you want to show that you have come to a position on your own.

9   **Avoid mixing metaphors and exaggerating claims.**

The intent of an analogy or metaphor is to represent an object or idea in a way that sheds new light on it (see Sections 2.2 and 6.5). However, by mixing metaphors and analogies, you may cloud the point you are making. For instance, mixing the maxims "The early bird may catch the worm" with "But sometimes it counts its chickens before they are hatched" may sound catchy, but your audience may have difficulty deciphering all the implicit references you are making.

You should avoid exaggerating a comparison, overemphasizing an emotional appeal, or using an overly dramatic delivery (see Sections 2.1, 2.2, and 7.2). These unnecessary embellishments may appear bombastic or phony and make your audience uncomfortable and wary of your sincerity.

10   **State a term or the name of an institution before using its common abbreviation or acronym.**

Make sure your audience recognizes an abbreviation or acronym by first introducing the term, name, or phrase it refers to. For instance, you could say, "According to the American Civil Liberties Union, or the ACLU, . . . " Once you have designated what the abbreviation represents, use the abbreviation consistently throughout your speech.

Consider abbreviating the names of texts, such as a scholarly book or government document, that you refer to throughout your speech. Likewise, simplify long and awkward professional or scholarly terms.

6.3 Revising Your Style

The guidelines offered here will help you assess your style when preparing your speech's final draft. This important part of your preparation provides you an opportunity to clarify your organization, strengthen your evidence, and enhance the aesthetic quality of your speech. Hence, make sure you allot enough time to assess your speech's style before you begin practicing your oral delivery.

1 **Before completing your final draft, take a break from writing your speech.**

Often, this time allows you to create some distance between you and your speech so that you can view your speech more critically when preparing your final outline or manuscript.

2 **When you begin working on your final draft, concentrate first on revising your speech's overall organization.**

When reviewing the organization of your speech, ask yourself these questions (see Chapter 4):

- Is the speech missing any major points or pieces of evidence?
- Does the speech sound unified?
- Will my audience recognize how my main points relate to my thesis statement?
- Is there a better way to organize my speech?
- Are there ways to make my speech flow more smoothly?

You should also take some time to compare the organization, content, and flow of your speech to those of other speeches you have heard or read. Last, when reviewing your speech, try to read it as if you were an audience member hearing the speech the first time.

3 **After reviewing your speech's overall organization, assess the various parts of your speech.**

Determine whether you support each point fully, or whether you are belaboring a point. Eliminate or consolidate excessive information, such as too many statistics or an extended explanation. Likewise, if you have several arguments relating to the same point, keep only the most important one and quickly summarize the others.

4 **Enhance the speech's style.**

Work to increase the effectiveness of your introduction and conclusion, create smoother transitions, strengthen your evidence, clarify the logic of your arguments, correct your grammar, and make your language more precise and eloquent (see Chapters 2 and 4). Shorten sentences that are too long, add more descriptive terms, and incorporate figures of speech to add rhetorical flair to your speech (see Section 6.5). Once you have made these changes, review your whole speech again, and check to see if you have covered everything you set out to discuss.

6.4 Oral Citations

Because your audience is not privy to your outline or manuscript, the only way they will recognize the sources of your information is through an oral citation. By documenting your research sources with an oral citation, you establish the legitimacy of your evidence and strengthen your credibility as a researcher (see Section 2.1). To determine how and when to use oral citations, follow these guidelines.

1   Cite those sources that you quote directly, summarize, or paraphrase.

You do not have to cite facts or ideas that everyone knows or that you find in several sources. However, you must provide an oral citation when quoting a text directly or when summarizing or paraphrasing information from a source. Regardless of whether you use an oral citation, you can be accused of **plagiarism** if you copy or simply rephrase a source's language (words or phrases) or style (sentence composition or arrangement of points).[8] Thus, when summarizing or paraphrasing a source, work from your own understanding of the information, and use your own words and compositional style to state the idea. Then use an oral citation to show where the information was obtained.

As in written composition, you will need to cite your source every time you refer to information obtained from the source. Even when you are moving from one point to the next while using the same source you must cite the source each time. Likewise, when first discussing information from one source and then a second, and finally, returning to your first source, you will need to use an oral citation for each instance.

2   Use an oral citation to establish the trustworthiness or timeliness of your source.

As a general rule, you should refer to the source's author, the name of the article and publication, and the date of its publication. However, you may want to cite the publication date only if the timing of the publication is important because it shows that your source was the first to expose a piece of evidence or because it shows that the information was known when someone says that it was not.

3   Be as brief as possible.

When citing a source for the first time, give all the important information. After this, abbreviate your reference with a key word or words by using just the name of the primary author or selected words from the title, and then use this abbreviation throughout the rest of your speech. Do not cite the page numbers of a source unless you are discussing a controversy relating to the text itself, or unless everyone in your audience is very familiar with the text.

Another way to simplify your citation is to eliminate any unnecessary information from your citation. Thus, state only those elements of the reference most relevant to your point and your audience. For example, you can refer to a newspaper article written by a staff writer by citing only its title, date, and name of the newspaper. Likewise, if your source is written by a well-known author and published in a major news periodical, you may want to give only the name of each, because your audience would have no trouble locating the source.

4   Acknowledge your source either before, after, or in the middle of a statement or quotation.

Vary the style of your oral citation to avoid a monotonous speech. For instance, begin one citation by saying, "According to George Will's, November 17, 1998, *Newsweek* editorial. . . ." Begin the next by stating, " 'The question is not . . . ,' as syndicated columnist Paul Giguot argues in the November 20th edition of the *Wall Street Journal*, 'but whether. . . .' " Then close your next quotation with a citation such as, "as was stated on the front page of the *New York Times* on November 21,. . . ." When the evidence you are citing is new or uncommon, or it goes against your audience's prior understanding, err on the side of providing your citation before your evidence to enhance the credibility of your evidence.

5   Avoid saying *quote* and *unquote*.

This technique should be used rarely and only for added emphasis. Instead, acknowledge the quotation by changing your voice: pause before the quotation, and then, when quoting the text, change your inflection, volume, and rate as if you are speaking with the author's voice. After stating the quotation, pause again and then return to your original speaking voice (see Section 7.2).

6   Refer to information gathered from a web site by giving the web site's title.

A web site's title is its official name, and it usually appears at the top bar of the browser's window (see Section 1.5). If audience members wish, they can find the site using a search engine. For instance, you could say, "According to *Heritage Foundation Online*, ..." However, for a web site that is continually revised, you may want to give more information so that an audience member can find specific web pages more easily. Hence, you might say, "In its August 19, 1998, on-line article entitled 'Clinton's Troubles Aren't Over Yet,' CNN's *Allpolitics* states. . . ."

6.5 Figures of Speech

Figures of speech, figures of thought, and tropes are words, phrases, and statements that can enhance your style's artistic or logical quality. **Figures of speech** play on the aesthetic properties of language by emphasizing similarities and differences between the sound quality of words or phrases. **Figures of thought** communicate ideas in a logical or orderly fashion by repeating similar ideas or contrasting opposite ones. **Tropes** substitute one word for another in order to express the meaning of the substituted word in a more poetic or unusual way. In general, all three figures make your ideas more appealing and memorable. You can use these figures in any speech and at any time in a speech; however, they are used most often and effectively to synthesize ideas or make an emotional appeal in the conclusion of a persuasive or ceremonial speech.[9] To present figures effectively, practice enunciating them clearly and emphatically and delivering them in a smooth, rhythmic cadence (see Section 7.2).

Because figures are not used commonly, you may have difficulty recognizing and constructing them. Along with studying the figures presented here, another way to familiarize yourself better with figures of speech is to analyze how other authors and speakers such as Shakespeare, Abraham Lincoln, Susan B. Anthony, John Kennedy, and Martin Luther King have used them (see Section 6.5).

1   Alliteration.

The repetition of words beginning with the same consonant sound is often used to create a poetic effect.

EXAMPLE
Once the seeds of this sordid story were sown, Klien simply substituted the pseudonyms.

2 Anadiplosis.

Starting a sentence with the same word or phrase that ended the preceding one. This immediate repetition brings order and logical coherence to your point.

EXAMPLE
The volunteers who participate in Big Brother programs devote their time to thousands of inner-city children in need of mentors. Mentors such as these restore hope to children by showing them that someone out there cares for them and will be there for them in the future.

3 Anaphora.

The repetition of a word or phrase at the beginning of consecutive clauses or sentences. This figure makes your sentence sound rhythmic and your ideas logical. Consider using this figure to unify a list of items or ideas you are discussing.

EXAMPLE
By smoking, cigarette smokers risk their own health; by smoking indoors, they risk the health of those around them; and by smoking in public, they risk the health of the nation as a whole.

4 Antanaclasis.

Repeating a word or root word but using it in two different senses. Although it is often used to lend humor to a pun, this figure of speech can also stress the different ways in which the same word can be interpreted.

EXAMPLE
The city council should not bow to pressure from those lobbying to put the monument in the park's mall. Just because there is some empty space there, doesn't mean the space is empty.

5 Antithesis.

Establishing an idea by constructing a sentence (or sentences) with contrasting words, phrases, or clauses. This figure builds a single point by asserting an idea and then denying its opposite.

EXAMPLE
Some may say that race doesn't matter, whereas others believe that it is all that matters.

6 Assonance.

The repetitive use of words that have the same vowel sound. Like alliteration, this figure of speech can add a poetic rhythm to your phrasing.

EXAMPLE
It seems that American politics today relies on three principles: lie, deny, and vilify the other guy.

7 Asyndeton.

The use of a series of words with no connective words such as *and, or,* and *but.* Eliminating conjunctions from your sentence conveys a sense of urgency or signifies a repetitive action.

EXAMPLE
The time to protest is now—by tomorrow, our opposition will be organized; by next week, they will be all over the press with halfhearted excuses and apologies; by next month, the public will be following another story.

8 Chiasmus.

Reversing the order of words or phrases in a sentence to highlight contrasting ideas. When chiasmus is used effectively, your audience becomes pleasantly surprised as you express contrasting ideas with a limited number of words.

EXAMPLE
One former alcoholic said it best when he told me, "I didn't drink to survive, I survived to drink."

9 Climax.

The repetition of successive words or phrases at the beginning and end of sentences. This figure represents your ideas in logical order and can build to an exciting end.

EXAMPLE
If we don't mend broken windows, then we will never bring people back into our urban communities. If we don't attract people to our urban communities, then we will never attract business to relocate in our urban centers. And if we don't get business to relocate in our urban centers, then American cities will never again be the thriving economic and cultural centers that once were the envy of the world.

10 Enallage.

The conscious use of grammatical mistakes such as mispronouncing or misusing a word, or using grammar improperly or using the wrong part of speech. Enallage can call attention to an otherwise normal statement. Like slang words, this figure should be used sparingly, and you should call attention to it by emphasizing the word or words you are using incorrectly (see Section 7.2).

EXAMPLE
Politicians seem to do lots of *talkin'*, but not much *listenin'*.

11 Epanalepsis.

Beginning and ending a sentence with the same word or phrase. This figure exemplifies logical thought and calls attention to the repeated word or phrase.

EXAMPLE
As my father used to always say, "You got to do what you got to do."

12 Epistrophe.

The repetition of the same or similar words at the end of a series of phrases or sentences. Using this figure of speech brings consistency to your ideas and a poetic sense to your wording.

EXAMPLE
I have lived by the word of God, and I will die by the word of God.

13 Hyperbole.

Exaggerating a claim for rhetorical effect. The exaggeration should be used to emphasize a point rather than to mislead your audience.

EXAMPLE
If you were told once, you were told a million times, there is no free lunch.

14 Malapropism.

Using an incorrect word that sounds similar to the correct word. Often, you replace the incorrect word with the correct word to call attention to your feigned slip of the tongue. As with enallage, emphasize this figure by raising your volume or changing your tone (see Section 7.2).

EXAMPLE
Along with abstinence, many health professionals *condom*—I mean, condone!—teaching safe sex.

15 Metaphor.

A word or phrase that suggests an idea by way of a likeness or analogy. Like the figurative analogy, metaphors often suggest a likeness between something that your audience is unfamiliar with and something natural or common (see Section 2.2). A metaphor also is similar to a simile; the difference is that by omitting such words or phrases as *as*, *as if*, and *like* that are used in a simile, the metaphor creates a more direct and immediate link between the object and what it resembles.

> **EXAMPLE**
> The stock market has been on a roller coaster ride for the last six months with no sign letting its passengers off.

16   Metonymy (Synecdoche).

A statement or phrase that substitutes a cause for its effect, a whole for its part, a part for its whole, a container for the contained, or a symbol for the thing itself. Although many metonymies are used in everyday speech, they can bring a poetic flourish to a phrase or statement.

> **EXAMPLE**
> Throughout the history of this country, many men have gone off to war and died for their flag.

17   Onomatopoeia.

Using a word whose pronunciation sounds like what it means. To increase its rhetorical effect, call attention to the figure by varying your vocal delivery to represent the sound realistically (see Section 7.2).

> **EXAMPLE**
> As the thunder cracked and the wind whizzed through the trees, the people of South Florida readied their homes for Hurricane Andrew's mighty gusts.

18   Parallelism.

The repetition of the same or similar phrases or sentences. Here again, this figure creates rhythm and suggests logical coherence.

> **EXAMPLE**
> Many world religions believe that you can reach true spiritual awakening only by renouncing all worldly ties. You must renounce your material possessions, renounce your family, renounce your friends, and renounce even your self.

19   Polysyndeton.

The frequent and emphasized use of connective phrases that tie successive words, phrases, or clauses together to highlight each of the items connected. Adding extra connecting phrases equalizes the importance of each successive word while creating a rhythmic cadence.

EXAMPLE

The American legal system must treat all citizens equally, no matter whether they are male or female, black or white, Jew or Gentile, Protestant or Catholic.

20 Pun.

A humorous expression usually created by using a term or phrase outside of its normal context. A pun is often created by using similar sounding words to express a contrast between different words, or by playing on words with similar meanings.

EXAMPLE

While fight enthusiasts were calling the second Tyson–Holyfield fight the "Fight of the Century" before it began, it will go down in the annals of boxing as "The *Bite* of the Century."

21 Rhetorical question.

A question or series of questions whose answer is readily understood and inferred by the audience. This figure is usually made by turning a generally accepted statement into a question so your audience considers the statement's meaning more fully. Remember to extend your pause after asking a rhetorical question to give your audience time to consider the question's implication (see Section 7.2).

EXAMPLE

Would you want a health care system that placed the government in charge of determining who would receive certain kinds of medical procedures? Would you want a health care system in which the government restricted what doctor you could see? Would you want a health care system in which, on top of dealing with doctors, hospital administrators, and insurance companies, you would have to contend with a government bureaucracy? Well, if you don't want such a system, then the senator's health care system isn't for you.

22 Simile.

An explicit comparison between unlike things made so that the characteristics of the one can be conveyed onto the other. A simile usually involves the use of the words *like, as,* or *as if.* Like a metaphor or metonymy, a simile allows you to stress the similar characteristics of the two things being compared.

EXAMPLE

His extramarital affairs hung like a great big albatross around his neck, preventing him from discussing family values during his political campaign.

7

Delivery

7.1   *Modes of Delivery*
7.2   *Elements of Vocal Delivery*
7.3   *Elements of Nonverbal Delivery*
7.4   *Enhancing Your Memory*
7.5   *Practicing Your Speech*
7.6   *Preparing to Speak*
7.7   *Reducing Speech Anxiety*
7.8   *Responding to Questions*

7.1 Modes of Delivery

Listed below are the four main modes of delivering a speech. Study each mode to determine which best suits your topic, delivery style, and speech situation. If time permits, try different modes of delivery when practicing your speech (see Section 7.5). Practicing these different delivery modes will both improve your delivery skills and increase your familiarity with your speech's text.

1   Extemporaneous delivery.

An extemporaneous delivery is given from an outline. It is the most common delivery mode because it offers you the chance to refer to an outline of your speech while allowing you to choose your words, construct your sentences, and vary your appeals when delivering your speech. Thus by speaking extemporaneously you can maintain a healthy balance between presenting your speech's text and modifying your delivery to fit the needs of your audience.

The other main advantages of an extemporaneous delivery are that it allows for increased eye contact and the ability to adapt your speech to your audience's nonverbal feedback (see Section 7.1). For instance, you can rephrase an explanation or provide an additional example when your audience appears confused, embellish an emotional appeal once you recognize its initial impact, or eliminate a point if you are running out of time (see Sections 2.1 and 2.2). Its main disadvantages are that it requires a great deal of preparation to make your main points flow together smoothly, and you must know when to speak from your outline and when to talk more directly to your audience. You also must avoid the temptation of trying to memorize an exact set of words, phrases, or statements that sound good when you are practicing your speech, for you may stumble or repeat yourself needlessly when trying to recall your ideas.

2   Manuscript delivery.

The manuscript delivery is most often used in speeches where stating your position, providing definitive evidential support, and wording your statements correctly are of utmost importance. As its name indicates, this mode of delivery is given from a written text that contains your whole speech.

While a manuscript explicitly sets forth all of your ideas, it limits your ability to adapt your speech to your audience's nonverbal feedback. As such, a manuscript delivery provides little opportunity for you to relay additional information, rephrase a confusing statement, or omit ineffective ideas. A manuscript delivery also may cause you to limit your eye contact and speak too quickly, and it may cause you to neglect other verbal and nonverbal delivery techniques. To avoid many of these pitfalls, refrain from simply reading your speech, speak slowly, and pronounce your words clearly. Likewise, remember to vary your tone, use facial expression and gesture effectively, and make eye contact with your audience whenever possible (see Sections 7.1 and 7.2).

3   Impromptu delivery.

Like improvisational theater, an impromptu delivery is unprepared and unrehearsed. It usually entails no research and uses neither an outline nor a manuscript.

The advantage of an impromptu delivery is that it is more informal and allows you to maintain eye contact with your audience. Moreover, it can highlight your knowledge of your topic and your sincerity. At the same time, however, it can expose your ignorance about your topic. Your lack of preparation also can make it difficult for you to state your thesis clearly, organize your speech and its main points adequately, present evidence thoroughly, and refer your sources properly (see Sections 2.2, 4.1, 4.3, 4.4, and 6.4). To avoid these problems, find places in your speech to restate your thesis statement and use review transitions to help you remember your main points (see Sections 4.3, 4.5, and 7.4).

4 Memorized delivery.

A memorized delivery is given without the help of either a manuscript or an outline. Usually it is used for short ceremonial speeches or speeches that you will give many times. Although you can memorize every word of your speech, it is better to commit only your outline to memory and then speak extemporaneously (see Section 7.4).

The main advantages of the memorized speech are that it allows you to maintain eye contact with your audience, and it can demonstrate your expertise with your subject. However, after continually delivering the same speech, your delivery may begin to sound dull and unenthusiastic. If this happens, rework parts of your speech and alter your delivery techniques (see Sections 7.2 and 7.3).

7.2 Elements of Vocal Delivery

It is easy to recognize how your vocal delivery plays a major role in the way you present yourself to your audience. Like your style, your delivery also is integral to the meaning you convey (see Section 6.1). Your vocal delivery is not just a way to embellish or ornament your ideas; rather, it plays a major role in how you communicate your ideas and, consequently, how your audience will comprehend and interpret them. Moreover, your delivery can help your audience follow your speech's overall organization and increase the appeal of your proofs (see Sections 2.1 and 4.1). To learn more about how to deliver your speech, study the elements of vocal and nonverbal delivery given here and in the next section (see Section 7.3).

1 Register.

Your **register** is the range of pitch, rate, volume, pauses, and enunciation used when delivering a speech. When giving a speech, try to stay within your **middle range,** which is somewhere between a conversational and formal style of speaking (see Sections 6.1 and 6.2). Your middle range should fit naturally with your voice and personality. Your delivery style and personal demeanor should be somewhat more formal than they are in conversation, but not artificial, affected, or pretentious. Your tone should be a degree lower than your conversational voice; your speed, a degree slower; your volume, a degree higher; your pauses, a degree longer; and your enunciation, a degree clearer (see the following subsections).

While keeping your delivery within this middle range, use **vocal variety** to avoid a monotone delivery. That is, alter your speed, volume, tone, and pauses to reflect the different elements of your speech.[1] For instance, cue your introduction and conclusion by using the same tone of voice, adopt a slightly lower tone and slower speed when stating your main definitions and explanations, and then speak more quickly and raise your pitch when relating an example or humorous anecdote. When presenting well-known facts or a short story, speak more quickly and in a light, conversational manner. For longer narratives, remember to use vocal variety to move your audience through the various stages of the story and the emotions you are attempting to evoke (see Section 2.2). Within a narrative, also try to depict hurried and fraught action by increasing your speed while representing more everyday or orderly actions with a slower, more methodical pace.

Vocal variety can also help you convey feeling and mood. For instance, if you want to instill a sense of anticipation and excitement about your subject, speak louder and more quickly, use greater changes in your inflection, and increase your gesturing. To reflect the serious nature of your subject, start and finish your speech in a more subdued manner, and use facial gesturing to reflect your sincerity and concern (see Section 7.3). Likewise, when warning or advising your audience about a serious matter, attempting to solicit pity, or expressing fear or shame, lower your tone, speak more slowly, and pause longer and more often. On the other hand, when arguing vehemently or placing blame on a culprit, raise your tone, increase your speed, and pause only for punctuation and to give your audience a chance to recognize the severity of the individual's ideas or actions.

2   Tone.

In music, pitch and tone are often used interchangeably, whereas in speech, your voice's tone is equated with your voice **inflection.** Your **tone** denotes the highness or lowness of your voice. By raising or lowering your tone, you can convey a variety of meanings.[2] For instance, consider lowering your tone to suggest an implied meaning, stress an important fact, or express a sincere conviction. You can also raise your tone when citing an example or telling a personal story.

You may want to change your inflection to stress certain words or phrases.[3] For example, use your tone to reflect the meaning of words such as *devote, caring, hateful,* and *patriotic.* Similarly, words and phrases that express the urgency of a situation, such as "the time is now" or "without hesitation," should be spoken quickly and forcefully, whereas those expressing a long, deliberate process, such as "after years of soul-searching" or "he moved cautiously," should be stated more slowly.

You also should repeat the same patterns of inflection when expressing similar ideas or parallel statements, and change your inflection to represent contrasting ideas in antithetical statements such as "To err is human, to forgive is divine" (see Section 6.5).

3   Rate.

The **rate** of your delivery refers to how quickly you are speaking. Although most people normally speak at a rate of 125 to 150 words per minute, slow down your rate when delivering a speech so that your audience can comprehend your ideas more easily.

How you vary your rate and pauses establishes the **rhythm** or **flow** of your delivery. Creating an effective rhythm demands maintaining some consistency as well as varying your speed (and other vocal elements), punctuating sentences and phrases with short pauses, and using your speed to indicate parts of your speech. As a general rule, speak more slowly at the beginning of your speech so that your audience can adjust to your delivery.[4] You should also slow your rate when stressing important points, abstract explanations, significant facts, or crucial statistics, and increase your rate when presenting familiar examples, figurative analogies, and short narratives. To build excitement in your conclusion and arouse your audience's emotions, move from speaking softly and slowly to speaking more quickly and loudly.

4   Volume.

Your **volume** is how loudly or softly you speak. Within your middle range, always raise your volume to just above your regular conversational voice, and remember to project your voice by bringing air from your diaphragm and chest, rather than just speaking from your throat. Projecting your voice will place less strain on your throat and allow you to be heard by all your audience members.

In general, increase your volume when stressing an important point, making a critical argument, emphasizing a definition, or expressing a strong conviction. Lower your volume when offering a helpful subpoint, expressing an empathic emotion, or building a suspenseful story. In addition, raise or lower your volume to call attention to a word or phrase. You also will want to speak more softly (and slowly) in parts of some speeches, such as a eulogy, and more loudly when delivering parts of other speeches, such as the climactic ending of an introductory speech (see Section 5.6).

5   Enunciation.

Enunciation entails pronouncing words and sentences properly. The main reason why a speaker mispronounces words is that he or she is speaking too quickly as a result of being nervous. Avoid mispronouncing words by controlling your speech anxiety and by making a conscious effort to slow down and pronounce each part of a word or sentence clearly (see Section 7.7).

To improve your enunciation, practice pronouncing difficult or commonly mispronounced words. For instance, practice pronouncing words with an *ing* suffix so that you do not leave off the last *g* and make sure to say *want to* and not the slang *wanna*. Similarly, make sure that you are pronouncing short and long vowels properly, such as the *a* in *bat* and *cape;* and soft and hard consonants, such as the *c* in *cap* and *catch.* Another way to ensure that proper pronunciation is to **round the sounds** by exaggerating your mouth's movements when forming a word.

Proper enunciation also involves placing the proper inflection on words and sentences. By changing your inflection, you can change the meaning of a statement. For instance, you can alter the implied answer to the question, "Should we blame the tobacco companies or smokers for the high levels of lung cancer in this country?" by stressing either the words *tobacco companies* or *smokers*. In general, your inflection should be lower at the end of a declarative sentence to reflect its truthfulness, but higher at the end of a question to signify its speculative character. However, questions that begin with an interrogative such as *Why*, or imperatives that begin with the command *Never*, should begin with a strong inflection.

Try to avoid several common problems with enunciation. First, do not slur your words or speak too softly at the end of a sentence. These problems usually result from a lack of breath. Hence, remember that the length of a sentence should be no more than the length of one of your breaths, and you should always pause at the end of a sentence. Second, to avoid mispronouncing words, do not string together too many multisyllable words and long sentences. If you are using a long, complex sentence, remember to speak slowly and stress its internal punctuation with pauses. Third, if you are having trouble placing the proper inflection in a sentence, underline the word or phrase written on your outline or manuscript that you need to stress.

With regard to regional dialect, some audience members believe such speech patterns bring character to a speech, whereas others, rightly or wrongly, believe they represent a lack of education or preparation. Thus, you must decide whether and to what degree you should rid your voice of its conversational character or regional flavor.

However, you always should avoid such speaking patterns if they cause you to enunciate your words unclearly and make your speech incomprehensible.

6   Pauses.

A **pause** is a brief moment of silence between words, sentences, important points, or parts of your speech. Pauses serve a variety of functions: (1) They indicate grammatical marks that are not evident in an oral medium, such as colons or semicolons; (2) they give your audience an opportunity to consider what you have just said and what you will say next; (3) they allow your audience to absorb the impact of an important point or savor a figure of speech or narrative; (4) they help create a smooth, intelligible rhythm by providing breaks between units of thought such as clauses, phrases, and sentences; and (5) they give you a chance to breathe and collect your thoughts before moving to your next point.[5]

You also should use a longer pause after your introduction and before your conclusion so that your audience can more clearly distinguish the main parts of your speech (see Section 4.1). Likewise, pause after a rhetorical question to allow your audience time to consider the question's implication (see Section 6.5). Finally, try to eliminate filler words such as *um, ah,* or *OK* by pausing, collecting your thoughts, and then continuing your sentence (see Section 7.7).

7.3 Elements of Nonverbal Delivery

The following nonverbal aspects of your delivery do not simply complement the vocal elements given in Section 7.2; rather, they are an integral part of your overall delivery. Like your delivery's tone, volume, and speed, your stance, gestures, and facial expressions can help you convey meaning, represent your speech's organization, and establish a rapport with your audience. As with your vocal delivery, you should express yourself nonverbally in ways that reflect your personality and yet are more formal than your usual conversational style. To become more comfortable with expressing yourself nonverbally, concentrate on accentuating those parts of your nonverbal delivery that feel most natural to you. Then work on incorporating other types of movements and facial expressions into your delivery. For instance, if you would like to increase your gesturing, think about how you normally gesture in everyday conversations, and watch other people's gestures when they are at the podium or talking. From these observations, select gesturing patterns that you fit your delivery style, and try to incorporate them into your delivery (see Section 7.5).

1   Dress.

The clothes you wear when speaking can be either casual or somewhat formal. When deciding how to dress, consider the occasion of the speech, your role as a speaker, and your audience's expectations.

Whatever you wear, dress comfortably so that you can move easily. Avoid wearing stiff, tight clothing and noisy, uncomfortable shoes. Likewise, your collar or tie should not be so tight that it restricts your breathing.

Do not wear a hat with a brim when you are speaking because it may make your audience uncomfortable if they cannot make eye contact with you. If you have a tendency to play with your hair, jewelry, or pocket change while you speak, you may want to pin your hair back, remove your jewelry, or empty your pockets.

2   Posture.

The term *posture* has two essential meanings: (1) your body's arrangement when you are standing; and (2) your disposition toward something. It is no wonder then that how you stand while speaking often reflects your attitude toward your speech and audience. To make sure you are sending the right message, always maintain a good posture. A good posture entails standing straight but not rigidly, and squaring your shoulders to your audience, even when you are moving from side to side. Keep your feet at shoulders' width apart and place one foot slightly forward, if you like. Because this is the most comfortable way to stand, it may prevent you from shuffling your feet and locking your knees, which speakers often do when they become uncomfortable.

To stress a point, lean forward or, conversely, convey your dismay or repulsion toward something by leaning backward. However, avoid rocking on your heels as well as swaying from side to side, standing on one foot, and slouching over the podium.

3   Gestures.

Gestures are motions of your body or limbs that, either singularly or combined with speech, express meaning. The basic technique of hand gesturing has three stages: First, begin with your hands either resting on the podium, clasped together, or at your sides; second, initiate the gesture or a series of gestures; and third, return your hands to their original position.

An endless array of gestures can help you convey meaning.[6] For instance, by holding up one, two, or three fingers, you can indicate which main point you are discussing; by bringing your hands together or apart, you can represent unity or disunity; by moving your hand

(and arm) to the rhythm of your speech, you can emphasize a point; and by making a fist or opening your hands, you can convey a sense of conflict or conciliation. You can also use gestures to mimic an action or feeling you are discussing, such as the dotted brush stroke of a pointalist painter, or wiping your forehead to convey a sense of relief. However, you do not want to appear overly theatrical by imitating grand movements or overusing this technique. You can represent a sincere conviction or emotion by placing your hand on your chest; or point into the audience when discussing a value they hold or away from them to refer to ideas and sentiments others hold and which the audience oppose.

As with vocal elements of your delivery, you will want to use certain patterns of gesturing to communicate similarities and differences in meaning. For example, create an imaginary grid in the space in front of you, and point to the same place whenever you are referring to the same idea, person, or thing. Then gesture in the opposite direction when referring to an opposing idea.

Finally, try to use an adequate amount of gesturing when speaking, neither too little nor too much—both can be distracting to your audience. Likewise, avoid nervously scratching your face and arms, waving your arms, or putting your hands in your pockets (see Section 7.7).

4   Movement.

There are three main forms of body movement: (1) You can move to either side of the podium to talk more directly to a part of your audience, (2) you can move to different parts of the room to establish a more intimate connection with your audience, and (3) you can walk toward and away from your visual aid. Unless you are a very experienced and confident speaker, you should never stray too far from your podium. This is especially important when you are using an outline or manuscript.

As with gesturing, use movement to convey the meaning of your speech. For instance, move closer to your audience when trying to build a feeling of trust or camaraderie, and move away from them to signify amazement or disbelief. Never, however, rapidly pace throughout your speech or use movement to burn nervous energy (see Section 7.7).

5   Facial expressions.

Like gestures, facial expressions convey meaning. As in everyday conversation, use your facial expression to amplify the intent and feeling of your message. For instance, smile at your audience when you begin your presentation, shake your head when you disagree with an opposing argument, give an inquisitive look when something sounds wrong, and smirk when saying something sarcastic. Lower your eyebrows to show sadness, or raise them to express happiness, surprise, or shock.[7] Likewise, lower your head to express sorrow or modesty, and turn slightly to one side, raise your head, and puff out your chest to indicate someone's overwhelming pride or elitism.

6 Eye contact.

Make eye contact with individual audience members and your audience as a whole. Maintaining eye contact with your audience allows you to convey meaning and to read their nonverbal feedback so that you can adjust your speech. Thus, when you see that most of your audience appears confused, spend more time explaining your point.

When seeking to establish eye contact, do not look over the heads of your audience or at their feet. Rather, look into their eyes. Make eye contact both by scanning your whole audience and by looking at individuals in every section of the room. To avoid becoming nervous, concentrate on making eye contact with those individuals who are giving you positive nonverbal feedback.

You should also use your eye contact to accentuate the meaning of your statements. For instance, when explaining something that affects everyone, pan your whole audience. Then, when discussing something that you know is of particular interest to an individual in your audience, make direct eye contact with that person.

Finally, consider the best times to make eye contact with your audience and when you should concentrate on your speech's text. For example, since your initial summary and transitional statements tell your audience something about your presentation's organization, these are good opportunities for eye contact (see Section 4.3). Realize that you do not have to maintain constant eye contact with your audience. If you become nervous or if you lose your place, pause briefly, breathe, and relax. Then look down at your notes or manuscript and speak directly from your speech's text. After regaining your confidence and the rhythm of the speech, look up from your notes and reestablish eye contact with your audience (see Section 7.7).

7.4 Enhancing Your Memory

Along with invention, organization, style, and delivery, memory was one of the five main elements of classical rhetoric. Today, however, the role of memory in rhetoric has lost much of its significance. Nevertheless, when speaking extemporaneously or from memory, the ability to recall your ideas still plays an important role in speaking (see

Section 7.1). Consequently, use the following guidelines to help you re-call the major elements of your speech.

1   **Build your memory by concentrating first on your speech's overall organization, and then on its individual parts.**

Start by reviewing the main parts of your speech; that is, study its introduction, body, and conclusion (see Section 4.1). Next, practice de-livering your speech from a key word outline (see Section 7.5). After you have gained a sense of its general structure, work on recalling the specifics of its main parts.[8] Begin with the most important parts of your speech—the main functions of your introduction, your body's main points, and the main functions of your conclusion. Then, from within the framework you have just built, try to recall the other parts of your speech that complete and tie your speech together, such as your subpoints, transitions, and secondary themes (see Sections 4.1, 4.5, and 6.1). Last, try to recall as much of the whole speech as possi-ble from your key word outline or memory. Remember that the more you practice your speech, the more you will know and recollect it when speaking.

2   **Do not try to memorize every word of your speech.**

Trying to recall every word may cause you to stumble through your speech and repeat yourself needlessly. Instead, try generally to recall the basic idea behind each of your main points and pieces of ev-idence (see Sections 2.2 and 4.1).[9] If you are having trouble recalling your introduction, try first to remember its four main functions, and then recall how you planned to fulfill each function with respect to your topic. Similarly, concentrate on recalling the main elements in a story's chronology rather than memorizing the entire story (see Sec-tion 2.2). Then allow yourself to reconstruct the story as you speak, choosing the words and sentence structures you want to use along the way.

3   **To maintain consistency in your speech, remember what you have already said when deciding what to say next.**

This consistency entails considering how to relate a previous idea to a subsequent one, how to weave an example or story throughout your speech, and when to use review transitions to help you recall ear-lier points and tie them to later ones (see Sections 2.2 and 4.5). Also, re-member to make your sentence's subjects and predicates relate grammatically, alternate sentence structures to avoid a monotonous style, and use approximately the same amount of time to discuss each main point (see Sections 6.1 and 6.2).

4   Use parallel sentences, mnemonic devices, and other rhetorical techniques to help recall your points.

Use parallel statements to introduce each of your main points or as transitions (see Section 6.1). Employ other figures of speech to help you recall your ideas and make them more memorable to your audience, and use pauses to collect your thoughts (see Sections 6.2, 6.5, and 7.1).

To also help you recall your ideas, use the classical rhetorical technique of visually equating each main point or a series of subpoints with a place or piece of architecture.[10] Likewise, weave a metaphor, analogy, or motif throughout your speech that helps you recall its various points. For instance, when discussing Ted Turner's career in broadcasting, you can refer to the metaphor of "the house that Turner built" throughout your speech and use the different rooms to recall the role of each of Turner Broadcasting's subsidiary companies. Begin by describing Turner Broadcasting as the roof under which all the subsidiaries are housed; the Cable News Network (CNN) as the house's foyer, because it introduced most people to Turner's media conglomerate and provided the passageway to his other news station; the Turner Network Television (TNT) as the family room, because it offers family entertainment, and so on.

Another technique is to use symbols to help recall your ideas. For instance, imagine a silly hat or article of clothing on different politicians to represent their various qualities or unfulfilled campaign promises. For instance, visually place a child's hat with a propeller on top of a presidential candidate whom most believe lacks the required knowledge of domestic and foreign affairs, while you have another candidate wear an overly starched shirt to represent his or her lack of personality.

5   Develop distinctive subpoints that are easy to recall.

Although it is easy to recall larger parts of your speech by using a parallel structure, using more specific examples, descriptions, or analogies makes it easier to remember specific subpoints (see Section 2.2).[11] Thus, represent on your outline each of your subpoints with a special word or phrase that will stimulate your memory.

7.5 Practicing Your Speech

The guidelines given in this section offer techniques for practicing your speech. Although the amount of time you will need to practice will depend on your familiarity with your topic and the level of your speaking skills, you should begin practicing your speech at least two or three days before you deliver it. This schedule will give you plenty of opportunities to revise your speech's text and refine your delivery.

1   **Begin by simply reading over your presentation and making revisions or mental notes as to how you want it to sound.**

Before practicing your delivery, study your speech's text and make further revisions (see Section 6.3). Then determine what points you want to stress and how you want your speech to sound as a whole. Try to establish the rhythm or flow of your speech by concentrating on the relationship among your thesis statement, main points, and supporting evidence (see Sections 2.2 and 4.1). Finally, consider how you will use transitional statements to add clarity and coherence to your speech (see Section 4.5).

2   **Practice your delivery.**

In your first few practice rounds, you should stop whenever necessary and refine your delivery. Then, as you become more familiar with your text, begin practicing without stopping for revisions. This practice technique will force you to make immediate changes while maintaining a fluid rhythm. It will also allow you to practice giving your speech within your assigned time limit. If your speech is too long, eliminate whole points, summarize background information, and find ways to shorten unnecessarily long explanations, descriptions, and narratives (see Sections 2.2 and 6.1). If you find your speech is too short, determine how you can develop your main points further or when to explain information more thoroughly.

In general, you should practice your speech three to five times without stopping before giving it to a small, preliminary audience. If practicing in front of a mirror is helpful, do so. However, if this technique makes you uncomfortable, do not use it. Consider recording yourself on audiotape or videotape as well as having someone else read your manuscript to you. Both of these techniques allow you to gain some critical distance from your speech, thereby allowing you to revise your speech and delivery more objectively.

3   **Use a key word outline in some of your early practice rounds to help you memorize parts of your speech and practice explaining ideas and formulating sentences.**

When speaking extemporaneously or from memory, do not try to memorize specific words, phrases, or statements in your speech (see Sections 7.1 and 7.4). This attempt at memorization may cause you to stumble during your speech as you try to recall these exact words again. Instead, use a key word outline to help you recall your main points and establish the flow of your delivery.

4   Attempt to relate whole ideas, not just words or sentences.

Listen for the organizational and logical relationship between the various parts of your speech. Make sure that your main points are well supported by their subpoints and that your arguments are valid or strong (see Sections 2.3 and 4.1). Listen for places where you will need to use transitions to clarify the relationship between ideas (see Section 4.5).

5   Practice the vocal elements of your delivery by varying your voice.

Practicing your vocal delivery allows you to create a physical memory of your mouth's movements as you speak. This physical memory helps maintain the rhythm of your speech and also comes in handy if you become nervous in front of an audience.

Practice varying your pitch, rate, and volume to convey your ideas, emotions, and intentions effectively (see Section 7.2).[12] Take a passage from your speech and use various vocal techniques to express yourself more or less seriously, emotionally, or emphatically. You can also increase your vocal variety by taking a passage from your speech or a simple sentence such as "The dog is on the mat" and playing around with increasing and decreasing your speed, volume, pitch, and so on. Although this technique may appear silly, it allows you to find some comfortable and useful vocal patterns that you may not have recognized previously. If you are still unsatisfied with your delivery, consider taking a favorite poem, speech, or passage from a book and try changing the vocal elements of your delivery to give the text different meanings.

In addition, listen for places where you need to slow down to emphasize a point, speed up to discuss a minor point, and change your voice inflection to connote a certain idea. Likewise, practice enunciating your words clearly and pausing to catch your breath.

6   Practice your gesturing and the other nonverbal elements of your delivery.

Begin by studying your own nonverbal techniques and those of others, and try incorporating them into your delivery (see Section 7.3). Then practice exaggerating these movements so that they can be seen by a large audience. If you would like to increase the amount of bodily gesturing and facial expressions you use, practice your speech with

two or three times the amount of gesturing your normally use, and select those gestures you find most comfortable and effective. If a gesture does not feel natural to you, do not force it because doing so could
distract both you and your audience.

You should also practice making eye contact with your audience.
Work on making eye contact during those parts of your speech, such
as between your introduction and body, where your speech's organization provides a good opportunity to look at your audience (see
Section 4.1). Moreover, find familiar passages in your speech that you
can discuss without looking directly at your notes or manuscript. Remember to use your eyes and facial expressions to convey sincerity,
surprise, dismay, and other feelings. Practice looking at whole sections of your audience and then at different individuals in the various sections of the room.

7 Choreograph any movements that are integral to your speech.

Practice critical gestures that help you express your ideas. Also
prepare your movement to and from your speaking aids as well as any
other movements you will use in a demonstration (see Section 3.6).

8 Recognize poor speaking habits, and try to correct them.

Listen to yourself speak and determine whether you are speaking
too softly or too quickly and whether you are mispronouncing words
or constructing sentences incorrectly (see Sections 6.1, 6.2, and 7.2).

If your voice is naturally high, lower it by relaxing your throat and
getting air from your diaphragm instead of your mouth. If your voice
is too low or nasal, try clearing your throat and nasal passages, relaxing your jaw, and bringing air from your chest rather than your diaphragm. If your low tone is caused by apathy or shyness rather than
physical reasons, increase your energy level and enthusiasm, speak
louder and more emphatically, and try to control your speech anxiety
or apathy (see Section 7.7). Also, if your throat is sore, gargle with salt
water and use throat lozenges in the days and hours before you speak.

If you are slurring your words or improperly omitting, substitut-
ing, or adding syllables to words, try to speak more slowly and continue practicing pronouncing your words (see Section 7.2).

Finally, try to eliminate any filler words and phrases such as *ah,
OK, all right, you know, like, um,* and *uh.* Speakers usually use such filler
words because they are nervous (see Section 7.7). Some speakers use
filler words because they are unsure how to begin stating an idea,
whereas others use them because they do not know how to complete
a thought. The best way to prevent yourself from using filler words is

to recognize when you use filler words and then make a conscious effort to pause and state your point directly.

9 Make a conscious effort to control nervous habits.

Listen to yourself speak, and work to eliminate any distracting mannerisms you have, such as rocking on your heels, slouching, crossing your legs, scratching your arms or face, or playing with your hair or jewelry (see Sections 7.3 and 7.7). If you do any of these things, make a conscious effort to stop them, and channel your energy into more meaningful movements and gestures.

10 After practicing your speech several times on your own, deliver it in front of a select audience of friends.

Ask a group of friends to listen to a practice round and make helpful comments. Choose friends who are not particularly knowledgeable about your topic so that they will catch ideas that you may need to clarify or explain in more detail. Friends who know a great deal about your topic will presuppose knowledge of ideas that your audience may not have. They may even suggest eliminating definitions, explanations, or examples that your audience may consider helpful.

When practicing your speech in front of this preliminary audience, present your complete speech without stopping. When you finish, ask your friends to comment on your speech's content and delivery. Ask for comments about your speech's main parts and ideas: For instance, ask whether your main points were clear and well supported, whether your points flowed together logically and smoothly, and whether your introduction was inviting and your conclusion effectively summarized your speech (see Sections 2.2, 2.3, 4.1, and 4.2). Then ask about your speech's style and delivery: Ask whether your friends thought particular words and phrases were helpful, if your sentences where too long, whether your delivery was clear and effective, whether you were maintaining enough eye contact, and whether you have any distracting mannerisms or nervous habits (see Sections 6.1, 6.2, 7.2, 7.3, and 7.7). Finally, practice your speech at least one more time, preferably an hour or two before you present it.

7.6 Preparing to Speak

The following procedures may help you prepare yourself to speak during the hours and moments immediately before your presentation. These techniques, along with those that will help you reduce speech anxiety, will help you relax and build your confidence as a speaker (see Section 7.7).

1   **Before speaking, find a place to relax and think about your speech.**

At this time, do not try to recall everything that you want to say in your speech. Testing your memory will only increase your level of anxiety. Instead, like the athlete who prepares by visualizing his or her successful shot, pass, or run, use this time to picture yourself giving a successful speech. Think about how you will stress your main points, express your transitions, and make your speech flow smoothly (see Section 4.1, 4.5, and 7.2).

2   **Prepare your voice by performing a warm-up exercise or two.**

For instance, roll consonant sounds like *rrrrrr* or *blblbl* while varying your tone and volume (see Section 7.2). Do the same by working up and down the musical scale or by lowering your tone for each word in a phrase such as "boo, hoo, hoo" and by raising your tone when repeating another such as "I'm hap, hap, happy!" Using such phrases also provides the opportunity to practice expressing feelings and emotions. To practice your enunciation, quickly repeat a tongue twister such as "Mother makes me make my bed" or a group of similar sounding words such as "slit, shot, slot."

3   **Prepare your body with warm-up exercises.**

Engaging in warm-up exercises before you speak will make your movements and gesturing feel more comfortable when you are speaking (see Section 7.3). Loosen your body by moving your shoulders up and down and shaking and rotating your limbs. Similarly, relax your facial muscles by miming big kisses or chewing too many pieces of gum. If you have any nervous habits, such as waving your hands, crossing your legs, or tossing your hair, allow yourself to engage in these actions, and even exaggerate such movements several times before speaking (see Section 7.7). This will help you expend nervous energy and allow you to concentrate on your speech.

4   **Establish a comfortable breathing pattern with a few relaxation exercises.**

One breathing exercise you can try is taking short breaths, slowly at first, and then gradually increasing your speed and the amount of air you are breathing.[13] When performing this exercise, keep your mouth slightly open, and breathe from your diaphragm. Another exercise starts with inhaling and filling your diaphragm with air. Next, concentrate on slowly moving the air up through your chest cavity and throat while allowing your chest to expand and your shoulders to move back. Finally, slowly exhale and let your shoulders move forward and your chest and diaphragm deflate. Repeat this exercise a few times. You also can perform this exercise by saying *ah* as you exhale while maintaining a smooth and clear flow of the sound. Because these exercises cause you to breathe from your diaphragm and not from your throat, you should have more oxygen to breathe and, consequently, more energy to speak. These exercises should also help reduce your speech anxiety (see Section 7.7).

5   When you arrive in the room, walk around to become more familiar with your speaking situation.

Arrive early for your speech, and try to reduce the strangeness of the situation and audience by becoming familiar with both. Acclimate your body to the room's temperature and lighting, acquire a feel for the podium by walking around and adjusting it, and prepare your visual aids. Moreover, make eye contact with some audience members even before you begin speaking. Try to gain a sense of your audience's overall mood, and look for people who use a lot of facial expressions in conversation and who may therefore provide good nonverbal feedback while you speak. If you are nervous, look for audience members who appear pleasant and open-minded and, thus, may react to your speech favorably.

6   Once you are ready to begin, look at your audience to gain their attention.

Acknowledge them by nodding or smiling. Once they recognize that you are about to begin, look down at your notes briefly so that you can adjust your eyesight to reading them, then look up, reestablish eye contact with your audience, and begin your speech.

7.7 Reducing Speech Anxiety

Psychologists, communicologists, and the general public agree that public speaking is one of the biggest fears of most people.[14] Its main symptom—speech anxiety—is an elevated feeling of stress and nervousness that occurs either immediately before or during a speech. A modest amount of nervousness is normal, and to some extent beneficial, because it increases your awareness of the speaking situation. However, extreme speech anxiety can undermine your effectiveness. Regardless of whether your fear is caused by the speaking situation or by elements of your own personality, you can reduce your speech anxiety by following the guidelines and techniques given here.[15]

1   **You will be more confident and have less speech anxiety if you are well prepared and practice your speech a great deal.**

Research and prepare your speech until you are satisfied with its content and composition (see Chapters 1, 2, 4, and 5). Then practice your speech until you can recall your ideas easily while maintaining a smooth delivery (see Section 7.5). If you have prepared and practiced your speech to the best of your ability, give yourself credit for the work you have done. Acknowledging your own hard work will build your confidence and convince you that your situation is not as bad as you are imagining. Also, realize that many of your audience members will recognize the effort you put into your speech and will sympathize with your fear of speaking. Finally, do not dwell on your past failures as a speaker. Instead, recognize that you will have good and bad speaking days. Know that the more times you speak, the less anxiety you will have, so try to make the most of every opportunity you have to speak in front of an audience.

2   **Have your introduction well prepared so that you begin strongly.**

Getting off to a good start can drastically reduce the amount of speech anxiety you experience throughout the rest of your speech. Therefore, practice your introductory statements often so that they flow smoothly.

3   **When you feel yourself becoming nervous, focus on the ideas in your speech and away from the fact that you are speaking to an audience.**

Speech anxiety may occur if you are concentrating too much on your speaking situation or your irrational fears about speaking in front of an audience rather than the topic that you are speaking about. If anxiety occurs, pause briefly, relax, look down at your notes, and speak directly from your notes. Try to rebuild your confidence by concentrating on your speech, instead of your audience, and work to reestablish your rhythm. Then after regaining your confidence and flow, make eye contact with your audience again (see Section 7.3).

4 **If your speech anxiety causes you to lose your place or have a mental block, try summarizing your last point to see if your summary helps you recall your next point.**

Speech anxiety may cause you to become so unsettled that you lose your place or forget what to say next. If this problem occurs, try summarizing the point you just made. This summary may help you remember your next point or give you some time to find it on your outline or manuscript.

5 **Breathe comfortably when speaking.**

A major cause and effect of speech anxiety is not having enough air to breathe. When you are nervous, you sometimes forget to breathe properly. A lack of air causes several nervous symptoms: It raises your body temperature, makes your heart beat faster, and restricts your throat. These symptoms not only cause an increase in speech anxiety, but also may cause your voice to tremble, your pitch to rise, and your volume to decrease. Therefore, remember to breathe sufficiently and speak at a slow and steady rate. Pause and take deeper breaths between the major parts of your speech as well as short, full breaths between sentences (see Section 7.2).

6 **Avoid increasing your rate of delivery when you become nervous.**

Nervousness may make you unconsciously attempt to remove yourself from the speaking situation as quickly as possible. Consequently, you may try to shorten your speech by speaking too quickly or by cutting out a main point. If you speak too quickly, you may mispronounce your words, shorten your pauses, and breathe improperly. To counteract these nervous symptoms, remind yourself that by speaking quickly, you are only making matters worse. Then tell yourself to slow down, pause when necessary, and enunciate clearly (see Section 7.2).

7 **Limit your use of filler words.**

Sometimes speakers use filler words such as *you know* and *OK* because they want constant confirmation from their audience. If you have this nervous tendency, stop yourself from using such words or phrases, and simply pause instead. You could also use a more formal statement such as "Is everyone following this?" as a way to ask for your audience's approval.

Another nervous habit some speakers have is ending a statement with a vague phrase such as "and things like that" or "you know what I mean." Using such phrases is usually a sign that you are concentrating too much on your audience or that you are unprepared. To avoid this problem, catch yourself before using the phrase, and concentrate on stating your point explicitly. Here again, you may want to avoid making eye contact for a brief moment so that you can express your thoughts more easily (see Section 7.2).

8 **If being nervous causes such symptoms as sweaty palms or shaky hands or legs, try to relax, breathe slowly and deeply, and move your muscles.**

If these symptoms occur before speaking, take a short walk beforehand, or engage your limbs in movements and rub your hands lightly. To relieve this tension, you even may want to repeat tightening and then relaxing those muscles that shake. When speaking, use gestures to engage your body in slight movements that will keep your blood flowing (see Section 7.3). You also can relax your throat and shoulders by yawning and rolling your head slowly.

To stop your hands from shaking, place them gently on the podium and try to relax for a moment. Do not grip the podium tightly, for this grip will only cause your hands and limbs to become weaker and shake even more when you release them. Once your shaking is under control, begin gesturing again.

9 **If your mouth and throat become dry, move your jaw back and forth, swallow several times, and keep your mouth closed before speaking.**

Smacking your lips when speaking is often a symptom of trying to create saliva because your mouth is dry. To avoid this problem, drink some water or chew gum before you speak, but remember to remove your gum before speaking. You should also bring water to the podium if you think you will need it. Pausing to take a drink of water is a common and accepted practice that should not disrupt your speech or reduce your credibility. Finally, if being nervous causes you to burp, eat lightly and avoid carbonated beverages on the day of your speech, and then take deep breaths and relax immediately before speaking.

10 **Do not let distractions make you nervous.**

If there is a minor distraction, such as an outside noise or someone entering the room, simply continue speaking or pause briefly, but do not draw attention to it. If a major disruption breaks the flow of your speech, such as someone yelling in the hallway or your visual aid falling off its easel, acknowledge (or apologize for) it or try to make a humorous remark. Allow for a brief pause to let the incident pass, and then return to your speech. Finally, do not become distracted by a disruptive audience member or one that is giving you negative nonverbal feedback. Focus your attention on the whole audience, and look for audience members who are giving you positive feedback.

7.8 Responding to Questions

After presenting your speech, you may have the opportunity to field questions from your audience. The following guidelines will help you prepare to answer potential questions.

1 **Prepare for potential questions by being as critical as possible about your speech when you are reviewing the final draft of your outline or manuscript.**

Try to determine every possible alternative position that someone could take in response to your arguments, and consider ways to undermine or refute these positions. Also determine ways to restate your main points, redefine your terms, rephrase your explanations, and develop potential examples that will clarify your ideas. Then practice any possible answer you may give. This process not only will prepare you to answer questions, but it also will help you revise and strengthen your speech.

2 **Direct your audience's questions to a point that you were unable to discuss thoroughly in your speech.**

If you need to bring up a point during your speech but cannot discuss it fully because of time constraints, briefly explain the point, and then offer to explain it further during the question-and-answer period if anyone is interested.

3 **If necessary, take notes on your audience's questions and comments.**

Outline their comments and your potential answers. If you are asked several questions, take notes so that you remember each one. You can answer them in the order in which they were asked or in the order of their relative importance. If time is limited, acknowledge your time constraints, and limit your answers to the most important questions.

4 **Always answer a question in the clearest, most concise manner possible.**

Begin your answer by first restating what you have said in your speech, and then make any additional statements relevant to the question. Although your answers should be brief and lucid, they must be developed enough to answer the question. When answering a question, look first at the person who asked the question, and then expand your eye contact to include the whole audience (see Section 7.3).

5   **Maintain a positive demeanor when answering a question.**

Show that you want to treat the person's question fairly and reasonably. Remember that your intent is to clarify or defend your point, not to promote yourself or degrade the questioner. Likewise, you should never respond harshly to a questioner, even one whose question is mean-spirited. If the questioner is attacking you, control your emotions so that you can think and speak clearly. A malicious response may hurt your credibility, but a reasonable one may undermine your attacker.

6   **If a question is unclear, ask the audience member to rephrase it, or try to restate it in terms that he or she accepts.**

Your request to have the question restated will show that you are trying to treat the person's questions fairly. Do not take advantage of a poorly stated question by dodging its basic intent. By doing so, you risk losing credibility. If you believe a question is not relevant, briefly explain why it is so and look to your audience for nonverbal confirmation of your reasoning.

7   **Respond gracefully to counterarguments, and then show why your argument is stronger.**

Point out the strengths of a questioner's arguments, and explain why his or her claim is appealing. Cite authorities who may agree with the claim or provide further evidence for it. To establish some commonality between your positions, show why you may agree with certain elements of his or her claim.

After building up the argument, gently tear it down. Clarify the reasons why your argument is stronger and offers greater insight into your topic. Refer to places in your speech that provide evidence refuting the claim, introduce additional evidence that would negate the claim, and address the flaws in the questioner's argument.

If the questioner does not accept your answer, allow him or her to reply again, and then offer a final response. If the questioner is still dissatisfied with your answer, respectfully respond by "agreeing to disagree" and, if you like, offer to continue the discussion after the question-and-answer period has been completed.

8 If you do not know the answer to a question, simply say so.

Do not risk having your answer refuted or looking foolish by giving an incorrect answer. If possible, try to explain what you believe would be a logical response to the question, or indicate where the questioner may find an answer to the question.

9 Never allow your questioner to limit your response.

Do not allow yourself to be forced into a yes-or-no response. This is usually an attempt to lead you into contradicting yourself when the person asks a follow-up question.

Likewise, avoid being placed in a false dilemma where the questioner offers only two possible answers that reflect extreme positions and no middle ground (see Section 2.5). Instead, state that there are other alternative responses and that your position is somewhere between the two extremes. For instance, if someone asks, "Why is an owl more important to you than people's livelihood?," explain why you do not consider that saving habitats and saving jobs are mutually exclusive goals.

If someone asks you a loaded or complex question, that is, one that either portrays you in a negative light or gives you only two negative options as possible responses, identify why the question is tainted or unduly limiting, and then state your position (see Section 2.5). For example, say someone asks, "Because you want to legalize marijuana, would you smoke it with your children or have them buy it at the grocery store?" State that, regardless of your own personal avocations, legalizing marijuana is a sound public policy, particularly if we restrict people under twenty-one from buying and smoking it.

Finally, if someone suggests that your proposals are too idealistic or that opposing parties will never accept your proposals, briefly restate how your ideas can be put into practice, or suggest ways in which the parties can negotiate a compromise.

10 When necessary, control the question-and-answer period forcefully yet discreetly.

Do not allow a hostile audience member, heckler, or long-winded respondent to take control of the floor. Ask hecklers to wait their turn to ask a legitimate question. Likewise, tell a hostile audience member that even though he or she may find your answers unacceptable, he or she does not have the right to disrupt the session and prevent others from asking questions. Here again, you could respond by agreeing to disagree, and then quickly move on to the next question. When you recognize that someone is trying to give a speech, at the first opportunity interject something such as, "You have already raised some interesting points so let me address one or two of them."

If the audience member still will not yield after having had an opportunity to speak, either make clear that you have the last say on the subject, or ask the moderator (or instructor) to intervene.

Student Speeches

Informative Speeches

Speech of Explanation

Beth Preston's informative speech on coffee offers her audience a good deal of new information on a familiar topic. Although she uses a variety of evidence, such as descriptions, narratives, and testimonies, her main intent is to explain how coffee was discovered and how its consumption has affected religious, political, and economic activities throughout history (See Sections 2.2 and 5.2). Notice how Beth builds her credibility both by acknowledging her love for her topic and her multiple oral citations to scholarly and popular books, periodical articles, and web sites dealing with coffee (see Section 2.1). She also makes her topic appealing by relating events, activities, and puns familiar to her audience in her title, introduction, last main point, and conclusion (see Sections 2.1 and 6.1).

Thanks a Latte!

Beth Preston

"Morning, Johnny. The usual? That will be $4.29." This is what I said every morning this summer when I worked at Starbucks. It got me thinking, how can someone spend $4.29 a day on coffee? First, I must confess that I am a coffee addict. I love the stuff. But $4.29 every day on coffee? That averages to about $30 a week, $120 a month, and $1,440 a year! That's a lot of money; that's a lot of coffee! This caused me to wonder if it was always like this. Has coffee always been this popular, or is this a recent trend? In order to understand better this growing phenomenon, let's first go back to where it all began and explore the discovery of coffee. Second, we will look at its history and its peculiar role in religion and politics. Third, I will discuss coffee's growth and decline in the United States and its reemergence as a leading industry in today's economy. Thus, I invite you to join in the journey as we observe the growth of this little bean, from goat feed to coffee king.

It all began in the eighth century in the tropical highlands of Ethiopia with Kaldi and his sheep. According to Geocities.com's web site, "A Brief History of Coffee," Kaldi was a shepherd who let his sheep stay in the pastures at night. One morning Kaldi noticed that the sheep stayed awake after grazing in wild fields and consuming unknown red beans. This intrigued Kaldi, and he soon discovered that the beans had the same effect when he ate them. He told local monks about this strange new bean, and the monks studied and experimented with the bean. They ground the dried beans and boiled the resulting powder and *voila,* coffee! The monks passed this newfound recipe to various monasteries, and though coffee was thought to have some medicinal uses, it mainly helped keep the monks awake during prayer.

Coffee spread from Ethiopia to Mecca and Yemen by traveling merchants via trade routes across the Gulf of Aden. There was extensive planting and harvesting of coffee in Yemen. By the sixteenth century, coffee had become a major part of the culture in Mecca. However, the governor of Mecca felt threatened by this new addition to his country. So threatened in fact, he closed down coffeehouses due to rumors that coffee drinkers were writing satirical songs about him. Coffee was such an influential "bean" of unrest, that it affected even family life during this time period. As noted in Heather Bourbeau's *Washington Monthly* article of October 1999, during the sixteenth century, a Turkish woman could divorce her husband if he refused to provide a sufficient amount of coffee.

Coffee had effects in other countries as well. In *The Coffee Book,* Dicum and Luttinger write that in Rome, priests wanted to ban coffee as an atheist drink. However, Pope Clement VIII baptized coffee, thus making it a "truly Christian beverage." In fact, the Pope is rumored to have said, "This Satan's drink is so delicious that it would be a pity to let the infidels have exclusive use of it. We shall cheat Satan by baptizing it."

In the late 1600s, the Turkish ambassador to France introduced Louis XIV to the magical little beans. Louis XIV in turn supported the consumption of coffee by his citizens. He enjoyed it so much that he tried to transport a young coffee plant from East Indies, but his attempts failed. Five years later, a French general's efforts proved more successful, and soon coffee poured into Europe.

Coffee became a popular trend around London and Paris. Barrels of the beans were being imported from Egypt. Coffeehouses thrived during the late 1600s until the mid 1800s. Although coffeehouses first were rest stops that provided refreshments for weary local merchants, they quickly developed into the center for social, economic, political, and literary discussion. Many, in fact, likened coffeehouses to "penny universities" because of the stimulating conversation one could receive for a penny dish. Each coffeehouse catered to a certain clientele. According to Margaret Woolfolk's 1990 *British Heritage* article entitled "The Penny University,"

> Every trade and profession had its particular meeting place. The prominent wits conversed with men of letters at Will's while lawyers and scholars gathered at the Grecian or Nando's. Physicians and the

> London clergy favored Child's in St. Paul's Churchyard. . . . The Cocoa
> Tree was a meeting place for London's Tories, while St. James's Cof-
> fee House was a meeting place for Whigs.

As you can see, these members of the emerging English bourgeois class
frequented coffeehouses whose conversations focused on issues and events
dear to the hearts of their clientele. Even the influential insurance and stock
exchange firm Lloyd's of London began as a coffee house where merchants met
and negotiated shipping contracts for goods coming in and out of London.
Alison Olson's 1991 *History Today* article, "Coffee House Lobbying," provides a
fascinating account of the coffeehouses which barred the names of different
American colonies. In these coffeehouses, English politicians and businessmen
met, delegated trading rights, and planned colonial policy.

These coffeehouses were politically and culturally influential in other
ways. For instance, by the early 1700s, the conversations in the coffeehouses
were so important that critics like Addison and Steele began publishing *The
Spectator* and *The Tatler* to provide their readers with a glimpse of conversations that took place in the various London coffee houses. According to the
German philosopher and sociologist Jurgen Habermas, these moral weeklies
edified this growing middle class with book and theater reviews as well as
commentary on the social and cultural mores of their times. Habermas even
goes so far as to say that coffee and the houses in which it was served provided a major impetus for the emergence of a "public sphere" of open discussion that we still hold as a necessary part of all democratic societies. But as
trends come and go, so did the influence of coffee. By the late 1700s, the importance of coffee waned due to the popularity of tea which, unlike coffee,
could be grown in England. Coffeehouses too lost influence as more exclusive
political clubs and parties began to form and take on a more direct role in
English parliamentary government.

But coffee soon found it's way to America. Willian Ulker, an early histo-
rian of the beverage, holds that the American Revolution was plotted and
conceived over a cup of Joe. Daniel Webster even turned a coffee shop in
Boston into the headquarters of the American Revolution. Ulkers, as quoted
in the August 1999 edition of *Business Week,* states that coffee "has been
the world's most radical drink in that its function has always been to make
people think."

Coffee played an important role in other wars as well. In the Civil War, a
union solider was given thirty-six pounds per year. That is three times the current consumption level. The reason for so much coffee drinking was that, like
the monks we met earlier, coffee kept the soldiers awake. However, problems
arose, as these soldiers became addicted to coffee's main stimulant: caffeine.
You see, caffeine is a chemical stimulant that triggers increased levels of brain
activity. However, once our brain adapts to the stimulant, it wants that effect
all the time. Without it, side effects such as headaches and fatigue can occur.
This is why so many people around the world seek the brew immediately after
waking in the morning.

Despite its addictive quality, coffee still was in high demand throughout the early twentieth century. *Business Week* in fact claimed that the British sent packets of coffee into "coffee-deprived" areas of Nazi-controlled countries in hopes to make them wish for Allied victory. However, after World War II, coffee fell in popularity mainly due to its new caffeine competition: Coca-Cola. As you probably know, Coke, and other soft drinks like it, has a sweeter taste as well as the caffeine that so many people became addicted to.

Yet once again, coffee has taken a turn for the better in consumption and sales. The new coffee trend began when three friends in Seattle started a coffee shop in 1971—Starbucks—and it has been growing ever since. Howard Schultz, Starbuck's CEO, was a coffee machine salesman and saw the potential for the company itself and for the coffee industry. Starbucks and many other Generation X coffee shops emphasized quality, variety, and clever marketing. They provided comfortable and trendy cafes for a variety of people, such as students, locals, tourists, and business people, to sip their brew. Today, coffee is the world's second most valuable commodity, second only to oil.

As we review coffee's history, we can see the main factors that have stirred the coffee phenomenon. First, coffee's stimulating quality was and is recognized by monks, militias, and millions of people alike. Second, it had the support and approval of many powerful leaders such as Pope Clement VIII and Louis XIV. Third, coffee and the houses that served the brew had a great influence in many political and cultural developments that began in the eighteenth century and are still with us today. Finally, the new coffee trend, began by companies like Starbucks, has made coffee into one of the most identifiable and profitable commodities in today's economy. These four factors have played an important role in the development of coffee. So to Kaldi and his sheep that discovered this magical little bean and the three men responsible for Starbucks—Thanks a latte!

Outline
   I. Introduction
      A. Story about a typical morning at Starbucks: 1. $4.29 a cup, $30 a week, $120 a month, $1,440 a year!
      B. Was it always this way? Was it always this popular?
      C. Look at the discovery of coffee, its history and role in religion and politics, its growth and decline in the United States, and its reemergence as a leading industry.
  II. Body
      A. Discovery and early history: It began in the eighth century in the tropical highlands of Ethiopia with Kaldi and his sheep.
         1. Sheep stayed awake after grazing on wild fields and consuming unknown red beans.
         2. Told local monks about this strange new bean.
            a. Monks studied and experimented with berries.
            b. Ground dried berries and boiled the resulting powder: coffee!

      c. Passed to various monasteries to help keep the monks awake during prayer.

      d. Also used for medicinal purposes.

   3. Coffee spreads to Mecca and Yemen via trade routes across the Gulf of Aden.

      a. Governor of Mecca threatened and closes coffeehouses.

      b. Heather Bourbeau's *Washington Monthly* article of October 1999, sixteenth-century Turkish women could divorce their husbands.

B. Coffee enters into Europe.

   1. *The Coffee Book,* Dicum and Luttinger, in Rome, priests want to ban coffee.

      a. Pope Clement VIII baptized coffee as a "truly Christian beverage." "This Satan's drink is so delicious that it would be a pity to let the infidels have exclusive use of it. We shall cheat Satan by baptizing it."

   2. Late 1600s coffee became popular. Turkish ambassador brings it to Louis XIV. Louis XIV transports coffee plant from East Indies.

      a. French general is more successful five years later.

C. Coffee becomes popular and political. Thrives late 1600s until the mid 1800s.

   1. Coffeehouses: From rest stops to "penny universities."

      a. Each coffeehouse catered to a certain clientele. Margaret Woolfolk's 1990 *British Heritage* article entitled "The Penny University": "Every trade and profession had its particular meeting place. The prominent wits conversed with men of letters at Will's while lawyers and scholars gathered at the Grecian or Nando's. Physicians and the London clergy favored Child's in St. Paul's Churchyard. . . . The Cocoa Tree was a meeting place for London's Tories, while St. James's Coffee House was a meeting place for Whigs."

      b. Lloyd's of London.

      c. Alison Olson's 1991 *History Today* article, "Coffee House Lobbying." Politicians and merchants of American colonies met in coffeehouses.

   2. Cultural influences of coffeehouses.

      a. Addison and Steele began publishing *The Spectator* and *The Tatler.*

      b. Jurgen Habermas, moral weeklies edified this growing middle class and coffeehouses created "public sphere."

      c. Late 1700s coffee less important because of tea, political clubs, parties, and parliamentary government.

D. Coffee in America.

   1. Willian Ulker: Daniel Webster turned Boston coffee shop in revolution headquarters.

      a. *Business Week,* August 1999, coffee "has been the world's most radical drink in that its function has always been to make people think."

2. Civil War: Union solider receives thirty-six pounds per year. Three times current consumption level. Coffee kept the soldiers awake, yet they became addicted to stimulant: caffeine.
   a. Caffeine triggers increased levels of brain activity. As brain adapts, it wants that effect all the time. Without it, headaches and fatigue can occur.
E. Twentieth-century history of coffee.
   1. *Business Week:* British send packets of coffee into "coffee-deprived" areas of Nazi-controlled countries.
   2. Coffee falls in popularity: Coke is sweeter and has caffeine. Then coffee increases in consumption and sales.
   3. Seattle, 1971: Starbucks. Howard Schultz, Starbuck's CEO was a coffee machine salesman.
      a. Generation X coffee shops provide comfortable and trendy cafes for variety of people.
      b. Coffee is second most valuable commodity, second only to oil.
III. Conclusion
   A. Summary:
      1. Coffee's stimulating quality recognized by monks, militias, and people.
      2. Coffee supported by powerful leaders: Pope Clement VIII, Louis XIV.
      3. Coffee and coffeehouses influence political and cultural developments that began in the eighteenth century.
      4. Starbucks and other companies have made coffee into one of the most identifiable and profitable commodities in today's economy.
   B. Closing:
      1. To Kaldi and his sheep that discovered this magical little bean and the three men responsible for Starbucks—Thanks a latte!

Bibliography

Heather Bourbeau, "Book Review: Uncommon Grounds," *Washington Monthly.* October 1999, 54.

"A Brief History of Coffee," <http://www.geocities.com/'Colusseum/Turf/8736/history.htm>.

Gregory Dicum and Nina Luttinger, *The Coffee Book* (New York: New Press, 1998).

Jurgen Habermas, *The Structural Transformation of the Public Sphere* (Cambridge, MA: MIT Press, 1989), 32–33.

"History of Coffee," *The Economist,* July 1999, 10.

Allison Olson, "Coffee House Lobbying," *History Today,* January 1991, 35–42.

Mark Pendergrast, *Uncommon Grounds: The History of Coffee and How it Transformed Our World* (New York: Basic Books, 1999).

"Rise and Fall and Rise of Coffee," *Business Week,* August 1999, 13.

Margaret Woolfolk, "The Penny University," *British Heritage,* June/July 1990, 50–54.

Speech of Demonstration

Kathy Chulkas introduced her public speaking class to part of her ethnic heritage by demonstrating the Greek wedding dance called the *kalamatianos* (see Section 5.2). She begins her speech by chronicling the development of the circle dance, a precursor to the wedding dance. In her second point, she displays and describes the ethnic costumes worn by the bride and groom and the musical instruments used to perform the wedding song. She then plays the traditional wedding song, further adding to the ethnic flavor of her speech. Finally, Kathy demonstrates the wedding dance. During her demonstration, notice how Kathy effectively uses signpost transitions and a review summary to help her audience follow the steps of the *kalamatianos* (see Section 4.3).

The *Kalamatianos*

Kathy Chulkas

Opa! This expression is commonly shouted when Greeks dance at festive occasions like an engagement, wedding, or community festival. If you ever attended the Greek Festival at the Greek Orthodox Church in downtown Greenville [SC], you would hear this expression as we dance the *kalamatianos,* or Greek wedding dance. Today, I would like to demonstrate the *kalamatianos* for you. Before performing the dance, I will discuss the history of the dance, as well as the music and costumes that accompany it. I hope that by the conclusion of my speech, you will come to appreciate an important part of my Greek heritage.

Because of archeological evidence found in Greece, we know of the ancient origins of circle dances. In the National Archeological Museum in Athens, Greece, there are vases decorated with figures of dancers. These dancers are participating in circle dances resembling the dances that many Greeks still perform today. Similarly, frescoes, which are wall paintings done on wet plaster, have been discovered in ancient buildings all over Greece depicting circle dances such as the *kalamatianos*. In the days of this ancient art, dance was a form of religion, prayer, worship, and faith.

During the Classical Age of Greece, religious, dramatic, and popular dances were performed in temples, theaters, and stadiums. According to Cecile Golbert, the author of *International Folk Dance at a Glance,* some thirty of these dances can be traced to the present day. It was during this period that the *kalamatianos* was formally organized.

As it evolved, the Greek wedding dance not only embraced traditional circle choreography, but also developed a traditional costume for the bride and groom. Both of these costumes are highly decorative. The groom wore the *fustanella* [exhibit], a garment made up of many elements including a skirt, jacket, and shirt. The skirt is fully pleated to enhance the groom's leaps and turning movements. The sleeveless jacket is usually red, blue, or purple and is richly embroidered with gold or silver. This jacket is worn over a white shirt with ballooning sleeves that create a very expressive arm movement when the groom tosses his arms as he dances.

Just as the groom wears the *fustanella,* the bride wears the *amalia* [exhibit]. Her skirt is long with layers and pleats that, as you can imagine, make the turns and movements of the *kalamatianos* not only easier, but also more pleasing. Her coat is short and usually made of red velvet. Her fez, a cone-shaped felt hat, is decorated with Turkish coins that form her dowry. Because her clothing is made of long, thick material and she is weighed down by lots of jewelry, there is little jumping in the bride's dancing.

Not only is the *kalamatianos* rich in tradition, but its music is unique because of its unusual rhythms and instruments. The music combines the clarinet, violin, and drum or tambourine. Probably the most unusual instrument is the *bouzouki* [exhibit], which is smaller than a guitar and has a higher pitch. A final special element of the *kalamatianos* is the song that accompanies the dance. The lyrics are "Beautiful is the bride, her dowry and her company, those which give her happiness. We wish happiness in the groom's eyes, which have picked the bride." Here is the song performed in its native Greek [play song].

Now that I have discussed the history, costumes, and music of the dance, I would like to show you the dance itself. Before I demonstrate the steps of the *kalamatianos,* I need to give you some background information on its choreography. The dancers are in a semicircle with their arms intertwined. The circle moves counterclockwise, led by the end dancer. While the leader holds onto the next dancer with his one hand, in his open hand he holds a handkerchief that he waves as he does leaps and twists.

It is in this semicircle formation that the steps to the *kalamatianos* take place. I'll now show you the basic steps of the *kalamatianos,* and you can follow along with your handout if you like [demonstrate]. The first six steps are very similar to walking sideways. First, begin by taking one step to the right with your right foot. Second, place your left foot in front of your right foot. Third, take another step to the right with your right foot. For the fourth step, again place your left foot in front of your right foot. Fifth, step to the right with your right foot again. Sixth, place your left foot in front of your right. As you can see, it's very similar to walking sideways. But now, for the seventh step, move both feet simultaneously. It's a little bit tricky, so watch carefully. As you move your left foot in front of your right foot, lift and lower your right foot back into its place. The eighth step simply returns your left foot back to a normal standing position. With the ninth step, place your right foot in front of your left foot while you lift and then lower your left foot. Finally, return your right foot to its normal standing position. That's all there is to it! I'll show you again what all the steps look like in sequence. Right to the right, left in front. Right to the right, left in front. Right to the right, left in front while you lift and lower your right foot. Stand normally. Right in front and lift and lower left. Right foot back to place. That's the *kalamatianos.*

In conclusion, I have told you about the history of Greek dance, including its representation on ancient vases and frescoes. We then looked at the *fustanella* and *amalia,* which are the traditional wedding costumes of the groom and the bride. We also listened to the traditional Greek wedding song. Finally, I showed you the steps in the *kalamatianos.* I hope that you have enjoyed this demonstration of the most popular dance in Greece. Hopefully, the next time you attend a Greek wedding or festival, you will feel comfortable dancing the *kalamatianos* with all of your new Greek friends.

Outline

I. Introduction
   A. *Opa:* Greek festival.
   B. Greek wedding dance: *kalamatianos*
   C. I would like to demonstrate the *kalamatianos* for you.
      1. History, music, costumes.
      2. Demonstrate the dance.

II. Body
   A. History of Greek Dance.
      1. Evidence in Greece: Ancient origins of circle dances.
         a. National Archaeological Museum in Athens: Vases with dance figures; frescoes or wall paintings; religion, worship, and prayer.
      2. Cultural evidence: Religious, dramatic, and popular dances were performed in temples, theaters, and stadiums.
         a. Cecile Golbert, *International Folk Dance at a Glance:* Thirty dances traced to the present day.
         b. *Kalamatianos* descends from the prehistoric circle dances, not formally organized until the Classical Age.
   B. Costumes.
      1. Groom: *fustanella.*
         a. Pleated skirt that allows for leaps and turning movements.
         b. Sleeveless jacket: red, blue, or purple, embroidered with gold and silver.
         c. White shirt with very full sleeves.
      2. Bride: *amalia.*
         a. Long skirt with layers and pleats.
         b. Short coat usually made of red velvet.
         c. Fez: Turkish coins form dowry.
         d. Clothing made of thick material.
         e. Weighed down by coins and jewelry.
   C. Music
      1. Intriguing in its unusual rhythms.
      2. Instruments used in the song:
         a. Clarinet, violin, drum, or tambourine.
         b. *Bouzouki:* Smaller than a guitar with higher pitch.
      3. Song for the dance: "Beautiful is the bride, her dowry and her company, those which give her happiness. We wish happiness in the groom's eyes, which have picked the bride."

    D. Demonstration of *kalamatianos*
        1. Background information.
          a. Semicircle moves counterclockwise.
          b. Leader is the person on the far end of the circle waving a
            handkerchief.
        2. Basic Steps in *kalamatianos*.
          a. Take one step to the right with your right foot.
          b. Place your left foot in front of your right foot.
          c. Take another step to the right with your right foot.
          d. Place left foot in front of your right foot.
          e. Right foot to the right.
          f. Left foot in front of right.
          g. At the same time, lift and then lower your right foot back into
            its place.
          h. Return left foot to normal standing position.
          i. Place right foot in front of left foot while you lift and lower
            left foot.
          j. Return right foot to normal standing position.
          k. Repeat steps 1–10.
III. Conclusion
    A. Summary.
        1. History: Vases and frescoes.
        2. Dress and Music: *fustanella, amalia, bouzouki*.
        3. Steps in the *kalamatianos*.
    B. Invite audience to dance at a Greek festival or wedding.

Bibliography
Audry Bambra and Muriel Webster. *Teaching Folk Dancing* (London: The Anchor
    Press Limited, 1972).
Peter Buckman, *Let's Dance* (New York: Paddington Press, 1978).
Cecile Golbert, *International Folk Dances at a Glance* (Minneapolis: Burgess,
    1974).
Marcia Snider, *Folk Dance Handbook* (North Vancouver: Hancock House
    Publishers, Limited, 1980.)

Persuasive Speeches

Mixed Speech Types

    Amy Lang approached her persuasive speech on the relationship
between pornography and sex crimes not by adopting any one model
of persuasive speaking, but by adapting a variety of persuasive speech
types and arguments to analyze both empirical studies and issues related to her topic (see Sections 2.3 and 5.4). To begin her speech, Amy
uses an inductive argument to relate three examples of convicted sex

criminals who were addicted to pornography. But her evidential support does not stop there. Acknowledging the difficulty of making a direct causal link between pornography and sex crimes, Amy then goes on to cite numerous studies that indicate a strong relationship between exposure to pornographic material and the potential to commit sex crimes. Next, Amy points out the faults of studies and arguments that try to downplay the effects of pornography on sexual crimes. She then ends her speech by asking her audience to help reduce the increasing number of sex crimes against women by joining antipornography campaigns. When reading Amy's speech, notice how well she explains the manner in which the studies were conducted and what can be surmised from their results. Finally, pay attention to how Amy uses clear summary transitions to review her evidence and arguments and tie her speech together (see Section 4.5).

Is Pornography Harmful?

Amy Lang

Is pornography really harmful? Is there really cause to regulate it? Judge for yourself.

Bob Lee Boog, Jr., raped at least ten women at knifepoint over a five-year period in the Capitol Hill area of Salt Lake City. Boog told the Utah Board of Pardons that pornography had contributed to his depravity. Boog said, "I was romanticizing the female anatomy to the point that they were an object to me and not a human being." Boog is presently serving a fifteen-year prison sentence.

Randy Joseph Wedding was sentenced to 320 years in jail after confessing to sexual assaults on six female rental agents as they showed him apartments in the Phoenix area. At his trial, Wedding, dubbed the "Rental Agent Rapist," admitted to a seventeen-year addiction to hard-core pornography. His obsessive habit cost him $200 to $300 a month.

Ramon Salcido, the Northern California man accused of killing two of his three daughters, his wife, and four other people, rented pornographic videos two or three times a week.

The cases of these three men just sample the countless number of violent acts, such as child molestation, sexual assault, rape, and even murder that are linked to pornography. While it is difficult to prove a direct causal relation between pornography and sex crimes, today I will present evidence showing a strong connection between the two and will seriously question research studies and arguments to the contrary.

Scientific or empirical evidence is so esteemed in our culture that it sells products and wins arguments. However, the empirical results of the research done on the effects of pornography have been reported inaccurately in the past and have led society to believe that the effects of pornography are harmless. Berl Kutchinsky, a criminologist and pornography advocate at the University of

Copenhagen, claims that when the Danish government lifted all restrictions on pornography in 1969, the number of sex crimes decreased. However, this widely cited study failed to differentiate between various types of sex crimes such a rape, indecent exposure, and attending peep shows. Because these sex crimes were lumped together into one category, the fact that rape actually increased was masked. What also was overlooked was that increased tolerance for sex crimes, such as sex with a minor and public nudity, may have contributed to the drop in reported sexual offenses.

There are also those who, like New York psychologist Patrick Suraci, believe that pornography fulfills a societal need by serving as a "safety valve" for potential sex offenders. Yet a study by two University of New Hampshire researchers, Larry Baron and Murray Strauss, has helped dispel the myth that pornography serves as an outlet for those who may otherwise commit a sex crime. Baron and Strauss's nationwide study found that where pornographic magazine circulation rates were high, rape rates were also high. In the same way they found that where circulation rates were low, the rate of rapes were low.

Like most studies on the effects of crime, there are multiple factors that may influence someone's potential to become a criminal. Thus, it would be very difficult for any study to show a direct link between pornography and sex crimes.

However, by looking at the behavior of sexual offenders themselves, we can find a strong association between their exposure to pornography and their subsequent crimes. Bill Marshall, the director of a sexual behavior clinic in Ontario, interviewed 120 men who had raped women or molested children. According to Mark Nichols of *Maclean's*, "[Marshall] concluded that in twenty-five percent of the cases, pornography appeared to be a significant factor in the chain of events leading to a deviant sexual act." In some cases, men initially looked at pornography with no intention of committing a sex crime, but then would go out and assault a woman or a child. Others deliberately used pornography to "prime" themselves to commit these acts. This study has been replicated in other prisons, and the same results have been found. Interviews with sexual assault victims in a San Francisco rehabilitation center also support these findings. Moreover, one out of every four rape victims says her attacker had specifically mentioned his use of pornography as she was being raped. Twenty-two percent of child molestation victims also said that pornography was either mentioned or used during the crime perpetrated against them.

While these studies show that close to a quarter of all sex offenders have had extensive exposure to pornography, some psychologists, such as Victor Cline of the University of Utah, believe that pornography almost always plays a role in sex crimes. According to Wes Goodman of *USA Today*, Cline's research has identified four stages linking pornography to sex crimes. "First, a person—almost always a man—becomes addicted to pornography. Second, he escalates to more explicit, 'kinky' material. Third, he becomes desensitized to the pornographic materials that originally were perceived as shocking or taboo; in time, they become acceptable and commonplace. Finally, he acts out the behaviors viewed in pornography."

These four stages can clearly be seen in the case of a twenty-six-year-old Japanese man named Tsutomu Miayazaki. Miayazaki was so addicted to pornography that three walls of his room were lined from floor to ceiling with shelves that held more than 4,000 pornographic videos. When these extremely explicit videos became mundane, Miayazaki began videotaping nude girls. Eventually, he began killing the women he videotaped. Before confessing to the slaying of four girls, he mailed the bones of one girl back to her parents and beheaded another, leaving her torso in the woods.

These research findings and the examples of sex offenders such as Boog, Wedding, Salcido, and Miayazaki all point to a highly demoralizing relationship between sexually explicit materials and violent acts toward women. Barring the evidence tying pornography to sex crimes, there is also the more general concern that extensive exposure to pornography desensitizes people. Support for this argument comes from a study conducted by Dolf Zillmann and Jennings Bryant. In their experiment, Zillman and Byrant maintained a control group who were not exposed to any pornography and then exposed two other groups of men and women to either an intermediate or a massive amount of nonviolent pornography. After viewing or not viewing pornography, the subjects were asked to recommend a prison sentence for a man who was convicted of raping a female hitchhiker. The study found that those who were exposed to pornography recommended shorter prison sentences than those who were not exposed to it. In fact, the massive exposure group recommended sentences only half as long as those who were not exposed to pornography. This experiment thus supports the claim that pornography does have a desensitizing effect on both the men and women who are exposed to it.

However, in the face of such evidence, there are still those, even some feminists, who believe that pornography has no effect on how women are viewed. According to *U.S. News and World Report,* some feminists believe that antipornography feminists "do immeasurable harm to women by making them out as helpless victims who require the protection of the state." In fact, there are even some pro-pornography feminists, like Camille Paglia, who claim that pornography improves a woman's role in society because it further establishes her sexual dominance over men. Paglia, for instance, interprets strippers as having control over the men who watch them dance. For Paglia, "the more a woman takes off her clothes, the more power she has."

I find the first of these two arguments to be invalid and the second, simply ludicrous. First of all, if, as the evidence I have provided shows, some women are raped and killed as a result of a man's pornographic fantasies, there is a strong case for having the government step in and protect women. I ask you, do members of Congress make the United States appear helpless when they advocate increased defense spending to protect our national security? I think not. As for Paglia's arguments and those of feminists like her, I can only say that a woman's role in society should be based on the fact that she is a human being with inalienable rights. These rights should allow her to pursue her personal freedoms and material well being just as they do any man. Implying that a woman should use her sexuality to gain power not only demeans women, but also puts them, morally and physically, in a very vulnerable position.

If you think that such trends in our thinking about sexuality are moving in the wrong direction, then you will probably be even more dismayed by the increasing amounts of pornography available in our society. In his March 1994 *USA Today* article, Goodman reports that, in a study on the pornography industry, researchers have found "a dramatic increases in the amount of violent sex in both soft- and hard-core pornography available in Western societies." In a 1986 study done on pornography by the attorney general's office, peep shows comprised the largest portion of the United States pornography market with an annual net profit of $2 billion. Similarly, a 1989 study found that the pornography video industry was valued at $380 million. And in January 1989 alone, there were 712,000 dial-a-porn calls reported by only one phone company, Pacific Bell. This market has only increased since then.

Based on our knowledge of the strong link between pornography and sex crimes, the implications of the vastness of this industry should not only alarm us, but also should stir us to action. In Cincinnati for instance, *U.S. News and World Report* states that a local citizen's group, Citizens for Community Values, polices the sale of pornography and pressures city and state government to rid Cincinnati of pornographic video stores and strip clubs. As a result of their work, "ninety percent of the region's 2,600 magazine outlets sell no adult publications at all." By its name alone, one can no doubt tell that the Citizens for Community Values is a conservative group. However, there are also feminist groups out there, like Women Against Pornography, fighting the ill effects of this industry. Hence, regardless of your own political affiliation, if you want to help combat the negative effects of pornography, I encourage you to do your part by becoming involved in a local organization, like the Citizens for Community Values or Women Against Pornography. Find a group whose agenda you can agree with, and work with its members to help fight the plague of pornography that is infesting our cities and towns.

In conclusion, while no direct causal relationship has been found between pornography and sex crimes, the evidence appears overwhelming that there is a strong link between the two. I hope that the number of examples and studies I have given documenting the negative effects of pornography has convinced you that more than being a safety valve for sexually deviant behavior, pornography is a primer for sexual predators. Finally, I encourage all of you to join local groups who are fighting the pornography industry. Remember the sexual crime you may be preventing could be directed at you or someone you love.

Outline
  I. Introduction
    A. Is pornography really harmful?

B. Examples.
   1. Bob Lee Boog, Jr., raped 10 women at knifepoint in 5 years in Salt Lake City.
      a. "I was romanticizing the female anatomy to the point that they were an object to me and not a human being."
   2. Randy Joseph Wedding: "Rental Agent Rapist." 320 years in jail.
      a. Seventeen-year addiction to hard-core pornography costing $200 to $300 a month.
   3. Ramon Salcido: Accused of killing two of his three daughters, his wife, and four other people. Rented pornographic videos two or three times a week.
C. Today, I will present evidence showing a strong connection between pornography and sex crimes and dismiss arguments to the contrary.

II. Body
   A. Problems with scientific evidence and arguments for pornography.
      1. Patrick Suraci, New York psychologist: Pornography is a safety valve.
      2. Berl Kutchinsky, a criminologist and pornography advocate, University of Copenhagen: Danish government, lifted all restrictions on pornography in 1969, and sex crimes decreased.
         a. Problem with study: Failed to distinguish between various types of sex crimes such a rape, indecent exposure, and attending peep shows.
         b. Masks the fact that rape actually increased.
      3. Larry Baron and Murray Strauss, University of New Hampshire. Study found that where pornographic magazine circulation rates were high, rape rates were also high. Also, where circulation rates were low, the rape rates were low.
   B. Studies that do show a link between pornography and sex crimes. Mark Nichols, *Maclean's*.
      1. Bill Marshall, director of a sexual behavior clinic in Ontario. Interviewed 120 men who had raped women or molested children.
         a. "He concluded that in 25% of the cases, pornography appeared to be a significant factor in the chain of events leading to a deviant sexual act."
         b. Cases where men initially looked at pornography with no intention of committing a sex crime, but then "go out and assault a woman or a child."
         c. Men use pornography to "prime" themselves to commit criminal sexual acts.
      2. San Francisco rehabilitation center findings.
         a. One of every four rape victims said their attacker mentioned his use of pornography.
         b. 22 percent of child molestation victims said that pornography was either mentioned or used during the crime.

C. Evidence that pornography plays a role in sexual illness.
   1. Victor Cline, psychologist, University of Utah: Four stages of illness. Wes Goodman, *USA Today*.
      a. "First, a person—almost always a man—becomes addicted to pornography.
      b. Second, he escalates to more explicit "kinky" material.
      c. Third, he becomes desensitized to the pornographic materials that originally were perceived as shocking or taboo; in time, they become acceptable and commonplace.
      d. Finally, he acts out the behaviors viewed in pornography."
   2. Example: 26-year-old Japanese man, Tsutomu Miayazaki.
      a. Room filled with pornographic pictures and 4,000 videos.
      b. Miayazaki began videotaping nude girls.
      c. He began killing the women he videotaped.
D. A major concern of pornography: Desensitizes people.
   1. Evidence of desensitization: Experiment by Dolf Zillmann and Jennings Bryant. Those who were exposed to pornography recommended shorter prison sentences than those who were not exposed to it.
   2. Argument against pro-pornography feminist.
      a. *U.S. News and World Report:* Some feminists believe that anti-pornography feminists "do immeasurable harm to women by making them out as helpless victims who require the protection of the state."
      b. Camille Paglia: Pornography improves women's role in society because it further establishes their sexual dominance over men. "The more a woman takes off her clothes, the more power she has."
      c. Against Paglia: Women's role: Human with inalienable rights. Paglia demeans and puts women in a vulnerable position.
E. Evidence of more pornography: Wes Goodman, *USA Today*, March 1994.
   1. Marshall and Barbaree: "There have been dramatic increases in the amount of violent sex in both soft- and hard-core pornography available in Western societies."
      a. Attorney General's Office study on pornography: Peep show made $2 billion net profit annually.
      b. *Wall Street Journal:* 1989 study: Pornography video industry worth $380 million. In January 1989, 712,000 dial-a-porn calls at Pacific Bell.
F. Call to action:
   1. Cincinnati's Citizens for Community Values polices pornography sales and pressures local government. *U.S. News and World Report:*
      a. "90% of the regions 2,600 magazine outlets sell no adult publications."
   2. Feminist groups: Women Against Pornography.
   3. Encourage audience members to join groups fighting pornography.

III. Conclusion
  A. Summary:
    1. No direct causal relationship. Still, the evidence appears over-whelming that there is a strong link between the two.
      a. Examples and studies document problems of pornography.
      b. Encourage audience to join local groups fighting pornography.
  B. Closing statement:
    1. Remember the sexual crime you may be preventing could be di-rected at you or someone you know.

Bibliography

Larry Baron and Murray Strauss. *Four Theories on Rape in American Society* (New Haven, CT: Yale University Press, 1989).

Wes Goodman, "Pornography, Peep Shows, and the Decline of Morality," *USA Today* (Magazine), March 1994.

Herbert Wray, "Is Porn Un-American?" *U.S. News and World Report,* 3 July 1995.

Mark Nichols, "Viewers and Victims," *Maclean's,* 11 October 1993.

Camille Paglia, "Interview," *Playboy,* May 1995.

Policy Speech

Combining evidence from news magazines, educational journals, and her own personal experience, Stephanie McClelland offered her classmates a convincing policy speech on the merits of service learning (see Section 5.4). Stephanie begins her speech with strong audience appeals stated in the form of questions (see Section 2.1). These questions lead her to offer a claim that does not reject the status quo policy outright, but rather argues for modifying the present policy in ways that will increase the potential that students have a positive educational and community experience. In her speech's body, Stephanie first explains the problems associated with mandatory service learning and then outlines how these problems can be solved. She closes her speech with a clear summary of her main arguments, while offering evidence from studies that show the advantages resulting from service learning (see Sections 4.1 and 4.2).

Learning to Serve and Serving to Learn

Stephanie McClelland

Have you ever been sitting in a class and wondered, "What does any of this have to do with the real world?" I'm sure many of you have. Well, today more and more universities are trying to bridge the gap between students' classroom activities and their professional interests by offering internships in businesses, government agencies, law firms, hospitals, and other places of potential employment. Although the advantages of such "experiential learning" activities are readily apparent, how many of you have considered what lessons may be learned from working in a homeless shelter, a nursery for crack cocaine babies, or a halfway house for adults with mental disabilities? Service learning is the general name given to public school and college programs that send students out into their communities to work as volunteers. Like an internship, these programs can provide firsthand experiences to students in such fields as social work, medicine, or psychology. Recent research has shown that service learning offers a variety of educational, personal, and civic benefits to students. Today, I want to argue that schools and universities should incorporate more service learning opportunities into their curriculums. However, to ensure that students have a positive experience, I will insist that participation in these programs be voluntary, that the student's community service is tied to some type of classroom activity, and that the programs include occasions for students to reflect upon their experiences.

In 1991 Maryland became the first state to mandate that students complete seventy-five hours of community service sometime between the sixth grade and graduation. Soon after, the city of Miami began requiring seventy-five hours of service, and in 1996 Chicago began demanding forty hours from its students. In fact, a 1996 survey by the Center for Human Resources found that nationally almost one-fifth of the students surveyed said they attended schools that mandated some form of community service.

However, there seems to be a basic contradiction in these programs. These programs are based on volunteer community organizations, such as Habitat for Humanity or the Salvation Army. Such organizations use volunteers so that they can spend more of their limited budgets on providing services. Also, these organizations believe that if community service is to enrich the volunteers' lives, volunteers must want to help their community. Making community service mandatory violates this essential principle. However, advocates of mandatory community service say that the students' work can help rebuild broken communities, and these programs show students that they can make a difference. Yet involuntary volunteerism may cause students to resent their mandatory community service. This resentment often limits the potential that students will find their work enriching and rewarding. It may even make students feel bitter about their community rather than connected to it.

Mandating that large populations of students perform community service also has its practical problems. As Rahima Wade, editor of a guide for service learning programs, writes, "Service learning can be a logistical nightmare. Funds, transportation, scheduling, volunteer help, supplies—all these and more can face a teacher who attempts to establish a service learning experience for her class." In addition, many urban schools find that they cannot afford to create a good community service program for their students. These schools do not have the staff to keep up with all the paperwork needed to verify that students did their community service.

Another factor to consider is that it has never been demonstrated that mandating community service ensures that students actually perform the community service. The National Center for Education Statistics studied schools with organized community service projects. They discovered that those schools mandating community service had only a fifty-six percent participation rate due to loopholes in the system, while schools that provided services as an option had a fifty-two percent participation rate. For schools that required students to perform service, but gave no help in arranging the projects, there was a mere nineteen percent participation rate.

A third problem with mandatory community service programs concerns the voluntary organizations in which students are placed. According to Karl Pence, President of the Maryland State Teachers Association, "many community service agencies are not equipped to take on this onslaught of volunteers." Some agencies have become overwhelmed trying to accommodate students desperate to complete their hours. In *NEA Today,* Bonnie Gardner states that many agencies simply chose to opt out of these programs because they weren't able to adequately supervise the teenagers or keep up with the paperwork that many schools required of them.

A final problem facing mandatory community service is a legal one. Marie Bittner, in her 1994 *Clearing House* article, "The Constitutionality of Public School Community Service," recounts the first court case challenging the legality of mandatory community service. Two high school students in Bethlehem, Pennsylvania, challenged their high school's graduation requirement on two grounds: one, it violated their First Amendment right of free speech by forcing them to accept the belief that "serving others and helping the community are what life is about"; and two, it violated the Thirteenth Amendment of the Constitution that forbids slavery and involuntary servitude by forcing students to perform a job against their will. The students, however, lost their case. On the one hand, the courts ruled that community service is not a form of speech nor does engaging in community service force students to adopt altruistic beliefs. On the other hand, because, as Bittner writes, "involuntary servitude could only result from labor compelled by the use of threat of physical force or imprisonment," the graduation requirement did not violate the Constitution.

While Bittner discusses other possible rulings that may still find mandatory service to be unconstitutional, I will concede the legality of mandating community service. Yet, by giving students the choice to participate in service learning programs, we can eliminate many practical problems as well as prevent further legal challenges.

Along with making these programs truly voluntary, I believe that service learning will reach its full potential only if such experiences are tied directly to the school's curriculum. Students must be given the opportunity to reflect upon their experience in some type of classroom activity. According to Gardner's *NEA Today* article, while some Maryland schools offer "entire courses built around a service project," other schools "simply expect students to find their own volunteer opportunities." While I applaud Maryland for giving school districts the flexibility to experiment with various types of programs, every program should closely monitor their students' experience to increase the likelihood that their community service results in a positive educational experience.

The best service learning programs begin with students working with teachers and counselors to define the learning objectives of their community work. As you might expect, often times these goals are associated with a student's program of study or a class he or she is taking. For example, Gardner writes, "Cosmetology students style hair for retirement home residents . . . or a social studies class may put on a play about racism." At the university level, San Francisco State University offered fifty courses during the 1997–1998 school year that included a community service component. Furman University, too, has joined in this trend toward service learning. I experienced service learning firsthand through Dr. Halva-Neubauer's Introduction to American Government class in which we were required to complete three hours of service a week at the Greenville [SC] Literacy Association.

Giving students the opportunity to discuss and reflect upon their experiences is another necessary component of service learning. John Dewey, the American philosopher and author of *Democracy and Education,* called for education to be deeply rooted in experience, yet he acknowledged that experience is not always educational. Experiences often create controversy, and if the controversy is not reflected upon, then the original experience can be misleading, even harmful. Ironically, it can produce a lack of sensitivity and responsiveness in the student. Thus, unlike community service programs that send students out to the community and then leave them to unravel that experience on their own, providing an opportunity for students to reflect upon their experience is an essential part of service learning. Robert Bringle and Julie Hatcher, directors of Indiana and Purdue University's Office of Service Learning, agree with Dewey when they conclude that these activities should include opportunities to assess changes in students' values, beliefs, and attitudes as a result of their experiences.

For my political science class, Dr. Halva-Neubauer had us participate in reflection sessions every two weeks. In these sessions, my classmates and I discussed our experiences at the Greenville Literacy Association. We also wrote papers about what we had learned. I found these sessions and assignments to be very beneficial in promoting a deeper understanding of citizenship, which was one of the class's main issues. My work at the Greenville Literacy Association was not only an eye-opening experience, but the classroom sessions gave me the opportunity to reflect upon what I did, debate the causes of illiteracy and the merits of government programs, as well as discuss the personal growth we all experienced as a result of our work.

In conclusion, I am happy to report that today, many schools around the nation are adopting voluntary service learning programs rather than mandating community service. Mandatory community service simply forces many unwilling students to have experiences within their communities. However, good service learning programs give students the chance to serve their communities, further their course work, and reflect upon their experiences. Evidence shows that the results of such programs are quite positive. Joe Follman, the director of Florida Learn and Serve, says that his two-year study of 50,000 students found that service learning increases grades and attendance and reduces discipline problems. Moreover, a four-year study by the University of Virginia

shows a forty-percent reduction in teen pregnancy among students who partic-
ipated in the St. Louis Teen Outreach Program. Psychologist Joseph Allen believes this reduction results from the program's ability to raise the students'
self-esteem and change their attitudes about the world. Allen says that "when
[students] learn to take care of others, they learn to take care of themselves."
Perhaps this is a lesson we should all learn.

Outline
I. Introduction
   A. "What does any of this have to do with the real world?"
      1. Internships in businesses, government agencies, law firms, hospi-
        tals, and so on
      2. Advantages of such "experiential learning": homeless shelter,
        nursery, halfway house.
   B. Service learning is based on programs that send students into their
      communities as volunteers.
      1. Research shows that service learning offers educational, per-
        sonal, and civic benefits to students.
   C. Today, I want to argue that schools and universities should incorpo-
      rate more service learning opportunities into their curriculums.
      1. Participation must be voluntary, service must be tied to classroom
        activity, and programs should include occasions for reflection.
II. Body
   A. History of mandatory community service.
      1. 1991, Maryland mandates seventy-five hours of community ser-
        vice between the sixth grade and graduation.
      2. Miami requires seventy-five hours. 1996, Chicago demands forty
        hours.
      3. 1996 survey, Center for Human Resources: Almost one-fifth of
        students attended schools that mandated community service.
   B. Basic contradiction in these programs.
      1. Based on volunteer community organizations: Habitat for Hu-
        manity or the Salvation Army.
      2. Volunteers allow groups to spend their budgets on services.
        a. Volunteers must want to help their community.
      3. Making community service mandatory violates this essential
        principle.
        a. Mandatory service may cause students to resent their service.
        b. Limits the potential that students will find their work reward-
          ing. Makes students feel bitter about their community.
   C. Practical problems.
      1. Logistics
        a. Rahima Wade: "Service learning can be a logistical nightmare.
          Funds, transportation, scheduling, volunteer help, supplies—
          all these and more can face a teacher who attempts to estab-
          lish a service learning experience for her class."
        b. Urban schools lack the staff for paperwork.

    c. Mandating community service does not ensure that students perform the community service.

    d. National Center for Education Statistics: 56 percent participation rate in mandatory programs, 52 percent participation rate where service was an option, 19 percent where service was required but schools did not arrange projects.

  2. Voluntary organizations.

    a. Karl Pence, President of the Maryland State Teachers Association: "Many community service agencies are not equipped to take on this onslaught of volunteers."

    b. *NEA Today,* Bonnie Gardner: Agencies simply chose to opt out of these programs because of problems with supervision and paperwork.

  3. Legal issues.

    a. 1994, *Clearing House,* "The Constitutionality of Public School Community Service," Marie Bittner: Bethlehem, PA, high school students challenge requirement on two grounds: one, it violates First Amendment by forcing them to accept the belief that "serving others and helping the community are what life is about"; and two, violates the Thirteenth Amendment forbidding slavery and involuntary servitude.

    b. Students lost the case when courts ruled that community service is not a form of speech, nor does engaging in community service force students to adopt altruistic beliefs.

    c. Bittner: Because "involuntary servitude could only result from labor compelled by the use of threat of physical force or imprisonment," the graduation requirement did not violate the Constitution.

    d. Mandating community service is legal. However, voluntary service will eliminate many practical problems.

D. My proposal for service learning.

  1. Voluntary service with reflective component.

    a. Programs must be voluntary and tied to school's curriculum.

    b. Students must be given the opportunity to reflect upon their experience in some type of classroom activity.

    c. Gardner's *NEA Today* article: Maryland schools, some offer "entire courses built around a service project," but others "simply expect students to find their own volunteer opportunities."

  2. Best service learning programs.

    a. Students work with teachers and counselors to define the learning objectives.

    b. Gardner, "Cosmetology students style hair for retirement home residents . . . or a social studies class may put on a play about racism."

    c. San Francisco State University offered fifty courses during the 1997–1998 school year with a community service component.

      d. Dr. Halva-Neubauer's Introduction to American Government, three hours of service a week with Greenville [SC] Literacy Association.

   3. Reflective component.

      a. John Dewey, *Democracy and Education:* Education rooted in experience, experience is not always educational. Experiences that can create controversy must be reflected upon or it may be misleading, harmful, or produce insensitivity.

      b. Robert Bringle and Julie Hatcher, directors of Indiana and Purdue University's Office of Service Learning: Activities should include opportunities to assess changes in students' values, beliefs, and attitudes.

      c. My political science class: Reflection sessions every two weeks. Promoted a deeper understanding of citizenship, debated the causes of illiteracy and the merits of government programs, discussed our personal growth.

III. Conclusion

   1. Most schools are adopting voluntary community service, not mandating community service.

      a. Mandatory community service forces unwilling students to work in their communities.

      b. Service learning programs give students the chance to serve their communities, further their course work, and reflect upon their experiences.

   2. Research.

      a. Joe Follman, the director of Florida Learn and Serve, two-year study of 50,000 students: Service learning increases grades and attendance and reduces discipline problems.

      b. University of Virginia, four-year study: 40-percent reduction in teen pregnancy among students who participated in the St. Louis Teen Outreach Program. Joseph Allen: Programs raise students' self-esteem and change their attitudes about the world. "When [students] learn to take care of others, they learn to take care of themselves."

   3. Perhaps this is a lesson we should all learn.

Bibliography

Marie Bittner, "The Constitutionality of Public Schools Community Service Programs," *The Clearing House,* November–December 1994, 115–119.

Marian Rouse Finney, "Service Learning in Maryland: Making Academics More Relevant," *NASSP Bulletin,* October 1997, 37–45.

Bonnie Gardner, "The Controversy Over Service Learning," *NEA Today,* September 1997, 17.

Ben Gose, "Many Colleges Move to Link Courses with Volunteerism." *The Chronicle of Higher Education,* 14 November 1997, A45–A46.

Julie A. Hatcher and Robert G. Bringle, "Reflection: Bridging the Gap Between
     Service and Learning." *College Teaching,* Fall 1977, 153–158.
Maurice Howard, "Service Learning: Character Education Applied." *Educational
     Leadership,* October 1993, 42–44.
Colman McCarthy, "A Win–Win Situation: The Real Benefits of Volunteerism."
     Washington Monthly, June 1997, 34–36.
Marci McDonald, "How to Reduce Teen Pregnancy: Voluntary Community
     Service." *U.S. News and World Report,* 29 December 1997, 48–49.

Ceremonial Speeches

Speech of Introduction

Diasuke Yamamoto gave this fictitious ceremonial address to his public speaking class a week after the release of Suu Kyi (see Section 5.6). Although this speech is one of celebration, his writing reflects the serious nature of Suu Kyi and her commitment to democracy. Diasuke first reacquaints his audience with Suu Kyi's personal history and achievements, referring along the way to her father's struggle to bring democracy to their native country. He then recounts how Suu Kyi has inspired both Vaclav Havel and himself. By showing how Suu Kyi has influenced both world leaders and ordinary people alike, he familiarizes his audience with Suu Kyi's impact on the world. Diasuke ends his speech by relating his audience to a worldwide community of people who welcome Suu Kyi's release as a sign of progress in the struggle for democracy.

Introducing Suu Kyi

Diasuke Yamamoto

We shall remember the tenth of July, 1995, as our happiest day in more than half a decade. A week ago, the Burmese government finally released the world's symbol of conscience, Daw Aung San Suu Kyi, from her house arrest that started in July 1989. Defenders of democracy in Burma and around the world rejoiced when we heard that she was now free and that she still maintained her noble character and convictions, those very qualities that once scared the junta into detaining her for many years. Throughout her confinement she remained our best hope as the leader who could bring about freedom and democracy in Burma. Today, as a result of her release, she remains our beacon of hope for a new democratic Burma.

Suu Kyi started her bold struggle in 1988 when she joined with students of Rangoon University to mount a demonstration calling for democracy. Her calls for national reconciliation and democracy quickly caught the public's attention in a nation fraught with civil wars and repression. Fearful of her movement's growing popularity, the junta imprisoned and then tortured many prodemocracy advocates, and finally dared to put Suu Kyi under house arrest. Despite the junta's defeat by Suu Kyi's National League for Democracy in 1990, this military government has maintained its illegitimate rule over the Burmese people.

Some ask why Suu Kyi has been so committed to bringing about democracy in her country. The answer invariably begins with the fact that General Daw Aung San, her father, won Burma's independence from Britain, but was assassinated before his aspiration to democratize his country was realized. For this reason, Suu Kyi always maintained that it is her personal responsibility to work for the good of her country, just as her father attempted to do. Thus, in a letter to her husband, Michael Aris, she wrote, "I only ask one thing, that should my people need me, you would help me to do my duty by them."

Suu Kyi has emboldened not only her countrymen and women, but people who love freedom and democracy all over the world. I myself am one of the many who were inspired by her struggle. My admiration for her began when I read the speech she delivered upon winning a human rights award from the International Human Rights Law Group. As an eighteen-year-old freshman, I found her message enlightening, and her words have since become the driving force behind my studies in political science. Her inspiring work has even led the Czech President Vaclav Havel to declare that "Aung San Suu Kyi is not only speaking out for justice in her own country, but also for all those who want to be free to choose their own destiny. She is an outstanding example of the power of the powerless."

In honor of her courageous engagement in the human rights and democracy movement, this Burmese woman has been awarded many prizes and honorary doctorate degrees, the best known of which is, of course, the 1991 Nobel Peace Prize.

Now, with her release from confinement, the movement for human rights and democracy in Burma will begin again with renewed conviction and fervor. We shall not let Burma's past six years of tragic history repeat itself. Now is the time that we should listen to her voice and unite as one people to bring about democracy in Burma and all over the world. Now let us welcome Aung San Suu Kyi.

Outline

    I. Introduction

        A. July 10, 1995: World symbol of conscience released.

        B. Noble character and convictions scared the junta.

        C. In confinement: Our best hope.

        D. After her release: Our beacon of hope.

    II. Body

        A. Background.

            1. Rangoon University 1988.

            2. Movement's popularity grew.

            3. Junta imprisoned her, thereby stealing election.

        B. Suu Kyi's commitment to democracy.

            1. Father's influence.

                a. Burma's independence from Britain.

                b. Assassination.

    2. Letter to her husband, Michael Aris. Her responsibility to country: "I only ask one thing, that should my people need me, you would help me to do my duty by them."
- C. Admiration.
  1. Personal story: International Human Rights Law Group.
  2. Vaclav Havel: "Aung San Suu Kyi is not only speaking out for justice in her own country, but also for all those who want to be free to choose their own destiny. She is an outstanding example of the power of the powerless."
- III. Conclusion
  - A. 1991 Nobel Peace Prize.
  - B. Encourage audience to remember Burma's human rights and democratic movements.
  - C. Introduce Aung San Suu Kyi.

Eulogy

Josh McKoon's commerative speech to his grandfather displays many of the fundamental principles of ceremonial speaking and the eulogy (see Sections 5.5 and 5.6). Through personal narratives that illustrate his favorite memories of his grandfather to those that describe his grandfather's relation to others, Josh is able to tie himself to his subject and audience. Moreover, his amplification of his grandfather's kind and gregarious nature allows his audience to remember the man they knew and to reexperience their own relationship with him. Josh also uses both humor and various figures of speech, such as metaphor and alliteration, effectively, both to alleviate his audience's pain and elevate their sense of the occasion and the man they came to honor (see Section 6.5).

To My Grandfather

Josh McKoon

H. W. Overton. The *H. W.* is short for Hugh Wilson, but, as he would like to say, it stood for all the "Hot Water" he would get himself into. Well, whether you knew him as Hugh, H. W., or *Dootie,* as his grandchildren called him, you all knew my grandfather as a man who liked to stir the water just to see if others could swim the tide. Well Dootie, although today your waters have been calmed, your memory still rises within us all.

Hugh Overton was my grandfather, but he was much more than that. When I was a child, he was my playmate, as a teenager, my confidante, and as a young man, my mentor. I recall how, as a child, I could hardly wait for his visits, not just because of the new toys he would always have for us, but for his enthusiasm and energy. For after playing catch with me for hours, my interest in my new baseball glove would wane, but, like most kids, I still wanted to play. But unlike most adults who would have sent my brother and I off to play by ourselves, Dootie would sit us on his knee and play horsey—riding the bucking bronco of his left knee or the tamer steed of his right—until we fell asleep on his lap. I also remember how he always had activities planned for us, whether it was a scavenger hunt on the beach where he dressed as our guide, or the birthday party he planned for me with a magician that let me be his assistant.

But what I remember most about the times we spent together was the stories he would tell. Dootie was a consummate storyteller, from the stories about his days at Auburn with Shug Jordan, to whatever trouble the neighborhood kids got into last week, he always had a story to tell. Sometimes he told these stories just for a laugh. Sometimes he even told them twice! But sometimes his words just helped you get through your day. I remember one time at Mud Island in Memphis, we all were supposed to ride a monorail to get across to another side of the park. I refused, thinking the cable would snap and we would all fall to our doom. He took me aside, as he had done so many other times, and began to patiently reassure me that it was safe. "Do you remember the time you didn't want to go in the ocean because you were afraid of what was in there?" he said. " And did you try going in?" "And was everything okay?" "Yes," I replied, and not long afterward, I agreed to give the monorail a try. Not only did he calm my fears, but I insisted on riding the monorail throughout the rest of the day.

Dootie's energy and kindness were not just for his family, but for everyone that crossed his path. Seeing him meet someone for the first time was a sight to behold. At one instance he was greeting a perfect stranger, and at the next, they were laughing as if they were old friends. I hope that one day I have a fraction of the goodwill and gregarious nature that he put forward so effortlessly to anyone he was around.

Because of his energy and enthusiasm, my grandfather had an incredible sense of adventure, which he instilled in his children and grandchildren. He traveled with my grandmother and other relatives all over the United States and the world, from Juneau to Jerusalem, and from Far Hope to the Far East. Everything he did was imbued with that sense of anticipation of new challenges to be overcome and new discoveries to be made.

My grandfather always knew how to cheer me up when I was down. He helped us all overcome our fears and dream our dreams. He always made you feel as if you were someone important, someone special. Dootie, I know your travels have brought you to a much better place today, a place where your kindness and caring are as treasured as are our memories of you.

Outline

I. Introduction
    A. H. W. Overton. "H. W." Hugh Wilson or "Hot Water."
    B. Hugh, H. W., or Dootie, my grandfather as man who liked to stir the water just to see if others could swim the tide.
    C. Well Dootie, although today your waters have been calmed, your memory still rises within us all.

II. Body
   A. Hugh Overton was my grandfather, but he was much more than that. He was my playmate, as a teenager, my confidante, and as a young man, my mentor.
      1. I remember him playing horsey with my brother and I for hours— riding the bucking bronco of his left knee or the tamer steed of his right.
      2. He always had activities planned for us.
         a. Scavenger hunt on the beach.
         b. Birthday party with a magician.
   B. What I remember most was the stories he would tell.
      1. Sometimes he told these stories for a laugh; sometimes he told them twice! His words just helped you get through your day.
      a. Mud Island in Memphis and riding the monorail.
   C. His energy and kindness were not just for his family, but for everyone that crossed his path.
      1. Meeting someone for the first time. From perfect strangers to old friends.
      2. I hope that I have his goodwill and gregarious nature.
   D. Because of his energy and enthusiasm, my grandfather had an incredible sense of adventure, which he instilled in his children and grandchildren.
      1. Travels with grandmother and relatives: Far Hope to Far East, Juneau to Jerusalem.
      2. Everything he did was imbued with that sense of anticipation of new challenges to be overcome and new discoveries to be made.
III. Conclusion
   A. My grandfather always knew how to cheer me up when I was down.
      1. He helped us all overcome our fears and dream our dreams.
      2. He always you made you feel as if you were someone important, someone special.
      3. Dootie, I know your travels have brought you to a much better place today, a place where kindness and caring are as treasured as are our memories of you.

Notes

Preface

1. Aristotle, *On Rhetoric*, trans. George A. Kennedy (New York: Oxford University Press, 1991), 1.2.1.
2. George Kennedy, *Classic Rhetoric and its Christian and Secular Tradition from Ancient to Modern Times* (Chapel Hill: University of North Carolina Press, 1999), 2.
3. Aristotle, *Rhetoric*, 1.1.13.
4. Neither do the handbook's endnotes attempt to provide a comprehensive account of those sources that address the principle or technique at hand, for to do so would be an inexhaustible task. Rather, endnotes are used to document those sources that are specifically referenced, that contain information from which the handbook's explanations are adapted, or that indicate both a reference source and where the reader can go to find more information about the principle or technique being discussed. On rare occasions, when the handbook discusses an important principle, concept, or technique, or a term whose definition and use has changed in some significant way, the endnotes clarify the term's former use and reference works that exemplify the original conceptions and historical developments. Otherwise, I have done my best to present my own interpretation of the many principles, strategies, and techniques of speaking that can be found in most classical and contemporary books on rhetoric and public speaking.
5. Michael Leff, "Genre and Paradigm in the Second Book of *De Oratore*," *The Southern Speech Communication Journal, 51* (Summer 1986): 321.

Chapter 1

1. Stephan E. Lucas, *The Art of Public Speaking*, 6th ed. (Boston: McGraw Hill, 1998), 63–64.
2. The notion of an ideal or universal audience is usually attributed to Chaim Perelman, *The Realm of Rhetoric*, trans. William Kluback (Notre Dame, IN: University of Notre Dame Press, 1982), 14. For

an application of this notion to public speaking, see David Zarefsky, *Public Speaking: Strategies for Success* (Boston, MA: Allyn & Bacon, 1996), 112.

3. One of the earliest discussions of the psychological character of an audience can be found in Aristotle, *Rhetoric*, 2.1–2.17. For a more recent discussion, from which the information provided here was adapted, in part, see Bruce E. Gronbeck, Raymie E. McKerrow, Douglas Ehninger, and Alan H. Monroe, *Principles and Types of Speech Communication*, 13th ed. (New York: Longman, 1997), 87–91.

4. Although most public speaking books now include a discussion of how to analyze your audience's cultural characteristics, two of the most detailed and enlightening discussions, from which the information provided here was adapted, in part, can be found in Steven Beebe and Susan Beebe, *Public Speaking: An Audience-Centered Approach*, 3rd ed. (Boston: Allyn & Bacon, 1997), 82–86, 296–297, 387–388; Clella Jaffe, *Public Speaking: A Cultural Perspective* (Belmont, CA: Wadsworth, 1997), 58–63, 366–367.

5. David Zarefsky, *Public Speaking*, 109.

6. Aspects of this journalistic technique can be found in Quintilian, *Institutio Oratoria*, trans. H. E. Butler (Cambridge, MA: Harvard University Press, 1920), 5.10.32.

7. The information on electronic research presented here was prepared with the help of Kevin Sargent, Department of Communication Studies, University of South Carolina, and Steve Richardson, reference librarian, Furman University.

8. This list of print sources presented here was compiled with the help of Steve Richardson and Mary Fairbairn, both reference librarians at Furman University.

9. William A. Katz and Linda Sternberg Katz, *Magazines for Libraries: For the General Reader and School, Junior College, College University, and Public Libraries*, 9th ed., (New York: Bowker, 1997).

10. The information on evaluating web sites presented here and in the following pages was adapted, in part, from Andrew Harnack and Eugen Kleppinger, *Online! A Reference Guide to Using Internet Sources* (Boston: Bedford Books, 2000), 104–113.

Chapter 2

1. Many sources from both the classical and contemporary traditions offer similar advice about where and how to use the various types of appeals in the organization of a speech. One of the earliest sources, from which the information presented here was adapted, in part, is Aristotle, *Rhetoric*, 3.14–19.

2. The original definition of *logos* from which the information presented here was adapted, in part, can be found in Aristotle, *Rhetoric*, 1.2.6.

3. Rex Sanford, "The Georgia Flag: Pride or Prejudice," speech, Furman University, Greenville, SC, 1994.

4. The original definition of *ethos* from which the information presented here was adapted, in part, can be found in Aristotle, *Rhetoric*, 1.2.2–4.

5. Courtney Armstrong, "A Story to Tell," speech, Furman University, Greenville, SC, 1998.

6. The original definition of *pathos* from which the information presented here was adapted, in part, can be found in Aristotle, *Rhetoric*, 1.2.5.

7. Jeremy Koch, "The Freedom We Already Have," speech, Furman University, Greenville, SC, 1998.

8. The appeal to myths and stories included in the notion of normative proof presented here was adapted, in part, from the notion of *mythos* found in Michael Osborn and Susan Osborn, *Public Speaking*, 5th ed. (Boston: Houghton Mifflin, 2000), 396–398. For an insightful discussion of the role of *mythos* in ancient Greek culture, see Paul Veyne, *Did the Greeks Believe in Their Myths? An Essay on the Constitutive Imagination*, trans. Paula Wissing (Chicago: University of Chicago Press, 1988).

9. Graham Seagraves, "The Outerbanks of North Carolina," speech, Furman University, Greenville, SC, 1998.

10. For a more detailed discussion of comparative explanation and its relation to figures of speech such as an analogy, see [Cicero], *Rhetorica Ad Herennium*, trans. Harry Kaplan (Cambridge, MA: Oxford University Press, 1954), 4.45.59–4.47.61; Edward P. J. Corbett and Robert J. Connors, *Classical Rhetoric for the Modern Student*, 4th ed. (New York: Oxford University Press, 1999), 92–97.

11. Dana Jacobson, "Does Your Friend Have an Eating Disorder?" speech, Furman University, Greenville, SC, 1991.

12. Two classical explanations of the practice of division from which the information presented here was adapted, in part, are Plato, *Phadreus*, trans. R. Hackworth, *The Collected Dialogues of Plato*, Eds. Edith Hamilton and Hunington Cairns (Princeton, NJ: Princeton University Press, 1961), 266a5; and [Cicero], *Rhetorica Ad Herennium*, 4.40.52.

13. Kimberly Rice, "Making Your Own Compost Pile," speech, Furman University, Greenville, SC, 1992.

14. Dena Serpanos, "Ordaining Women into the Catholic Priesthood," speech, Furman University, Greenville, SC, 1994.

15. For one of the most extensive discussions of definition in a classical handbook from which the information presented here has been adapted, in part, see Cicero, *Topica,* trans. H. M. Hubbell (Cambridge, MA: Harvard University Press, 1949), 4.26–8.37.

16. For a discussion of how the etymology of a term can represent its continued significance see John Poulakos and Takis Poulakos, *Classical Rhetorical Theory* (Boston: Houghton Mifflin, 1999), 176. Their discussion of etymology leads one back to the more general description of etymology found in Quintilian, *Institutio Oratoria,* 1.6.28–43, 5.10. Another source from which the information on etymology presented here was adapted, in part, is Cicero, *Topica,* 8.35–9.37.

17. Anne Reeves, "The Unacknowledged Minority," speech, Furman University, Greenville, SC, 1997.

18. For an understanding of how Aristotle used the notion of categorical definition to categorize animals, plants, and other living organisms through their *genus, differentia, species,* and so on, see Aristotle, *On the Parts of Animals,* trans. D'Arcy Wentworth Thompson, *The Selected Works of Aristotle,* Ed. Richard McKeon (New York: Random House, 1941), 643–665. For further discussions of the rhetorical use of categorical definition, see Cicero *Topica* 6.28–8.34; Edward P. J. Corbett and Robert J. Conners, *Classical Rhetoric,* 34.

19. Michael Shuman, "Don't Eat Meat!" speech, Furman University, Greenville, SC, 1993.

20. Keith Elis, "What is a Yankee?" speech, Furman University, Greenville, SC, 1994.

21. For a discussion of visual description in Cicero, from which the information presented here was adapted, in part, see Beth Innocenti, "Towards a Theory of Vivid Description as Practiced in Cicero's *Verrine* Orations," *Rhetorica,* 12 (Autumn 1994): 355–381. One of the many useful references her article provides on the subject is [Cicero], *Rhetorica Ad Herennium,* 4.51.

22. Amy Fletcher, "A Walking Tour of the Capitol," speech, Furman University, Greenville, SC, 1995.

23. LeGette Phillips, "Domestic Violence," speech, Furman University, Greenville, SC, 1995.

24. Brad Harmon, "Recycling," speech, Greenville, SC, Furman University, 1997.

25. The information on statistical evidence presented here arose from conversations with Gil Einstein, Psychology Department, Furman University, who suggested adapting, in part, information on the subject from Fredrick Gravetter and Larry Wallnau, *Statistics for the*

Behavioral Sciences, 4th ed. (Minneapolis, MN: West, 1996), 3–7, 372–373, 500–503.

26. Sarah Rusciano, "CPR," speech, Furman University, Greenville, SC, 1997.

27. The information on examples presented here was adapted in part from [Cicero], *Rhetorica Ad Herennium*, 4.49.62.

28. Hayden Woolen, "Advocating Single-Sex Education for Women," speech, Furman University, Greenville, SC, 1995.

29. Anthony Smith, "Blaming the Victim," speech, Furman University, Greenville, SC, 1993.

30. Andre Sheppard, "Cafes for the Homeless," speech, Furman University, Greenville, SC, 1994.

31. Narratives are a fundamental component of the classical speech structure (see Section 5.4). For the differing discussions of narrative in classical rhetoric and poetry from which the information presented here was adapted, in part, see Aristotle, *Rhetoric*, 3.16.1–11; Aristotle, *Poetics*, trans. A. J. Jenkinson, *The Selected Works of Aristotle*, Ed. Richard McKeon (New York: Random House, 1941), 1455–1487; Cicero, *De Inventione*, trans. H. M. Hubbell (Cambridge, MA: Harvard University Press, 1949), 1.19.27–21.31. For a more contemporary discussion of narrative rationality from which the information presented here also was adapted, in part, see Walter R. Fisher, *Human Communication as Narration: Toward a Philosophy of Reason, Value, and Action* (Columbia, SC: University of South Carolina Press, 1987); Karyn Rybacki and Donald Rybacki, *Communication Criticism: Approaches and Genres* (Belmont, CA: Wadsworth, 1991), 106–129.

32. Christie Matthews, "Migrant Law Reform," speech, Furman University, Greenville, SC, 1993.

33. Anthony Smith, "Should Rap be Censored?" speech, Furman University, Greenville, SC, 1992.

34. Nicole Maglio, "The Russian Crisis," speech, Furman University, Greenville, SC, 2000.

35. For a list of analogies described as metaphors in a classical handbook, see Aristotle, *Rhetoric*, 3.10.7

36. Rex Sanford, "The European Community," speech, Furman University, Greenville, SC, 1993.

37. Hillary Farr, "Leni Riefenstahl: Hitler's Cinematic Genius," speech, Furman University, Greenville, SC, 1995.

38. John Ramey, "Why Gun Control Doesn't Work," speech, Furman University, Greenville, SC, 1995.

39. Dena Serpanos, "Greenpeace," speech, Furman University, Greenville, SC, 1994.

40. The information on nominal testimony presented here was adapted, in part, from the notion of prestige testimony presented in Osborn and Osborn, *Public Speaking,* 172.

41. Mandy Collinger, "Burn Free: Towards a New Forestry Policy," speech, Furman University, Greenville, SC, 1996.

42. Most contemporary definitions of deductive arguments focus on the inference from a general to a specific claim that is rendered from the definitions of reasoning and syllogism originally found in Aristotle, *Topica,* trans. A. J. Jenkinson, *The Selected Works of Aristotle,* Ed. Richard McKeon (New York: Random House, 1941), 1.1.100a.25; Aristotle, *Prior Analytics,* trans. A. J. Jenkinson, *The Selected Works of Aristotle,* Ed. Richard McKeon (New York: Random House, 1941); Aristotle, *Rhetoric,* 1.2.8–19. Yet some contemporary sources that define a deductive argument based on the author's intent to show that the conclusion follows necessarily from the premises have great rhetorical significance. Ironically, this aspect of the information presented here was adapted, in part, from Patrick J. Hurley, *A Concise Introduction to Logic,* 3rd ed. (Belmont, CA: Wadsworth), 30–35, 40–45.

43. A discussion of the categorical syllogism can be found in many books on logic, rhetoric, argument, and grammar throughout history. For the original ancient source and two contemporary sources from which the information presented here was adapted, in part, see Aristotle, *Prior Analytics;* Hurley, *Concise Introduction to Logic,* 174–180, 242–247; Austin J. Freeley and David Steinberg, *Argumentation and Debate: Critical Thinking for Reasoned Decision Making,* 10th ed. (Belmont, CA: Wadsworth, 2000), 134–138.

44. The information on the hypothetical syllogism presented here was adapted, in part, from Hurley, *Concise Introduction to Logic,* 32, 294–297.

45. In contrast to how deductive arguments are defined, most contemporary definitions of inductive arguments focus on the inference from specific premises to a general claim that is rendered from the definitions of induction or paradigm originally found in Aristotle, *Topica,* 1.105a.12.10–20; Aristotle, *Rhetoric,* 1.2.8–19. Yet some contemporary sources that define an inductive argument based on the author's intent to show that the conclusion follows probably from the premises make an important rhetorical point. Here again, this aspect of the information presented here was adapted, in part, from Hurley, *A Concise Introduction to Logic,* 30–35, 40–45.

46. Aristotle, *Rhetoric,* 1.2.19.

47. The original discussion of enthymeme from which the information presented here was adapted, in part, can be found in Aristotle,

Rhetoric, 1.28–1.21, 2.21–2.26.1. For one of the best contemporary analysis of the enthymeme, see Robert N. Gaines, "Aristotle's Rhetoric and the Contemporary Arts of Practical Discourse," in *Rereading Aristotle's Rhetoric,* Ed. Alan G. Gross and Arthur E. Walzer (Carbondale, IL: Southern Illinois University Press, 2000), 3–23.

48. Kerry Stubbs, "Multi-Cultural Approaches to Literacy," speech, Furman University, Greenville, SC, 1993.

49. For an explanation of arguments from signs as enthymemes, see Aristotle, *Rhetoric,* 1.2.16–18.

50. LeGette Phillips, "Domestic Violence," speech, Furman University, Greenville, SC, 1995.

51. The use of two-sided arguments has a rich and varied history from fifth-century B.C., in Greece to the late Roman Empire, where it emerges from principles of philosophy, organization, and style in such techniques as *antithesis* and *dissoi logi* to its understanding as a form of argumentation and rhetorical training pursued through such practices as the *dialectic, eristic, thesis,* and *controversia.* You can follow elements of this history by reading Richard Leo Enos, *Greek Rhetoric Before Aristotle* (Prospect Heights, IL: Waveland Press, 1993); Gilbert Ryle, "Dialectic in the Academy," *New Essays on Plato and Aristotle,* Ed. Renford Bambrough (New York: Rutledge and Kegan Paul, 1965), 39–69; Kennedy, *Classical Rhetoric;* M. L. Clarke, *Rhetoric at Rome: A Historical Survey* (New York: Routledge, 1996). For Cicero's description of using two-sided arguments in preparing legal arguments see Cicero, *De Oratore,* trans. E. W. Sutton and H. Rackham (Cambridge, MA: Harvard University Press, 1942), 2.24.102–103.

52. Otis Ballenger, "NAFTA," speech, Furman University, Greenville, SC, 1993.

53. The doctrines of *stasis* and *loci* are used to find evidence and arguments on many different types of issues. Application of these methods are found throughout this section as well as the information on argument strategies, the principles of persuasive speaking, and the speech of fact, value speech, and policy speech (see Sections 2.4, 5.3, and 5.4). The information on *stasis* and *loci* presented here was adapted, in part, from Aristotle, *Rhetoric,* 1.13.1–14.32, 3.15.1–4, Cicero, *De Inventione,* 2.4.14–2.51.154; Quintilian, *Institutio Oratoria,* 3.6, 7; Thomas M. Conley, *Rhetoric in the European Tradition* (New York: Longman, 1990), 32–33; Corbett and Conners, *Classical Rhetoric,* 124–126.

54. Nathan Karn, "Do School Uniforms Violate a Student's Right to Free Speech?" speech, Furman University, Greenville, SC, 1994.

55. The information on Toulmin's model of argument presented here was adapted, in part, from Stephen Toulmin, Richard Rieke, and

Allan Janik, *An Introduction to Reasoning*, 2nd ed. (New York: Macmillan, 1984), 23–77, 281–311.

56. Diasuke Yamamoto, "Strategies for Ending the Bosnian War," speech, Furman University, Greenville, SC, 1995.

57. The information on argument strategies or topics presented here and some of the argument strategies that follow were adapted, in part, from Aristotle, *Rhetoric,* 2.1.23. Although most classical rhetorical handbooks discuss argument topics, you can find some of the most developed discussions of topics in Aristotle, *Rhetoric,* 1.2.21–22, 2.1.1, 2.1.23, 3.15.1–4; Cicero, *Topica;* Quintilian, *Institutio Oratoria,* 5.10. For more contemporary discussions of topics, see Perelman, *Realm of Rhetoric,* 29–31; Corbett and Conners, *Classical Rhetoric,* 84–130.

58. Argument fallacies have been discussed and categorized in many different ways throughout the history of logic, rhetoric, and grammar. In fact, many of the Latin names for these fallacies still are used today and are presented here. The various argument fallacies that follow were adapted, in part, from Aristotle, *Rhetoric,* 2.24.1–10; [Cicero], *Rhetorica Ad Herennium,* 2.19–2.29.46; Hurley, *Logic,* 104–150.

Chapter 3

1. The information on computer aids presented here was adapted, in part, from Dan Cavanaugh, *Preparing Visual Aids for Presentations* (Boston: Allyn and Bacon, 1997), 4–5; Timothy J. O'Leary and Linda I. O'Leary, *Microsoft PowerPoint 4.0 for Windows* (New York: McGraw Hill, 1995), 24–25.

2. For a unique and interesting discussion of the visual display of information, see Edward Tufte, *The Visual Display of Quantitative Information* (Cheshire, CT: Graphic Press, 1983).

Chapter 4

1. Two important classical sources on the functions and techniques of a speech's introduction and conclusion, from which the information presented here was adapted, in part, are Aristotle, *Rhetoric,* 3.14.1–11, 3.19.1–4; and [Cicero], *Rhetorica Ad Herennium,* 1.3.4–1.4.6, 2.30.47, 3.6.12–3.8.15.

2. The information on introductory and concluding statements presented here was compiled with the help of Kevin Sargent, Communications Department, University of South Carolina. Here again, see also Aristotle, *Rhetoric,* 3.14.1–11, 3.19.1–4; [Cicero], *Rhetorica Ad Herennium,* 1.3.4–1.4.6, 2.30.47, 3.6.12–3.8.15.

3. In general, the ancient rhetorical handbooks used the term *proposition* when referring to the thesis statement as it is used here. The term *theses* was used for more of a theoretical or general question such as "What is the best form of government?" which, although it could be a proposition of a speech, it also could be a question used in the rhetorical exercise of the same name. For discussions on propositions and their place in a speech's partition, from which information presented here was adapted, in part, see Cicero, *De Inventione*, 1.22.32–1.23.33, Quintilian, *Institutio Oratoria*, 4.5. Also see the discussion of partition in the Classical Speech Structure found in Section 2.3. For two among many discussions of *theses* and their counterpart, *hypotheses*, which involve arguing a practical and specific question such as "Is democracy the best form of government for Athens?," see Cicero, *Topica*, 81–86; Quintilian, *Institutio Oratoria*, 3.5.5–18. And for two discussions of the rhetorical exercise involving arguing *theses*, see Quintilian, *Institutio Oratoria*, 2.4.24–25; Aphthonius, "Progymnasmata," *Readings from Classical Rhetoric*, Eds. Partrica P. Mateson, Philip Rollinson, and Marion Sousa (Carbondale, IL: Southern Illinois University Press, 1990), 283-288.
4. Hayden Wollen, "Salvador Dali: Artist of the Unconscious," speech, Furman University, Greenville, SC, 1995.
5. Jay Brown, "Preventing Heat Stroke," speech, Furman University, Greenville, SC, 1993.
6. Hayden Woolen, "Advocating Single-Sex Education for Women," speech, Furman University, Greenville, SC, 1995.
7. Anthony Smith, "Why Vouchers Don't Work," speech, Furman University, Greenville, SC, 1993.
8. Although most public speaking books classify patterns of organization, the information presented here was adapted, in part, from one of the clearest and most detailed discussions of organization found in Karyln Kohrs Campbell, *The Rhetorical Act*, 2nd ed. (Belmont, CA: Wadsworth, 1996), 249–274.
9. Quintilian, *Institutio Oratoria*, 7.1.10.
10. Quintilian, *Institutio Oratoria*, 7.1.11.

Chapter 5

1. Although most public speaking books discuss the speech of explanation, one of the best sources for this speech from which the information presented here was adapted, in part, is Zarefsky, *Public Speaking*, 408–409.
2. For a description of the definitional essay form from which aspects of my speech of definition was derived, see Annette T. Rottenberg,

Elements of Argument: A Text and Reader, 5th ed. (Boston: Bedford Books, 1997), 94–105.

3. Two of the best discussions of audience reception from which the information presented here was adapted, in part, can be found in Beebe and Beebe, *Public Speaking,* 397–400; Jo Sprague and Douglas Stuart, *The Speaker's Handbook,* 5th ed. (Fort Worth, TX: Harcourt, Brace, 2000), 270–276.

4. Similar advice is given to the legal advocate when speaking to a judge in Quintilian, *Institutio Oratoria,* 4.5.5.

5. The information on emotional appeals presented here was adapted, in part, from Aristotle, *Rhetoric,* 2.1–11; Quintilian, *Institutio Oratoria,* 6.2. Aristotle's presentation of the definitions and causes of various emotions in the second book of *Rhetoric* is considered by many to be the first systematic treatment of psychology in western thought and should be referred to for this reason alone. While Aristotle's description of emotions does offer some practical advice about how to make emotional appeals, the discussion of emotional and ethical appeals in Quintilian referenced above provides additional strategies and techniques for making such appeals (directed mostly to a judge in a legal court).

6. One of the most detailed, yet perhaps dated, discussions of humor in a classical handbook, from which the information presented here was adapted, in part, is Quintilian, *Institutio Oratoria,* 6.3.

7. Although various classical handbooks offer differing explanations of how to organize a speech, the information on the classical speech structure presented here was adapted, in part, from Aristotle, *Rhetoric,* 3.14.1–3.19.4; Cicero, *De Inventione,* 1.15.20–1.41.109; Quintilian, *Institutio Oratoria,* 4–6. Also, see Corbett and Connors, *Classical Rhetoric,* 260–288.

8. Monroe's motivated sequence is a standard persuasive structure that is found in most public speaking books. Because Monroe is a coauthor of the book being referenced, the information on this organizational structure presented here was adapted, in part, from Gronbeck, et al., *Principles and Types,* 175–193.

9. Quintilian, *Institutio Oratoria,* 7.2.1; Ronald J. Malton, "Debating Propositions of Value: An Idea Revisited," *CEDA Yearbook, 9* (1988): 10.

10. The information on speech of fact presented here was adapted, in part, from Malton, "Debating Propositions," 10–11; Freeley and Steinberg, *Argumentation and Debate,* 62–63.

11. Freeley and Steinberg, *Argumentation,* 46.

12. The information on the value speech presented here was adapted, in part, from Joseph S. Tuman, "Getting to First Base: *Prima Facie* Arguments for Propositions of Value," *Journal of the American*

Forensic Association, 24 (Fall 1987): 87–91: Chaim Perelman, *Realm of Rhetoric,* 26–30; Malton, "Debating Propositions," 2–4; Freeley and Steinberg, *Argumentation and Debate,* 62–63.

13. The information on the policy speech presented here differs somewhat from many of the explanations of the policy speech found in most public speaking and argumentation books. One standard interpretation of the policy speech from which some of the information presented here was adapted is Freeley and Steinberg, *Argumentation and Debate,* 63–64.

14. J. Michael Sproule, *Speechmaking: An Introduction to Rhetorical Competence* (Dubuque, IA: Wm. C Brown, 1991), 437.

15. David Zarefsky, *Public Speaking,* 461.

16. Amplification was a standard technique of classical epideictic or ceremonial speaking. Although ancient sources offered different explanations of amplification, the two classical and one contemporary source from which the information presented here was adapted, in part, are Aristotle, *Rhetoric,* 1.9.38–1.9.39; Quintilian, *Institutio Oratoria,* 8.4.1; Poulakos and Poulakos, *Classical Rhetorical Theory,* 166–170.

17. One of the best known treatments of the emotional responses to death, from which the information on the eulogy presented here was adapted, in part, is Elizabeth Kubler-Ross, *On Death and Dying* (New York: Macmillan, 1969).

Chapter 6

1. The imitation of models was a central feature of rhetorical training in antiquity and still retains its importance today, as does the discussion of imitation found in Quintilian, *Institutio Oratoria,* 10.2.

2. The themes of clarity and appropriateness are found throughout classical handbooks, as in Aristotle, *Rhetoric,* 3.2.1; and [Cicero], *Rhetorica Ad Herennium,* 4.12.17.

3. The discussion of the various styles of speaking is developed most fully in Roman rhetoric. The information on various styles presented here was adapted, in part, from [Cicero], *Rhetorica Ad Herennium,* 4.8.11–4.11.6.

4. The information on word usage presented here was adapted, in part, from Dionysius, "Rhetoric of Style," *Readings from Classical Rhetoric,* Eds. Partrica P. Mateson, Philip Rollinson, and Marion Sousa (Carbondale, IL: Southern Illinois University Press, 1990), 302–304.

5. For a more detailed description of word usage, from which the information presented here was adapted, in part, see Corbett and Conners, *Classical Rhetoric,* 349–366.

6. Here again, the insight into how to use words effectively was found in Corbett and Conners, *Classical Rhetoric,* 351.
7. The information on creating new terms presented here was adapted, in part, from Quintilian, *Institutio Oratoria,* 7.3.
8. The standards for documenting a source and techniques for avoiding plagiarism, from which the information presented here was adapted, in part, can be found in Diana Hacker, *A Pocket Style Manual,* 3rd ed. (Boston: Bedford Books, 2000), 144–147.
9. This list of figures of speech was compiled with the help of Anne Leen, Classics Department, Furman University. One of the most comprehensive classical sources of figures of speech is [Cicero], *Rhetorica ad Herennium,* 4.13.19–4.56.69. An extensive modern source is Arthur Quinn, *Figures of Speech: 60 Ways to Turn a Phrase* (Davis, CA: Hermagoras Press, 1982).

Chapter 7

1. Most contemporary public speaking books still discuss delivery in the manner presented here. However, many of the basic precepts on delivery, from which the information presented here was adapted, in part, were established in such classical sources as [Cicero], *Rhetorica Ad Herennium,* 3.11.19–25; Quintilian, *Institutio Oratoria,* 1.3.61–65.
2. The information on using a variety of voice inflections presented here was adapted, in part, from Quintilian, *Institutio Oratoria,* 11.3.160–177.
3. One of the most detailed discussions of delivery in a public speaking book can be found in Paul L. Soper, *Basic Public Speaking,* 3rd ed. (New York: Oxford University Press, 1963). His particular suggestions on voice inflection, from which the information presented here was adapted, in part, are found on pp. 139, 154.
4. The information on varying your speaking rate presented here was adapted, in part, from Quintilian, *Institutio Oratoria,* 11.3.160–177.
5. Here again, some of the information on the use of pauses presented here was derived from Soper, *Basic Public Speaking,* 135, 140.
6. Although much of what ancient sources tell us about bodily gestures would appear a bit odd to contemporary audiences, some of their suggestions are still helpful, such as those adapted from Quintilian, *Institutio Oratoria,* 11.3.85–90.
7. Unlike their advice about bodily gestures, most of what ancient sources say about the techniques of facial gesturing still retain their usefulness and significance, such as those adapted from Quintilian, *Institutio Oratoria,* 11.3.69–80.

8. Rarely do contemporary sources discuss techniques of memory as the ancients did, no doubt because speaking from memory was the only accepted mode of delivery of their time. The information on the memory techniques presented here was adapted, in part, from Quintilian, *Institutio Oratoria*, 11.2.27–29.

9. This advice on recalling elements of your speech presented here was adapted, in part, from Quintilian, *Institutio Oratoria*, 11.2.48–49.

10. The memory techniques explained here can be found in Quintilian, *Institutio Oratoria*, 11.2.11–23; and [Cicero], *Rhetorica Ad Herennium*, 3.16.29–3.23.39.

11. The memory technique presented here was recommended by Gil Einstein, Psychology Department, Furman University.

12. Although many contemporary public speaking books discuss similar techniques for practicing your delivery, one of the most detailed discussions of these techniques from which the information presented here was adapted, in part, is Soper, *Basic Public Speaking*, 142–157.

13. The breathing exercises discussed here can be used to calm yourself before almost any stressful activity or situation. For a more detailed discussion of these breathing exercises, from which the information presented here was adapted, in part, see Soper, *Basic Public Speaking*, 136–137.

14. Michael T. Motley, " 'Taking the Terror Out of Talk," *Psychology Today* (January, 1988): 46.

15. For more information on the causes of and potential remedies for speech anxiety and other forms of communication apprehension in general, see James C. McCroskey, *An Introduction to Rhetorical Communication*, 7th ed. (Boston: Allyn & Bacon, 1977), 39–62; Virginia P. Richmond and James C. McCroskey, *Communication Apprehension, Avoidance, and Effectiveness*, 5th ed. (Boston: Allyn & Bacon, 1998).

Index

Acronyms, 192
Analogy, 54–56
 figurative, 55–56
 literal, 54–55
Argument, 59–81
 causal, 71–72
 deductive, 61–68
 enthymeme, 70–71
 inductive, 68–70
 legal, 75–78
 from signs, 72–73
 Toulmin's model of argument,
   78–81
 two-sided, 73–75
Argument fallacies, 87–93
 accident, 88
 after this, therefore because of this
   (*post hoc, ergo propter hoc*), 89
 against the person (*ad hominem*),
   91
 appeal to authority, 89–90
 appeal to ignorance, 90–91
 appeal to the people (*ad populum*),
   90
 appeal to tradition, 90
 begging the question, 93
 complex question, 92
 composition, 88
 division, 88–89
 equivocation, 89
 false dichotomy, 91
 hasty generalization, 88
 red herring, 92
 slippery slope, 91
 straw man, 92
 weak analogy, 89
Argument strategies, 81–87
 before and after, 84–85
 best- and worst-case scenerios,
   86–87
 common maxims, 87

correlative ideas, 82
 crisscross consequences, 83
 greater and lesser, 82–83
 identical consequences and
   antecedents, 84
 less and more likely (*a fortiori*), 83
 means-to-ends rationale, 86
 method of residue, 85–86
 opposites, 83
 proportional relations, 84
 reduction to absurdity (*reductio ad
   absurdum*), 85
 same principle but different
   actions, 84
 sustainability, 86
 turning the tables, 85
Audience, analysis of, 4, 5–10
 demographic, 6–7
 psychological, 7–8
 cultural, 8–9
Audience, 5–6, 154–155
 ideal or universal, 5–6
 general public, 6
 mixed, 155
 neutral, 155
 receptive, 154
 unreceptive, 155
Appeals
 (*see* Proofs)
Audio aids, 108
 audiocassette decks, 108
 compact disc (CD) players,
   108
 microphones, 108

Bibliography, 140–143
Body, of speech, 119
Brainstorming, 10–11

Ceremonial speaking, principles of,
   174–176

Ceremonial speech, 176–182
  eulogy, 181–182
  speech of acceptance, 179
  speech of introduction, 177–178
  speech of presentation, 178–179
  testimonial, 181
  toast, 179–180
Charts, 101–103
  flowcharts, 103
  tables, 102
  word charts, 101–102
Claims, 80–81
  factual, 80
  policy, 81
  valuative, 80–81
Computer aids, 109–110
Conclusion, of speech, 119–127
Contractions, use of, 191
Cost–benefit analysis, 159
Credibility
  of source, 27–29
  of speaker, 35–36, 145–146,
    156–157
Critical listening and thinking,
  1–4

Databases, 16–17, 18–19, 21, 23
  academic and professional
    journals, 26
  news and current events, 26
  nonsubscription, 26–27
  special topics, 26
  types of, 26–27
Deductive argument, 61–68
  categorical syllogism, 63–65
  disjunctive syllogism, 65
  hypothetical syllogism,
    65–68
  syllogism, 62–63
Definition, 41–43
  categorical,42–43
  etymological, 42
  oppositional, 43
Delivery, 202–204
  extemporaneous, 202–203
  impromptu, 203–204
  manuscript, 203
  memorized, 204
Delivery, nonverbal, 208–211
  dress, 209
  eye contact, 211
  facial expression, 210–211

  gestures, 209–210
  movement, 210
  posture, 209
Delivery, vocal, 204–208
  enunciation, 207
  pauses, 208
  rate, 206
  register, 204–205
  tone (inflection), 205–206
  volume, 206
Description, 43–45
  objective, 44–45
  pictorial, 43–44

Electronic research, 18–23
  browsers, 21
  search engines, 22–23
  URLs (uniform resource
    locators), 22
  web sites, 21, 196
  webzines, 23
Ethnocentrism, 9
Evidence, 2, 38–58, 122–125,
    146–147, 156, 186
  analogy, 54–56, 124–125
  definition, 41–43
  description, 43–45
  example, 48–50
  explanation, 38–41
  narrative, 51–54, 123–124
  statistics, 45–48, 122
  testimony, 56–58, 122–123
Example, 48–50
  case study, 50
  factual, 49
  hypothetical, 49–50
Explanation, 38–41
  comparison, 39
  division, 39–40
  interpretation, 40–41

Figure of speech, 196–201
  alliteration, 196–197
  anadiplosis, 197
  anaphora, 197
  antanaclasis, 197
  antithesis, 197
  assonance, 198
  asyndeton, 198
  chiasmus, 198
  climax, 198
  enallage, 198–199

epanalepsis, 199
epistrophe, 199
hyperbole, 199
malapropism, 199
metaphor, 199–200
metonymy (synecdoche), 200
onomatopoeia, 200
parallelism, 200
polysyndeton, 200–201
pun, 201
rhetorical question, 125–126,
  201
simile, 201
Figure of thought, 196
Filler words, 221–222

General speech structure, 117–120
Graphs, 97–101
  bar graphs, 99–100
  circle graphs, 99–100
  line graphs, 97–98
Gender-neutral terms, 191

Hecklers, dealing with, 225–226
Humor, use of, 125, 160–161

Inductive argument, 68–70
  generalization, 69
  specification, 69–70
Informative speaking, principles of,
  144–148
Informative speech, 148–154
  speech of definition, 149–150
  speech of description, 151
  speech of demonstration, 151–154
  speech of explanation, 148–149
Internet, 16–17, 18–19, 21–23
Interviewing, 17, 29–32
Introduction, of speech, 117–119
  introductory statements, 120–127

loci, 76, 81

Main points, 119, 138
Media aids, 106–110
  audio aids, 108
  computer aids, 109–110
  projectors and video aids,
    106–108
Memory, ways to enhance, 211–213
Mnemonic devices, 213
Motif (*see* Theme)

Narrative, 51–54
  anecdote, 53–54
  personal narrative, 52–53
  report, 53
Narrative rationality, 51

Oral citations, 140, 194–196
Organization, 130–133
  anticlimactic, 133
  cause and effect, 133
  chronological, 131
  climactic, 133
  deductive, 132
  inductive, 132
  parallel, 132
  problem and solution, 133
  spatial, 131
  topical, 131–132
Outlining, 18, 137–143

Paraphrasing, 194
Persuasive speaking, principles of,
  154–162
Persuasive speech, 162–173
  classical design, 162–165
  Monroe's motivated sequence,
    165–167
  policy speech, 171–173
  speech of fact, 167–168
  speech of value, 169–171
  stock issue speech, 167
Plagiarism, 194
Practicing your speech, 213–217
Preparing to speak, 217–219
Projectors and video aids,
  107–108
  overhead projector, 107
  slide projector, 107
  videocassette recorder (VCR),
    107–108
  video presenter, 107
Proofs, 33–37, 145–146,
  156–158
  emotional (*pathos*), 36–37,
    145–146, 157–158, 175
  ethical (*ethos*), 35–36, 145–146,
    156–157
  logical (*logos*), 34–35, 145, 156
  normative, 37, 158

Qualifiers, 160
Questions, responding to, 223–226

Research sources, 11–12, 17, 24–29
  almanacs, 25
  biographies, 25
  credibility of, 27–29
  databases, 26–27
  dictionaries, 25
  encyclopedias, 25
  government documents, 26
  government indexes, 26
  newspapers, 24
  periodicals, 24–25
  quotations, books of, 25
  types of, 24–27
rounding the sounds, 207

Speaker, credibility of, 35–36,
    145–146, 156–157
Speaking situation, 13
Speech anxiety, 219–223
Speech, main parts of, 2–3
Statistics, 45–48
  correlational study, 47
  descriptive, 46–47
  experimental method, 48
  inferential, 47–48
  mean, 46
  median, 47
  mode, 47
  poll, 47
  scientific inference, 47
  soft inference, 47
  survey, 47
  sampling error, 48
Style, 183–195
  composition, 188–192
  grammar, 188–192
  grand, 185
  middle, 185
  plain, 185
  principles of, 183–188
  revising your, 193–194
Stasis, 76
Subpoints, of speech, 119, 138
Sub-subpoints, of speech, 119, 138
Syllogism (*see* Deductive
    argument)

Testimony, 56–58
  authoritative, 56–57
  lay, 57–58

  nominal, 58
Text, 1
Theme, 186–187
Thesis statement, 118–119, 127, 154
  and preview summary, 127–130
Three-dimensional aids, 106
  cutaways, 106
  mock-ups, 106
  models, 105
Title of speech, 185
Topic, 10–18
  researching your, 14–18
  selection of your, 10–14
Topoi, 81
Toulmin's model of argument,
    78–81
  backing, 79
  claim, 80–81
  grounds, 78
  qualifier, 80
  rebuttal, 79–80
  warrant, 79
Transitions, 115, 134–137, 139,
    147–148
  chronological, 135
  oppositional, 137
  preview, 134
  qualifying, 136
  relational, 136
  review, 134–135
  signpost, 135
  spatial, 135–136
Tropes, 196
Two-dimensional aids, 96–105
  charts, 101–103
  graphs, 97–101
  handouts, 104–105
  maps, 96–97
  pictorial aids, 103–104

Visual aids, 94–116
  design of, 110–113
  media aids, 106–110
  purpose of, 94–96
  three-dimensional aids, 105–106
  two-dimensional aids, 96–104
  use of, 113–116

Warm-up exercises, 218